PRAISE FOR *THE TEST*

"Provocative, well-researched. . . . With the Common Core upon us, this timely book should be required reading for anyone concerned with education today."

—*Library Journal*, STARRED

"Thorough research and illuminating interviews. . . . With abundant data assembled in an accessible format, the book is a must-read for anyone in the educational system or any parent who has a child old enough to enter pre-school. . . . An informative and enlightening appraisal of the regimented tests that American schoolchildren of all ages are subjected to taking on a regular basis."

—*Kirkus Reviews*

[Kamenetz] digs deep into the business practices that govern current testing systems and policy . . . [she] offers several strategies to keep students balanced and calm while preparing for such exams."

—*Publishers Weekly*

"A readable, comprehensive overview of the historical background of testing, the policy considerations that have increased the occurrence of assessments, and problems this has caused. . . . Acknowledging the need for assessment and accountability while dismantling many of the myths introduced by testing companies, Kamenetz offers powerful arguments against high-stakes standardized testing and provides an impartial critique of the current obsession with testing. . . . A tremendous introduction to the field."

—*Choice*

"A must-read. *The Test* is a vital contribution to the growing debate about how to evaluate our students, schools, and teachers. And Kamenetz offers invaluable guidance to the people so often caught in the middle: parents."

—Tony Wagner, author of *The Global Achievement Gap* and *Creating Innovators: The Making of Young People Who Will Change the World*

"Anya Kamenetz's *The Test* is a fearless expose of how testing permeates our schools, our homes, even kids' psyches. People will be talking about this important, provocative book for years to come."

—Ashley Merryman, coauthor of *NurtureShock: New Thinking About Children* and *Top Dog: The Science of Winning and Losing*

"Kamenetz develops a powerful, independent argument against high-stakes standardized testing. More importantly, she shows parents, teachers, and students an array of creative and collaborative alternatives for engaging, real-world learning."

—Dale Dougherty, CEO, *Makermedia*

"*The Test* is a brilliant, passionate, insightful, and useful look at America's destructive obsession with high stakes testing. Anya Kamanetz yet again shows why she is one of America's truly original thinkers on how we should be educating the next generation—and how we are failing. If I still believed in grades after reading this book, I'd give *The Test* an A+."

—*Cathy Davidson*, director of the Futures Initiative at the City University of New York and author, *Now You See It*

THE
TEST

WHY OUR
SCHOOLS ARE
OBSESSED WITH
STANDARDIZED
TESTING—
BUT YOU DON'T
HAVE TO BE

ANYA
KAMENETZ

PublicAffairs
New York

Hardcover first published in 2015 in the United States by PublicAffairs™,
a Member of the Perseus Books Group
Paperback first published in 2016 by PublicAffairs

PublicAffairs books are available at special discounts for bulk purchases in the U.S. by
corporations, institutions, and other organizations. For more information, please contact
the Special Markets Department at the Perseus Books Group, 2300 Chestnut Street, Suite
200, Philadelphia, PA 19103, call (800) 810-4145, ext. 5000, or e-mail special.markets@
perseusbooks.com.

Book Design by Jack Lenzo

Library of Congress Cataloging-in-Publication Data
Kamenetz, Anya, 1980–
   The test : why our schools are obsessed with standardized testing—but you don't
have to be / Anya Kamenetz.—First Edition.
     pages   cm
   Includes bibliographical references and index.
   ISBN 978-1-61039-441-3 (hardback)—ISBN 978-1-61039-442-0 (e-book)
   1. Education—Standards—United States. 2. Educational tests and measurements—
United States. 3. Education and state—United States. 4. Academic achievement—
United States. I. Title.
   LB3060.83.K36   2015
   371.26—dc23
                                                                        2014035859

ISBN 978-1-61039-601-1 (paperback)
10 9 8 7 6 5 4 3 2 1

For Luria Stone,
who will set her own goals in life
and who teaches me every day.

CONTENTS

PART I
THE PROBLEM

INTRODUCTION

"**I**'m writing a book about school testing."
    "Thank goodness. It's about time."

That's the conversation I've been having again and again recently. As an education writer for the past twelve years and as a parent talking to other parents, I've seen how high-stakes standardized tests are stunting children's spirits, adding stress to family life, demoralizing teachers, undermining schools, paralyzing the education debate, and gutting our country's future competitiveness.

The way much of school is organized around these tests makes little sense for young humans developmentally. Nor does it square with what the world needs.

My husband edited together a two-minute time-lapse video of our daughter learning, over several months, to walk: standing up on wobbly legs, waving her hands with a "Woop!" crashing back down on her rear end, toddling a few steps into our outstretched arms, and, finally, crossing a room. It's pretty irresistible, if I do say so myself.

Parenting my daughter in the first years of her life has been a master class on human development. She is so driven to explore her environment and to express herself, to communicate with, please, and sometimes resist the people around her. She doesn't just walk—she walks toward something. She doesn't just speak—she speaks to someone. Mental, physical, emotional, and social milestones are all intertwined.

In the first year or four, children are hardly ever bored, unless they're hemmed in by "Nos." They stay in the proverbial state of flow, right on the edge of their abilities. Provided they get the emotional refueling they need to feel secure, they are always reaching for the next milestone, stumbling, teetering, and getting up again.

All the experts are constantly reminding parents that infants develop on their own timetables. The overall trajectory of growth and progress is more important than any particular snapshot in time. Furthermore, early learning is as much about creative expression and social engagement as it is about parroting any memorized patterns, like letters or numbers. Good preschools are little Paris salons—full of art, music, movement, rivalries, friendships, love, and, above all, imagination. They are also highly concerned with the practical matters of life, such as the use of forks, buttons, faucets. Folding laundry and washing dishes can be just as absorbing for toddlers as reading books and singing songs.

Yet just a few years later, when kids enter school, we start to limit our consideration of learning and development to a single hand-eye-brain circuit, forgetting the rest of the body, mind, and soul. It's math and reading skills, history and science facts that kids are tested and graded on. Emotional, social, moral, spiritual, creative, and physical development all become marginal, extracurricular, or remedial pursuits. And we suddenly expect children to start developing skills on a predetermined timetable, one that is now basically legislated on a federal level. This is what is called rigor and high expectations. But it's woefully out of date.

Still, as a parent, I have to admit that if you give my daughter a test—any test—I want her to score off the charts. Tests seductively promise to reveal the essential, hidden nature of identity and destiny. Everyone wants to see good numbers.

This is a book about reconciling that dilemma. If you can't manage what you don't measure, as the business maxim goes, how do we measure the right things so we can manage the right things? How do we preserve space for individual exploration while also asking our children to hit a high score? Is there any way to channel the collective thirst for metrics and data into efforts that actually make our schools and our communities healthier and our children more successful?

The modern era of high-stakes standardized testing kicked into gear at the turn of the twenty-first century, with federal No Child Left

Behind legislation mandating annual math and reading tests for public school children beginning in third grade. It has not been a golden age. Standardized testing has risen from troubling beginnings to become a $2 billion industry controlled by a handful of companies and backed by some of the world's wealthiest men and women.

The near-universally despised bubble tests are now being used to decide the fates of not only individual students but also their teachers, schools, districts, and entire state education systems—even though these tests have little validity when applied this way.

Attaching high stakes to the outcomes of individual tests is an error that economists call "Goodhart's law" and psychologists call "Campbell's law." This has been stated most simply as: "When a measure becomes a target, it ceases to be a good measure."

If you give people a single number to hit, they will work toward that number to the detriment of all other dimensions of success. The more you turn up the pressure to hit that number, the worse the distortion and corruption gets.

A recent example of Goodhart's law is the 2008 case of thousands of pounds of Chinese infant formula and milk powder adulterated with toxic melamine. Why would you add something like this to food in the first place? Melamine is a nitrogen-based industrial compound. Dairy products are tested for their protein content to ensure good nutritional quality. But most tests of the level of protein in food actually just check for the element nitrogen, as protein is the only wholesome source of nitrogen in food. So adding melamine powder to a food raises its apparent nutritional value. The food inspectors asked for a simple number—How much nitrogen is in this?—in place of a more complicated value—Is this a healthy food? And they got what they asked for.

In a 1976 paper, multidisciplinary social scientist Donald Campbell cited educational testing as a case of Goodhart's law. "Achievement tests may well be valuable indicators of general school achievement *under conditions of normal teaching aimed at general competence*," he wrote. "But when test scores become the goal of the teaching process, they both lose their value as indicators of educational status and distort the educational process in undesirable ways."

That undesirable distortion is exactly what is happening today.

The stakes for the state tests currently given annually in public schools are enormous. They determine eligibility for grade promotion and graduation. This shuts out large numbers of minorities, the poor, English language learners, and the learning disabled. They double as performance metrics for teachers, who are being denied tenure and even fired based on their students' scores. Schools that fail to meet test score targets are sanctioned, lose their leadership, or close; districts and states must give the tests and follow the rules or else lose billions of dollars in federal education aid.

These are only the most obvious, direct effects of testing. The indirect effects of judging our schools with these numbers ripple outward through society.

The Two-Income Trap was a best-selling book cowritten by Elizabeth Warren, now a senator from Massachusetts, with her daughter, Amelia Warren Tyagi. It was published four years before the mortgage crisis.

As Jill Lepore summarized in the *New Yorker*: "With two wage earners and low down payments, middle-class families took on bigger mortgages and contributed to an increase in the cost of housing, especially when families with children paid a premium for property in school districts with high test scores"—test scores that were newly available in the early 2000s thanks to No Child Left Behind and published in many districts.

The feedback loop is closed when rising real estate values result in higher property taxes, meaning even more money flows to the schools that post the best scores.

In the book Warren advocates a universal public voucher system to neutralize the unequal effects of local property taxes on school funding, a position she's since revised.

Of course there were many factors that contributed to the so-called Great Recession, but a lot of them, like this one, seem to trace back to an overreliance on numbers at the expense of good sense and heedless of the broader social implications.

In any case, the high-stakes madness is going to get worse before it gets better.

In 2015 the phase-in of the Common Core State Standards in forty-two states brings with it new, more difficult, and longer mandatory tests to nearly every classroom in the nation, up to five times a year. Scores are projected to drop sharply—the "Common Core Cliff"—and even more kids, teachers, and schools will be labeled failures as a result.

TEACHING TO THE TEST IS FAILING

The test obsession is making public schools, where nine out of ten American children are enrolled, into unhappy places. Benchmark, practice, field, and diagnostic exams are raising the total number of standardized tests up to thirty-three per year in some districts. Physical education, art, foreign languages, and other vital subjects are going on the block in favor of more drilling on core tested subjects. In one Florida high school a student reported that her brand-new computer lab was in use 124 days out of the 180-day school year for testing and test prep.

Like so many other Gen X and Gen Y parents, I'm committed to sending my daughter to a public school, both because private school would be a financial stretch for our family and because I have a strong personal belief in public schools as the building block of democracy. But I can't ignore what I've been hearing.

Parents are sending kids to public schools with high test scores and great reputations, only to come up against an unyielding rigidity that I trace directly back to The Tests. In poorer districts, teaching to the test is even more likely to replace the other activities that students desperately need.

The charter schools that are supposed to provide educational choice are captive to data-driven decision making that results in even more test score obsession to please lawmakers and private donors with good-looking figures.

I've heard from parents whose kindergartner was shy at first, so she got placed in the slow reading group. Or everything was fine until third grade, the first testing year, and then their son started getting stomachaches every night. Or their twins, who were reading grade levels ahead of the rest of the class, wanted to bring in their own books, and the teacher said no. Or their daughter is a great reader who overthinks the answers on multiple-choice questions. Or their son loves math but is frustrated by the long word problems with written explanations used to satisfy the Common Core State Standards. Whatever subject the kid hates the most, "targeted interventions" on that subject grow to take over all of school. Instead of customizing learning to each student, standardization dictates one best way. In the end it seems pretty much everyone gets left out.

MOM TRUTH

Here's what's so insidious about this test creep. It's something I didn't realize before I had my daughter: it's not just the child who takes the tests. I can tell you all day that I want my kid to be a natural learner, immersed in her passions, following her bliss, unfolding like a flower just at her own pace, but don't I know the exact day, week, and month when she said her first word? Don't my husband and I keep a Google doc tally of all of her milestones? Don't we use the G word—genius—unironically, several times a day, to label a child who's barely potty trained?

Rationally, I know how crazy this obsession with metrics and data is, how counterproductive. I could talk to you all day about developmental variations and multiple intelligences and student-driven learning. But I think it's a natural human instinct, brought to excess by the anxious times we live in, that just wants my daughter to be the winner, even when I know winning is beside the point, even when I know it would be good for her to lose sometimes. I know I'm not the only parent out there with these tiger tendencies. And I know this tension has got to be resolved somehow if we are to move forward.

As the mother of a preschooler, my highest priority is to protect her innate resilience, curiosity, and joy. One huge threat to that is sixteen years of high-stakes, high-pressure, highly regimented schooling and testing. I wrote this book to give you and me the tools to build a shield.

The Test is a tour of our test-obsessed culture. Part 1 is "The Problem." We'll look at the troubling history of standardized testing and the mystery of human intelligence: What is it, exactly, and does it really exist? Then we'll continue into the Cold War birth of today's testing mania and the toll it is taking across our education system.

The second half of the book is "The Solutions." I visit the schools, labs, and other sites where educators and innovators are moving beyond the limitations and distortions of today's high-stakes standardized tests. What if evaluation and feedback could be an integral, joyful part of the learning process? What if the data schools collect actually served our communities? This book has a positive vision for accountability that really works.

In the last chapter I'll give you an actionable set of strategies borrowed from fields like games, neuroscience, social psychology, and ancient philosophy to help children do as well as they can on tests and, more important, to use the experience of test taking to do better in life.

I use a simple acronym, TEST, to remember these win-win strategies.

- **Manage the *T*est:** Realize what the tests are for and how they work, and come up with a strategy to take them well.
- **Manage *E*motions and Energy:** Emotional intelligence and the mind-body connection can be cultivated for optimal performance in school and in life.
- **Manage *S*elf-Motivation:** Successful children set their own goalposts instead of abiding by external marks. Motivation and effort matter most. For these the child has to take the lead.
- **Manage your *T*one:** Instead of focusing on preparing your child, focus on your own attitude and the messages you're sending as a parent.

THE TESTING ARMS RACE

While we subject our offspring to endless measurement, what is really being tested? It's our values as parents—the kind of kids we want to raise and the kind of society we want to have. The testing obsession is damaging our education system. It is damaging our children.

But our society is locked into a testing arms race. The parents who have the most time, energy, and resources are afraid to stop playing the testing game for fear their children will be left behind. The schools that serve the children with the fewest resources are even more determined to push them toward standardized test performances that can somehow make up for everything else they lack.

Some parents will read this book and decide not to subject their kids to any more tests. Some will find ways to make the testing experience better. Some, I hope, will be inspired to work toward a collective solution. Whatever you choose, as parents we can—we must—transform our families' relationships to these tests.

- How do we keep our own parental anxieties in check to build corresponding resilience and calm in our children?
- How do we let our children be who they are while also motivating them to be the best they can be?
- How do we build a world where every child is challenged to achieve her own personal best?

The answer is not multiple choice.

TEN ARGUMENTS
AGAINST TESTING

O n a snowy morning in January, on the repurposed second
floor of a cavernous parochial school, the 135 sixth graders of
Leaf, a brand-new charter middle school in Brooklyn, are getting
ready for the first of six full school days of testing. (I've chosen a
pseudonym for this school and its students, administrators, and
teachers to ensure that they can speak freely.) The students aren't taking the real New York State standardized tests, which come in April,
nor are they taking the extra benchmark exams that are up to each
school to choose for their own diagnostic purposes. Leaf does those
in reading, social studies, science, and math in August, December,
and June—seven testing weeks a year out of thirty-six, a pretty typical schedule.

Instead, today is the English Language Arts (ELA) Mock Exam:
three days spent taking a practice reading test, to be followed by the
Math Mock Exam next week. Regular students will take the test for
ninety minutes each morning; the one-fifth of the students who have
a learning disability, English language learners, or ADD (Attention
Deficit Disorder) diagnosis get double time, up to three hours to
complete the test. In the afternoon the kids are "burnt," said Ms.
Berry, the principal, both from the questions and from sitting in total

and strictly enforced silence for three hours. So they'll spend the rest of each day doing meditation, playing games in the gym, drawing pictures, and watching movies.

It's a big investment of time and resources, and the results count for nothing. But Ms. Berry knows from experience that a top-to-bottom dress rehearsal is necessary in order to calm nerves and deal with any logistical issues that might come up before the big days. As we walk the halls the troubleshooting begins: one kid finished the first section in pen, which is verboten. A teacher has a cup of coffee; if a monitor dropped by from the city, that would be considered an infraction of the strict rules for proctors. In another classroom an inexperienced teacher needs a pep talk; she's unable to control her students' multiple requests to move their desks around the room "to concentrate."

The word of the day is anxiety. Parents are anxious about how their students' scores—one for "below standard," two for "basic," three for "proficient," and four for "exceeds proficient"—will look on their applications for competitive public high schools. They call to complain that Leaf is doing either too much test prep or too little. Some New York City public schools send home workbooks for months on end; others hold Saturday tutoring sessions every week of the year. Despite the six days of mock testing, Leaf is actually on the lighter end of the spectrum.

Teachers are anxious because 40 percent of their evaluations come from student scores on a combination of state and other standardized assessments. Ms. Berry is anxious because under New York City's charter school rules, if they don't demonstrate enough test score growth within each subgroup of minorities, English language learners, and learning disabled students, they'll be closed in five years.

Students pick up on their parents' and teachers' anxiety. Some stay home with stomachaches. Others stare into space or misbehave. "My mom worries about me a lot. So does my grandmother," says Lucas, a liquid-eyed sixth grader carrying a fantasy novel with a dragon on the front. When I ask what he thinks of the test, he says, "It's like a life-and-death situation. It decides whether you'll get to another grade. If not, people will be disappointed with you."

Leaf isn't the only school in the country that's consumed by anxiety over standardized testing. It's close to the norm. And as students, family, and school leaders scramble to comply with these requirements, sometimes they lose sight of the big picture: there's lots of evidence that these tests are doing harm, and very little in their favor.

Here is the case against high-stakes state standardized tests in math and reading as currently administered annually at Leaf and nearly every other public school in the nation:

1. We're testing the wrong things.
2. Tests waste time and money.
3. They are making students hate school and turning parents into preppers.
4. They are making teachers hate teaching.
5. They penalize diversity.
6. They cause teaching to the test.
7. The high stakes tempt cheating.
8. They are gamed by states until they become meaningless.
9. They are full of errors.
10. The next generation of tests will make things even worse.

1. WE'RE TESTING THE WRONG THINGS.

States are required to test just two subjects: math and language. Reading is emphasized over writing because the tests are mainly multiple choice.

Hugh Burkhardt is a British mathematician and international expert in both curricular design and assessment of mathematics. He has been a consultant on the development of the new Common Core tests. In his spare time he dabbles in elementary particle physics. When I ask him about the problems with tests as they are currently used in the United States, Burkhardt puts it this way, in a plummy accent: "Measurement error consists of two parts: systematic and statistical error. The systematic error in education is not measuring what you want to measure. . . . Psychometricians [test makers], who usually focus only on statistical error, grossly overestimate the precision of tests. . . . They just assess some bits that are easy to assess accurately."

In other words, to use a metaphor: if your telescope is out of focus, your problem is a statistical error. In Burkhardt's opinion the lenses we're using are sharp enough, but we are focusing on just a few stars at the expense of the universe of knowledge.

Are we measuring what we really want to measure in education? A flood of recent research has supported the idea that creative problem solving, oral and written communication skills, and critical thinking, plus social and emotional factors, including grit, motivation, and the ability to collaborate, are just as important in determining success as traditional academics. All of these are largely outside the scope of most standardized tests, including the new Common Core–aligned tests.

Scores on state tests do not correlate with students' ability to think. In December 2013 MIT neuroscientists working with education researchers at Harvard and Brown Universities released a study of nearly 1,400 eighth graders in the Boston public school system. The researchers administered tests of the students' fluid intelligence, or their ability to apply reasoning in novel situations, comprising skills like working memory capacity, speed of information processing, and the ability to solve abstract problems. By contrast, standardized tests mostly test crystallized intelligence, or the application of memorized routines to familiar problems. The researchers found that even the schools that did a good job raising students' math scores on standardized tests showed almost no influence over the same students' fluid intelligence.

Daniel Koretz, the Henry Lee Shattuck Professor of Education at the Harvard Graduate School of Education and an expert in educational testing, writes in *Measuring Up: What Educational Testing Really Tells Us*:

> These tests can measure only a subset of the goals of education. Some goals, such as the motivation to learn, the inclination to apply school learning to real situations, the ability to work in groups, and some kinds of complex problem solving, are not very amenable to large-scale standardized testing.

Others can be tested, but are not considered a high enough priority to invest the time and resources required . . . even in assessing the goals that we decide to measure and that can be measured well, tests are generally very small samples of behavior that we use to make estimates of students' mastery of very large domains of knowledge and skill.

So some important things we don't test because the tests aren't up to it. Some we could test but don't bother. And for the things we do test, the tests are actually too small a sample of behavior to make wide-ranging judgments.

2. TESTS WASTE TIME AND MONEY.

Not only do standardized tests address only a fraction of what students need to learn, but we're also spending ages doing it. At schools like Leaf, time given to standardized tests is more than the weeks spent taking the tests; it also includes practice tests, field tests, prep days, Saturday school, workbooks for homework. It includes afternoon periods full of movies for kids "burnt" from the tests. And standardized tests are not just state-mandated accountability tests. There are independent national assessments like Iowa Basic Skills Tests and the "Nation's Report Card," international tests like the Programme for International Student Assessment (PISA), diagnostic tests such as Dynamic Indicators of Basic Early Literacy Skills (DIBELS), supplementary subject tests in social studies and science, and local benchmark tests so districts can predict how their students will do on the state tests. In the later grades, of course, come the SAT and ACT and their accompanying practice and prequel tests, now starting as soon as seventh grade. Reports from across the country suggest that students spend about three days taking state tests in each of grades three through ten but up to 25 percent of the school year engaged in testing and test prep.

By the time a student graduates high school that could translate to 585 school days—three and a quarter extra school years that they could have spent learning instead of being tested on what they already knew or, worse, didn't know.

At the outer limits, in the Pittsburgh Public Schools in the 2013–2014 school year, students in kindergarten through twelfth grade took a total of more than 270 tests required by the state or district. The most tested grade was fourth, with 33 required tests, just shy of one a week on average. These included the state Pennsylvania System of School Assessment tests in math, reading, and science, for teacher evaluations; a three-part reading test; the DIBELS Next three-part reading tests; plus twenty more benchmark reading tests and four benchmark math tests created by district staff.

Ongoing and frequent assessment is part of good educational practice. Good teachers give lots of formative feedback—steady little nudges that let students know how they're progressing. But they draw on a full palette of assessment to do that: calling on the class during a lecture, pop quizzes, sending students up to the board to solve homework problems, daily journal entries, lab reports, peer evaluations and group critiques, research papers, presentations, and final exams. Standardized tests, however, restrict the palette to black and white. They aren't in teachers' control, so they aren't integrated into teaching and learning in the same way that formative feedback is.

Often the more a kid is struggling in school, the more time she spends taking standardized tests. Response to intervention (RTI) is a heavily assessment-driven approach to schooling that's being used to some extent in 60 to 70 percent of schools. Assessment is "at the front end" of RTI, said Louis Danielson, who was in the Department of Education's Office of Special Education Programs from 1976 until 2008.

With RTI, "Assessment," he said, "plays a key role in decision-making. You're screening to identify at-risk kids." Under RTI, at the beginning of first grade every student takes a reading test. Those who score at the low end are assessed every other week to determine whether they're making sufficient progress. If they aren't, after six to eight weeks they'll be eligible for more targeted interventions, like tutoring or small-group work. The testing continues, up to once or twice a week.

Richard Halverson, a professional of educational leadership at the University of Wisconsin-Madison who studies how technologies change schools, calls RTI "a national effort to make special ed into all of school—so all kids get assessed, all get learning plans, and the kids who struggle get assessed even more. It's the enshrinement of pervasive assessment as the model of education." Pervasive assessment is a nightmare version of school for most students. It's like burning thirsty plants in a garden under a magnifying glass, in the hope that they will grow faster under scrutiny.

That's the time factor. What about money? Are we spending too much on these tests, most of which goes to a handful of private companies? A 2012 report by the Brookings Institution found $669 million in direct annual spending on assessments in forty-five states, or $27 per student. But that's just the beginning.

The cost rises up to an estimated $1,100 when you add in the logistical and administrative overhead (e.g., the extra cost of paying teachers to prep for, administer, and grade the tests) plus the instructional time lost. Leaf, for example, employs a full-time testing coordinator, though it has fewer than two hundred students.

According to a 2006 analysis by Bloomberg Markets, over 60 percent of the test companies' revenue comes from prep materials, not the tests themselves. The profit margins on No Child Left Behind tests are as low as 3 percent, but practice tests and workbooks are more cheaply produced and claim as high as a 21 percent profit margin.

Many informed observers say we'd do better to have more expensive tests and fewer of them. "The reliance on multiple choice tests is a very American obsession," said Dylan Wiliam, an expert on the use of assessments that improve classroom practice. "We think nothing of spending $300–$400 on examining kids at the end of high school in England." It's a case of penny wise and pound foolish, critics like Wiliam say: you waste billions of dollars and untold hours by distorting the entire enterprise of school, preparing students to take crummy multiple-choice tests that cost only twenty-five bucks to grade.

3. THEY ARE MAKING STUDENTS HATE SCHOOL AND TURNING PARENTS INTO PREPPERS.

"The tests are boring!" complains Jorge, a sixth-grade student at Leaf. "You don't really want to sit in a chair for three hours. There's no breaks. You can't stand up and stretch, go to the bathroom, get a tissue, get a drink of water. It makes us really stressed, so we don't do as well."

A little bit of stress can be healthy and motivational. Too much or the wrong kind can be damaging and toxic. When you put teachers' and principals' jobs on the line and turn up the heat on parents, students catch the anxiety like a bug.

Claire Walpole, a Chicago parent, blogged about her experiences assisting her daughter's class with computer-based testing. Her daughter broke down on the way home on the second day. "'I just can't do this,' she sobbed. "The ill-fitting headsets, the hard-to-hear instructions, the uncooperative mouse, the screen going to command modes, not being able to get clarification when she asked for it. . . . It took just two days of standardized testing for her to doubt herself. . . . 'I'm just not smart, Mom. Not like everyone else. I'm just no good at kindergarten, just no good at all.'"

Especially in the elementary grades, teachers and parents across the country report students throwing up, staying home with stomachaches, locking themselves in the bathroom, crying, having nightmares, and otherwise acting out on test days. As a first- and second-grade teacher, giving mandated state tests, educational consultant Sara Truebridge said, "I never gave a test where I didn't have one child totally melt down. Just crying. These are second graders. They can't do it, they're nervous, they're tired, they're showing tics, they're not sleeping. And these may be the most gifted kids in the room."

Research dating back to the 1950s has shown that 25 to 40 percent of students suffer anxiety significant enough to depress test performance and that these anxious students perform 12 percent worse on average. The current thinking is that anxiety distracts people from the task at hand, as their minds are focused on negative thoughts about shortcomings and their imminent failure, and that this negative self-talk also interferes with working memory. All of these effects undermine the reliability of standardized tests to discern students' true competence. And as the tests draw more and more focus, they destroy students' enjoyment of school.

The anxiety doesn't end when students go home. The pressure of high-stakes tests is driving parents to act against their own values.

"Parenthood, like war, is a state in which it's impossible to be moral," wrote Lisa Miller in *New York Magazine* in 2013 in an article in which she describes sending a fourth grader to school with head lice so she could take the state-mandated English exam to get into competitive middle schools.

From striving immigrants to the very wealthy, it's becoming more commonplace for families across the country to spend thousands of dollars annually to help their kids prepare for the standardized tests that will get them into public gifted kindergartens, private schools, competitive middle schools and high schools, and, of course, college. Since the 1970s, among affluent families the total amount spent on out-of-school enrichment has grown from $3,500 a year to $8,900 a year, both in 2012 dollars.

For working-class parents whose kids are more likely to be labeled failing, school-mandated tutoring, afterschool programs, and Saturday and summer school sessions crowd out limited time and resources for extracurriculars or other enrichment. "She goes in the morning to the extra tutoring before school, she stays after school, she's pulled out during class," says Rosendo Soto, a firefighter in Texas, whose middle child is struggling with the tests. "We're on spring break now. I'm working intensively with her every day on math and writing expository stories and personal narratives. It's all geared toward these tests, tests, tests. She's nervous, fearful, and I have to remind her every day it's just school. I feel like we're sending her to be tortured."

The money parents spend on preparing kids for tests dwarfs what schools are spending to give them. The total test preparation, tutoring, and counseling market in the United States was estimated at $13.1 billion by 2015, and the global private tutoring market was estimated to pass a whopping $78.2 billion. That counts the companies like Kaplan, Princeton Review, and Grockit that hold classes, sell books, and offer online services, and the national and international chains like Kumon, Sylvan Learning, and Huntington Learning Center that accept kids as young as eighteen months old for pre-academic and after-school drilling and prepping. That estimate also includes money spent on private tutors, who can charge anywhere from $45 to $1,000 an hour, and independently operated "Saturday schools" or "cram schools" that are expanding from their traditional Chinese-, Korean-, and Russian-speaking immigrant roots to attract more and more mainstream American families.

What these dollar figures don't convey is the time, anxiety, and opportunity cost that come along with them. Instead of giving them time to pursue a creative passion, a sport, play outside, or just be together as a family, millions of stressed-out parents are frog-marching their kids through hours of the most boring kind of studying on top of the time they spend in school. No matter how much you want to convey to your children the spirit of fair play, the joy of learning for its own sake, the belief that they are more than a score on a piece of paper, sending them to test prep is an action that speaks far louder than words.

4. THEY ARE MAKING TEACHERS HATE TEACHING.

I want my child taught by proud, well-paid, highly engaged professionals. But high-stakes standardized tests deprofessionalize teaching because they give outside authorities the final say on how teachers should do their jobs. The testing company determines the quality of teachers' performance. In judging students' progress, the law gives test scores more weight than the observations of people who spend time with the kids every day.

Possibly the most politically charged application of standardized testing is the rapid growth in the use of these tests in teacher evaluation. Teachers used to be evaluated solely by their supervisors, and the vast majority historically got satisfactory ratings regardless of how well the school or their students were doing. Race to the Top, a 2009 Department of Education initiative under President Obama, instead rewarded states for evaluating teachers based on student test scores in the hope that this would be more objective.

According to the National Council on Teacher Quality, from 2009 to 2012 thirty-six states and the District of Columbia have changed the rules for teacher evaluation. Thirty states now require these evaluations to include "objective measures of student achievement," which in practice nearly always means test scores. Eighteen states and the District of Columbia actually base tenure decisions on the test scores of a teacher's students.

How do you judge a teacher based on their student's test scores? Not very well. Obviously you can't take a teacher whose students are the children of Hispanic migrant workers and simply compare their test scores to those of the teacher teaching the rich kids up the hill to figure out who is a better teacher. Value-added measurements were thus concocted. These take students' scores one year and their scores the next year (or, sometimes, their scores on the same test repeated in the fall and the spring) and compare them to a model that predicts how much they should have grown over that time period. The teachers' "value add" is how much the student actually gains compared to what was predicted.

There are a lot of holes in this approach. There is no value-added data at all on kindergartners through third graders, in the years before official testing begins, although some states have added yet more tests to rectify this problem. Should physical education, art, science, and social studies teachers be evaluated based on their students' math and reading skills? What about students who transfer into a class midyear? What about team teachers? What about specialists? What about students who are often absent? What if tests and/or cutoff scores change and test results drop district-wide as a result?

In a 2011 paper, "Getting Teacher Evaluation Right," the Stanford researcher Linda Darling-Hammond and three other education researchers concluded that value-added measurements should only be used alongside other means of evaluation and in a low-stakes way. Their research showed that ratings for individual teachers were highly unstable, varying from year to year and from one test to another.

A vivid example of the instability of value-added formulas is the story of Carolyn Abbott, the "worst" eighth-grade math teacher in New York City. Abbott taught math to both seventh and eighth graders at the Anderson School, a public school in Manhattan that pulls students from all over the city for its gifted and talented program. Her seventh-grade students performed in the 98th percentile on the 2009 state test. Based on their high scores, the value-added model predicted that these students would perform at or above the 97th percentile the following year.

But in 2010 Abbott taught this exact same class of students, now in the eighth grade. By this time these students were far ahead of the material covered on the state test, which they had learned in fifth grade at Anderson. They were preparing instead for a much tougher, high school–level Regents Exam in algebra and were busy applying to high schools. "The eighth-graders don't care; they rush through the exam, and they don't check their work," Abbott told the *Washington Post*. "The test has no effect on them. I can't make an argument that it counts for kids. The seventh-graders, they care a bit more."

So her eighth graders, who had been 98th-percentile performers as seventh graders the year before, slacked their way to "only" the 89th percentile in 2010. The value-added formula blamed Abbott for the relatively large drop in scores, thus anointing her the worst eighth-grade math teacher in New York. New York City's Department of Education, over the objection of the teachers' union, released its Teacher Data Report to major media outlets, and Abbott's name and rank were published far and wide. Abbott had the support of her administration and her students' parents, but the experience was so "humiliating" that she left teaching for a PhD program in mathematics at the University of Wisconsin-Madison. "It's too hard to be a teacher in New York City," she told one blogger. "Everything is stacked against you. You can't just measure what teachers do and slap a number on it."

"Teachers are demoralized and feel very powerless" because of test-driven accountability, said Randi Weingarten, president of the American Federation of Teachers, one of the two national unions. "Large numbers of teachers are retiring. The attrition rate in big cities is around 50 percent," up to a high of 70 percent after five years in Washington, DC.

The 2012 annual MetLife Survey of the American Teacher showed that the percentage of teachers who are "very satisfied" with their jobs had sunk to 39 percent, its lowest point since 1987. Half of teachers said they felt very stressed. Only a fifth to a quarter of teachers in other surveys express faith that tests are accurate reflections of their students' learning. "These are pretty shoddy tests," said Weingarten. "When everything becomes about data and testing, it wholly controverts the purposes of education."

Teachers are taking to YouTube, blogs, Tumblr, and Twitter to describe just how demoralizing standardized tests are to them personally. A veteran fourth-grade teacher in Florida resigned in May 2013 via YouTube. "I have experienced the depressing gradual downfall and misdirection of education that has slowly eaten away at my love of teaching," she said in her video. Curtains blow gently in the breeze behind her; her face is haggard. "Raising students' test scores on standardized tests is now the only goal. . . . Everything I loved about teaching is extinct." The video has over 600,000 views.

5. THEY PENALIZE DIVERSITY.

No Child Left Behind (NCLB), the major testing law, was intended to "close the achievement gap." It sought to hold schools accountable, not just for results averaged over all students, but also for the performance of each historically lower-performing group of students: the poor, African Americans, Hispanics, English language learners, and those with a learning disability.

The unintended consequence of that laudable intention is that the more of these subgroups a school has, the more chances it has to fail to make adequate yearly progress (AYP) targets. In other words, schools that serve the poor and ethnic minorities are more likely to fail NCLB tests and be punished or closed. The number of so-called turnaround schools spiked from around one thousand a year in the mid-2000s to a peak of six thousand in 2010–2011. The number of schools shut down has been more volatile, but it has risen from around one thousand a year in the early 2000s to between fifteen hundred and two thousand a year in the late 2000s. School reorganizations, granted, sometimes bring improvement, but in all cases they disrupt communities, and this is why they have sparked protests from Detroit to Newark to Chicago to Houston to Baltimore.

Leaders of diverse schools have two rational responses to this situation. The hard way is to redouble efforts to ensure the success of at-risk subgroups of students. The easy way is to cheat on the tests, or to somehow get rid of those subgroups.

The case of Lorenzo Garcia, the superintendent of the El Paso Independent School District, shows the lengths that some school leaders are willing to go in response to high-stakes testing policies— far beyond cheating, to actually interfering with the educations of hundreds of students in order to manipulate the statistics. Garcia collected $56,000 in bonuses for the outstanding improvement in scores posted by his overwhelmingly low-income, immigrant, Hispanic student population on the Texas tenth-grade test.

Over his six-year tenure from 2004 to 2010, as a federal court found, Garcia achieved this improvement in scores by systematically targeting lower-achieving students and stopping them from taking the tests. He and his coconspirators used a wide variety of methods. Students would be transferred to charter schools. Older students arriving from Mexico, many of whom were fleeing the drug wars in nearby Ciudad Juárez, were incorrectly placed in ninth grade. Credits were deleted from transcripts or grades changed to move students forward or back a grade in order to keep them out of the tenth-grade test. Because of the manipulation, enrollment at some high schools dropped 40 or 50 percent between ninth and tenth grades.

Those intentionally held back were sometimes allowed to catch up before graduation through "turbo-mesters," "earning" a semester's worth of credits in a few hours on the computer. Sometimes truant officers would visit students at home and warn them not to come to school on test days. And sometimes students were openly encouraged to drop out. El Paso citizens called their lost students "los desaparecidos," or the disappeared.

Linda Hernandez-Romero's daughter was one of those held back in the ninth grade. She dropped out of high school and had three children by the age of twenty-one. Hernandez-Romero told reporters, "She always tells me: 'Mom, I got kicked out of school because I wasn't smart. I guess I'm not, Mom, look at me.' There's not a way of expressing how bad it feels, because it's so bad. Seeing one of your children fail and knowing that it was not all her doing is worse." Rick Perry's Texas Education Agency found Garcia innocent of these allegations, but a federal prosecution resulted in $236,500 in fines and a forty-two-month prison sentence for Garcia.

Garcia's case is exceptional because it resulted in jail time. But this kind of systematic discrimination in response to high-stakes testing has been documented in at least three states for over a decade, as discussed in Chapter 3.

Not only do they motivate blatant discrimination, but high-stakes standardized tests also interfere with educators' ability to meet individual learning needs. Overall, 13 percent of schoolchildren are now labeled LD, for learning disabled. Under a high-stakes system both parents and schools have good reasons to push for an official diagnosis for any student who has trouble sitting perfectly still for ninety minutes every day for three weeks at a stretch. The diagnosis means extra time to take the tests, modifications, extra help, and resources. For schools, if more kids with mild learning differences end up slotted into the LD category, statistics dictate that scores will rise in both the general and LD groups.

But the long-term consequences of aggressively sorting, stigmatizing, and medicating kids are unknown. In particular, the number of kids on medication for attention disorders like ADD and ADHD has risen from 600,000 in 1990 to 3.5 million in 2013. Leading doctors who study this disorder have called the trends a "national disaster"—not a medical epidemic but rather one of overzealous treatment driven by a profit-seeking pharmaceutical industry.

The good test-takers are getting shortchanged too. Traditional standardized tests provide the most accurate information on students toward the middle of the intellectual bell curve. If a child either "hits the ceiling" with a perfect score or bottoms out on the test, her score will tell teachers very little about which areas she needs to work on. Not surprisingly, there is evidence that in the most test-driven school settings students who score well above or well below proficient get less individualized attention because teachers instead work intensively with the students who are just below proficient, or "on the bubble." Promoting a single standard of proficiency for every child may be efficient for policymakers, but it flies in the face of current educational theory, which celebrates the individual learning path of each child.

Allison Keil is the codirector of the highly popular Community Roots Charter School in New York City. Each class in her school is team taught and includes gifted, mainstream, and special needs students working together. She calls the tests distracting, demoralizing, and confusing for many of her students and their families. "A child with an IEP [individualized education plan, e.g., those with a learning disability] has specific goals. She may be working incredibly hard all year, meeting the promotional criteria that she and her teacher have set together, and then she gets a 1 (below proficient) on the test and feels like a failure. It's a huge disservice to the progress she's made."

Rebecca Ellis expresses the identical frustration. She is a single mother of a nine-year-old autistic boy named Jackson in Mandeville, Louisiana, north of New Orleans. I met them through a mutual friend at the raucous sidelines of a Mardi Gras parade; her younger, typically developing son was up on a ladder, trying to catch beads from passing floats, while Jackson ignored the racket, playing with a small plastic puzzle.

"I know today, in 2014, that Jackson is never going to pass one of these standardized assessments," she tells me. "He took the Iowa test last year and scored in the second percentile." It frustrates her that there is no official recognition of the real progress he is making, such as in interacting with other children, because there is no room for nuance in the standards. Rather than help him achieve his social development goals, the school's resources are diverted toward drilling him on math and reading concepts that are far out of his ken.

Standardization is the enemy of diversity. In our high-tech era, what humans have to offer is not robotic sameness but rather variation, adaptability, and flexibility. Rating students as 1, 2, 3, or 4 in a few limited skills does nothing to promote, support, or recognize that human value or individual potential.

6. THEY CAUSE TEACHING TO THE TEST.

In an ideal world better test scores should show that teaching and learning are getting better. But, as Daniel Koretz explains, standardized tests have never delivered on that simple promise. "If a test is well designed, good instruction will produce increases in scores," said Koretz. "But if the test is narrow enough, and you're incentiviz-ing teachers, many will stop doing the more general instruction in favor of the fairly modest amount of material that we can test well. NCLB focuses on easily tested portions of reading and math skills. Huge literatures say that's a fundamental mistake."

In his book Koretz identifies seven rational teacher responses to high-stakes tests. From most desirable to least desirable, they are:

1. Working more effectively (e.g., finding better methods of teaching)
2. Teaching more (e.g., spending more time overall)
3. Working harder (e.g., giving more homework or harder assignments)
4. Reallocation (e.g., shifting resources, including time, to emphasize the subjects and types of questions on the test)
5. Alignment (e.g., matching the curriculum more closely to the material covered on the test)
6. Coaching students
7. Cheating

How do we know which strategies teachers are applying? We can guess by looking at the types of tests we're using. Reliability is a basic concept in the profession of test making (known as "psycho-metrics"). A reliable test is one in which this year's test takers show pretty much the same distribution of scores as last year's test takers. Think back to high school: if you took the SAT more than once, say, in the fall and spring, you would have noticed that the two tests were virtually identical even if no single question was repeated. It wouldn't be fair to students if the fall 2014 test was very different from the spring 2015 test because that could lead to unpredictable variations in scores. In order to be reliable, then, tests must be at least some-what predictable or at least change slowly and gradually from year to year. And in order to be relatively cheap to administer, standardized tests currently have to be mostly multiple choice and gradable by computer. Multiple-choice, predictable tests are inherently more sus-ceptible to coaching and cheating. And high stakes applied to cheap tests drive even good teachers toward bad strategies.

A first-grade teacher described on a blog exactly how testing had hurt her and her students:

> Standardized tests actually make students stupid. Yes, stupid. Not only are the kids not thinking, they are losing the ability to think. In my zeal to get administrative scrutiny off me and my students, I mistakenly thought that if I give [administrators] the test results they want, then I could do what I know was best for my students. To that end I trained my students to do well in these tests. I taught them to look for loopholes; to eliminate and guess; to find key words; to look for clues; in short, to exchange the process of thinking for the process of manipulation.

Research suggests this teacher's experience is a common one. The Center on Education Policy reported in 2007 that 44 percent of districts cut time from activities such as social studies, science, art and music, physical education, lunch, and recess after NCLB. "We're seeing schools emphasize literacy skills and math to the detriment of civics, social studies, the arts, and anything creative," Wayne Au at the University of Washington Bothell, author of a separate study on the topic, told me. Au found that even in the tested subjects teachers lectured more and raced to cover more ground for the sake of exposing students to all the material potentially covered on the test. This meant fragmented, out-of-context presentation of information— more time spent with teachers talking and students sitting and listening.

7. THE HIGH STAKES TEMPT CHEATING.

The simplest way to improve a school's test scores is a #2 pencil with an eraser. You take the test papers, erase the students' incorrect answers and bubble in the correct ones. This is Daniel Koretz's seventh and least desirable response to testing.

It's very likely that something like this took place in 2007–2008 after Washington, DC, public school superintendent Michelle Rhee offered cash bonuses to principals with the greatest improvement in scores. Statistical evidence pointed to widespread fixing of test answers. But Rhee, who had built a national reputation on the numbers, refused to investigate and claimed not to have seen a memo detailing the cheating that was written by a whistleblower and later obtained by the press. (She refused to be interviewed for this book.)

In no way is Washington, DC, an isolated case. According to a Government Accountability Office (GAO) report issued in May 2013, officials in thirty-three states confirmed at least one instance of cheating in the 2011 and 2012 school years, and in thirty-two of those cases, states canceled, invalidated, or nullified test scores as a result of cheating. Again, this was over just two school years.

A 2012 investigation by the *Atlanta Journal-Constitution* showed that 196 school districts across the country exhibited test score patterns consistent with widespread cheating. In 2011–2013, thirty-five educators were indicted in an FBI investigation for allegedly tampering with test scores in Atlanta, where school leaders held "erasing parties" to change student scores at forty-four schools; Louisiana investigated thirty-three schools in the charter-dominated Recovery School District of New Orleans for suspiciously high levels of erasures, improper administration of the tests, and other infractions; and two elementary schools on Long Island were investigated for teacher coaching of third, fourth, and fifth graders.

University of Chicago economist Steven Levitt, of *Freakonomics* fame, analyzed statistical evidence of cheating in Chicago public schools. He found that "cheating by school personnel increased following the introduction of high-stakes testing, particularly in the lowest-performing classrooms." The groups most likely to cheat were classrooms that did badly the previous year and classrooms in schools with lower achievement, higher poverty rates, and more African American students, all characteristics associated with lower test scores.

"I'm not going to let the state slap them in the face and say they're failures," Damian Lewis, a teacher who participated in the Atlanta teaching scandal, told the *New Yorker*, explaining part of his justification for fixing answers. But at the same time, he said, "I couldn't believe what we'd been reduced to."

After he and other teachers began changing student answers on state tests at Parks Middle School, the predominantly poor, African American school falsely "met" its NCLB proficiency goals for the first time in 2006. They held a pizza party for the whole school. "Everyone was jumping up and down," Neekisia Jackson, a student, told the *New Yorker*. "It was like our World Series, our Olympics." She went on, "We had heard what everyone was saying: *Y'all aren't good enough.* Now we could finally go to school with our heads held high." The school became nationally honored for both its focus on data and its fabricated achievement.

When facing high stakes, students catch the cheating bug too, though not nearly as often as the people educating them. In the fall of 2012 twenty Long Island high school students were arrested for taking part in an SAT cheating ring; five of the students charged others up to $3,600 to sit for the exam. In the spring of 2013 students at more than 240 California schools broke the rules by posting pictures on social media while taking standardized tests, including pictures of test questions and answers. And in the spring of 2013 Nayeem Ahsan, a student at Stuyvesant High School, one of the best public schools in the nation, was caught texting hundreds of his classmates the answers on the state Regents Exams.

Widespread cheating should undermine our faith in tests as an objective measure of student progress. Instead, it undermines the process of education itself.

8. THEY ARE GAMED BY STATES UNTIL THEY BECOME MEANINGLESS.

More widespread and even more detrimental than the cheating that goes on at schools are the games that districts, states, and politicians play with the law's definitions of "proficiency" and adequate yearly progress. No Child Left Behind states that each school, district, and state must make "adequate yearly progress" in increasing the proportion of students in each subgroup that state tests deem proficient.

But the law did not define proficiency.

You might think that the psychometricians and learning specialists who create the tests also decide what "proficiency" means for a given test in a given grade. You'd be wrong.

Jeff Livingston is a senior vice president at CTB/McGraw Hill, one of the big four companies responsible for creating and marketing annual tests to states. An African American, he defends testing passionately as an instrument of equity. But he also paints a picture of states essentially ordering up tests to get the scores they want. "Respecting the local nature of education decisions, NCLB allowed every state to create its own assessment regime, cutoff scores, and measures of AYP," or adequate yearly progress, he said.

The assessment regime is the set of tests being given in each grade and state. The cutoff score, also known as the cut score, is the score that designates proficiency. "And so what happened then," Livingston explained, "is that you essentially had fifty state infrastructures in the process of putting together their own tests. You could have a state where 80 percent of kids are at or above grade level on the state tests but 20 to 30 percent are if you look at any nationally normed situation. And so it was in many ways a game to figure out who could create the test that met the minimum standards of adequacy without making the state education infrastructure look too bad, and I don't know that it ends up being especially helpful for students."

I ask him: Didn't the testing companies balk at participating in this kind of psychometric malpractice? Livingston chuckles. "Our job is to respond to what our customers ask us to do, and our customers are the representatives of their communities," he said. "I can't argue with a state board of education. We gave them precisely what they wanted in precisely the way that they wanted."

Doug Kubach, the CEO of Pearson School, the testing division of the largest education publishing company in the world, echoes this point: it's out of our hands; the buck does not stop here. "We're implementing the program and not designing or making decisions about it," he tells me. "At the end of the day it is the state and the people working for the state that make the cut score decision."

Unfortunately, when political leaders set educational standards they tend to act with political motivation. The Northwestern

Evaluation Association (NWEA) can put some flesh on that characterization. NWEA is a thirty-seven-year-old nonprofit testing company dedicated to low-stakes diagnostic testing meant to drive personalized instruction. Their tests are used in about half of the school districts in the country as well as 119 countries around the world. Over the last decade independent researchers have published a series of reports comparing NWEA test scores with state NCLB guidelines, and they have come to a single conclusion: there is no accountability in accountability measures. That's because there is no consistency in state standards.

In a 2009 report, "The Accountability Illusion," researchers took actual NWEA results in a sample of eighteen elementary schools and compared them to AYP targets for schools and population subgroups in twenty-six states. They concluded, "The way NCLB rates schools appears to be idiosyncratic—even random—and opaque. . . . In Massachusetts, for example, a state with high proficiency cut scores and relatively challenging annual targets and AYP rules, only 1 of 18 elementary schools made AYP; in Wisconsin 17 schools made AYP. Same kids, same academic performance, same schools—different states, different cut scores, different rules. And very different results."

The Common Core was initially conceived partly as an opportunity to replace the hodgepodge of state-created tests with those produced by two federally funded multistate consortia, Partnership for Assessment of Readiness for College and Careers (PARCC) and Smarter Balanced. But a dozen states, for cost or other reasons, are already balking at the tests the consortia produced and instead commissioning their own from other publishers. And even those states that use the tests from the big two consortia can still choose their own AYP targets, now covered by a hodgepodge of state waivers. So the basic problem—no consistent definition of proficiency—will persist.

9. THEY ARE FULL OF ERRORS.

Kubach, Pearson's CEO, rarely talks to the press. Our interview is rescheduled four times. When I get him on the phone he goes into great detail explaining the twenty- to twenty-five-step process by which test items are written and vetted by a series of committees. Then I ask him about the "pineapple question." He knows exactly what I'm talking about.

"Yeah, so the pineapple question . . . um," he pauses.

In 2012 the *New York Daily News* reported that students taking the New York state eighth-grade reading exam were asked to read a bizarre story about a talking pineapple that challenges a group of animals to a race. It doesn't budge. At the end the animals eat the pineapple. The students were then asked two multiple-choice questions:

Why did the animals eat the talking fruit?

Which animal was wisest?

This idiotic faux fable stumped teachers, students, and school officials alike. The pineapple story became a local scandal, forcing the state Education Department to officially announce that the question would not count against students. The most annoying part was that it wasn't even new. The story had appeared on Pearson tests in several states since 2006, drawing complaints year after year.

Kubach explained that this item, for some reason, went through a different review process from that used for the Common Core tests. He also said Pearson and New York State responded to the problems caused by the pineapple question. They changed the passage selection guidelines to reduce the use of "fables and fantasy stories"—no more ambiguous literature!

But the mistakes on tests are far more widespread than one bad pineapple. If your child starts taking math and reading tests in third grade, by the time she gets to seventh grade odds are she will have taken at least one test on which her score was bogus.

Each testing company employs a staff of psychometricians with advanced degrees, issues guidelines, and reviews most test items. But both the writing of actual test items, such as the pineapple question, and the grading of student writing is often farmed out to independent contractors making as little as $15 an hour. These workers, some of whom I've spoken with, aren't required to have relevant degrees or any experience in education. Add this to the expanded and accelerated production schedule of these tests, with tens of thousands of questions in circulation each year, and flaws in standardized tests, ranging from poorly written questions like the one above to outright mistakes, are disquietingly common.

In a yearlong investigation published in the *Atlanta Journal-Constitution* in September 2013, Heather Vogell studied more than 92,000 test questions given over two years to students in forty-two states and Washington, DC. The investigation revealed that almost one in ten tests nationwide contained significant blocks of flawed questions—10 percent or more of the questions on these tests had ambiguous or wrong answers. In other words, the percentage of flawed questions is high enough in one out of ten tests to place the fairness of the results in doubt. The National Board on Educational Testing and Public Policy reported that fifty high-profile testing mistakes had occurred in twenty states from 1999 through 2002.

If anything, essay questions on standardized tests are even more questionable than multiple choice. They are supposed to be the place to demonstrate deeper learning and communications skills, yet they are typically graded by temporary workers who spend about two minutes per essay. In 2014 the head of the College Board announced that essays would become optional on the SAT. The reason: essay scores are predictive neither of student grades nor success in college. A series of experiments by Les Perelman at MIT had shown that non-sensical essays could get high scores from graders if they used the right vocabulary and length.

10. THE NEXT GENERATION OF TESTS WILL MAKE THINGS EVEN WORSE.

The Common Core State Standards, touted as "fewer, higher and deeper" and emphasizing ideas like critical thinking and logical reasoning in English Language Arts and math, were introduced in 2010 by Achieve, Inc., a nonprofit with considerable backing from the Gates Foundation. They have a growing chorus of detractors: Oklahoma, Indiana, and South Carolina dropped the standards in the spring of 2014, leaving them in place in forty-two states, and they have been the target of right-wing protests from Glenn Beck and others. Educators' groups, teachers unions, parent groups, and others who oppose the Core tend to conflate it with the drift toward high-stakes testing.

But what about the tests themselves?

The federal government funded two state consortia to create the tests to the tune of $330 million. When the consortia, PARCC, and Smarter Balanced were announced in 2010, Education Secretary Arne Duncan said, "I am convinced that this new generation of state assessments will be an absolute game-changer in public education . . . many teachers will have the state assessments they have longed for—tests of critical thinking skills and complex student learning that are not just fill-in-the-bubble tests of basic skills but support good teaching in the classroom."

The consortium assessments were set to roll out in the 2014–2015 school year. Joe Willhoft, then the executive director of the Smarter Balanced assessment consortium, told me the Common Core tests will be more useful than older tests because they are given by computer, so teachers can see and apply the results more immediately.

Still, the new tests will have most of the same problems as the old tests. They are still cheap. The Smarter Balanced assessment package, for example, is estimated at $27.30 per student. This is cheaper than what two-thirds of states in the consortium are currently paying. They're cheap because they are still largely multiple choice and still cover limited subjects in limited ways. And because they are multiple choice and limited, they'll still be error-prone, coachable, and likely to distort the curriculum.

The Gordon Commission, an independent panel of experts, concluded in a 2013 review of the Common Core–aligned assessments: "The progress made by the PARCC and Smarter Balanced consortia in assessment development, while significant, will be far from what is ultimately needed for either accountability or classroom instructional improvement purposes." Linda Darling-Hammond, a Stanford researcher and a member of the Gordon Commission, clarifies, "They are for most states a step in the right direction, but they are limited and still in the US testing paradigm, which is different than you see in most countries: a sit-down test with lots of selected-response, multiple-choice questions, and a few open-ended questions . . . they are not as robust as the standards themselves call for and as some other countries do."

And the worst part is that these tests are still, by current law, intended to be high stakes. The high stakes becomes a real problem when you realize one more consequence of Common Core aligned assessments: the so-called assessment cliff.

These tests are harder by any measure than the ones they're replacing. Two states got a head start by giving Common Core–aligned assessments produced by Pearson. New York saw a 24 percentage point drop in ELA proficiency and a 33.8 point drop in math in the first year. In Kentucky the drop in both subjects was around 25 points.

Willhoft says the score drop-off is just a reality check that schools and districts need to face, stating, "Thirty to forty percent of our public school graduates must take remedial courses when they get to college." This number is in dispute: the National Center for Education Statistics, the government clearinghouse, lists the remediation rate for all first-year college students at 20 percent. But even if the real number is half what Willhoft quotes, it's too much.

Still, the predictive validity of the Common Core tests is not proven because they haven't yet been given to large numbers of students or correlated with the long-term success of those students. Just because they are harder doesn't prove that they align well with what students need to know or be able to do in college.

More important, there is no evidence that the effects of high-stakes tests—more teaching to the test, more cheating, more closing of schools and firing of teachers—will indeed prepare more students to succeed in college. In fact, we can be pretty sure it won't because that's what we've been trying with little success since No Child Left Behind was passed twelve years ago.

The Common Core poses another dilemma: these tests are in some ways even more standardized than the ones that came before them. Instead of fifty different curricular standards and fifty different tests in fifty states, there is just one set of standards and will potentially be just three or four Common Core tests in use across the country.

On the one hand, using fewer tests makes comparisons between states more valid.

If the same tests are given to millions of students, states won't be able to play so many games with the definition of "proficiency."

Even if each state sets its own cut scores, as McGraw Hill's Jeff Livingston and Pearson's Doug Kubach say they do, it will be easy to compare scores across state lines. This may be one of the reasons why a dozen states backed out of the test consortia in the spring and summer of 2014. As of June 2014 only 42 percent of the nation's students were set to take these tests the following spring; other states would either purchase Common Core tests from vendors like Pearson or hadn't yet decided.

At the same time, the greater alignment between curriculum and test as well as the smaller number of tests overall and school districts' need to swiftly adopt brand-new curricula and tests at the same time creates a major business opportunity. Education Secretary Arne Duncan has spoken about the Common Core creating a unified "marketplace." Companies like Pearson, Apple, Microsoft, and Google can sell the same tests, materials, curricula, and devices to schools nationwide.

The Common Core thus paves the way for education that is ever more test driven, that begins and ends with tests, where teaching to the test is the only option left because the textbook and the test were written and vetted by the same committees and published at the same time by the same company.

Where did these things come from? How did they become the law of the land? And how can we do better?

THE HISTORY
OF TESTS

THE PERSONAL EQUATION

In 1795, at an astronomical observatory in Greenwich, England, an astronomer named Nevil Maskelyne had an assistant, David Kinnebrook, who consistently reported times of stellar transit about one second later than Maskelyne's. Kinnebrook was fired for what must have looked like laziness. Friedrich Bessel, an astronomer and mathematician conducting research at Konigsberg, Prussia, read an account of the incident published in 1816. He was inspired to compare his own observations and those of two other astronomers. In 1823 Bessel reported an average, consistent variation from person to person of between 1.0 and 1.2 seconds. He developed two innovations to improve accuracy: first, a "personal equation" to correct for individual variation, and secondly, a better clock, one that ticked every half a second instead of every second. These two corrections improved the accuracy of astronomy quite a lot. They also introduced the idea of using statistics to measure and correct for the differences among people.

In fact, Maskelyne and Bessel were not the first to notice this strange pattern of human variation in timekeeping. Johann Carl Friedrich Gauss (1777–1855), known as the "Prince of Mathematicians," had created his own version of the personal equation to model the distribution of human errors in astronomical observation. This was the "Gaussian distribution," or the famous bell curve.

Notably, history is silent as to whether Maskelyne's recorded times or his assistant Kinnebrook's, one second later, were truer to the actual movements of the star. The man was fired, in essence, for not living up to an arbitrary numerical standard set by his superior— the first victim of high-stakes assessment.

Barely a decade would pass before both the bell curve and the concept of a personal equation underwent a subtle and important shift— from improving people's perception of performance with respect to an objective scientific phenomenon (e.g., the timing of an eclipse) to attempting to observe and measure objectively the people themselves.

A Belgian social scientist, Lambert Adolphe Jacques Quetelet, was the first to apply the bell curve beyond astronomy to what he called "the facts of life." He published a work in 1835 titled *A Treatise on Man, and the Development of His Faculties*, that maps out a kind of clockwork human universe, noting bell-curve patterns in crime, poverty, disease, marriage, suicide, birth and mortality rates, morality and immorality, and weight and height. (Quetelet developed the Body Mass Index, the measure of obesity that we still use today.) As a criminologist, he was among the first to calculate the statistical relationships between crime rates and poverty, age, alcohol consumption, and even local climates (people misbehave more in warm weather than cold weather).

His theory, which he called "social physics," was simple: survey the population, chart the variations on a curve, and at the top of the camel's hump, in the middle of the distribution, you will find the "average man." What begins to be assumed in Quetelet's writing is that being average, if not above average, is desirable. The normal becomes the normative.

ANTHROPOMETRY

Quetelet laid out the method for calculating the distribution of human intelligence in the early nineteenth century, but science still lacked any way to directly measure or define intelligence.

Folk archetypes allow, at a minimum, for the existence of at least three distinct kinds of smarts: the wise, the clever, and the talented or creative. The tricks of a Loki or an Anansi are very different from the sublime flute playing of Krishna, the scholarship of Thoth, or the strategy and skill of Athena.

"I neither know, nor think that I know" is Socrates's definition of his own wisdom in Plato's *Apology*. "Who is wise? He who learns from every person," says the *Pirke Avot*, a Jewish sacred book. In 1575 the Spanish philosopher Juan Huarte de San Juan described three very different and even contradictory qualities associated with intellect: "docility in learning from a master, understanding and independence of judgment, inspiration without extravagance." All of these dimensions of intelligence—creative talent, interpersonal cleverness, practical skill, prodigious memory, openness to experience, originality—ring true today, but they're still just as hard to quantify or compare.

Science focuses on what can be measured. In the nineteenth century anthropometry was the name given to the emerging practice of measuring people's physical characteristics such as weight, height, bone lengths, blood pressure, and so on. Among its notable applications was the Bertillon method of identification, a system of five body measurements, plus photographs, developed in France in 1879 and used to identify criminals for a few years before fingerprinting came along. The Bertillon method was the basis for the mug shot, still in use today.

DARWIN'S COUSIN

Francis Galton was a cousin of Charles Darwin and a child prodigy. He studied at Cambridge with Wilhelm Wundt, the "father of experimental psychology," who measured people's reactions to sensory stimuli such as hot and cold, hard and soft, and high and low tones. Wundt, in turn, had studied with Hermann von Helmholtz (1821–1894), a physicist and philosopher whose wide-ranging interests included the study of visual perception.

In 1884 Galton opened an anthropometric laboratory at the Kensington Museum in London. Between the years 1884–1890 he measured ten thousand people along lines set forth by Wundt, recording their "Keenness of Sight; Colour-Sense; Judgement of Eye; Hearing; Highest Audible Note; Breathing Power; Strength of Pull and Squeeze; Swiftness of Blow; Span of Arms; Height, standing and sitting; and Weight" as well as their eye and hair color—the better to identify "mongrel" characteristics. Among his other accomplishments, Galton coined the term "eugenics."

His 1889 book *Natural Inheritance* is a bewildering blend of racism and path-breaking social science. Both are family traits in the field of intelligence testing. Galton presents the foundations of regression analysis and the correlation coefficient, both essential tools across the sciences for describing the relationship between disparate variables. Regression analysis, at its simplest, involves drawing a "line of best fit" between two variables, visualized as X and Y axes on a graph, to understand the relationship between them. The coefficient of correlation between two variables ranges from -1 (if one occurs, the other never occurs) to 0 (no relationship) to +1 (if one occurs, the other one always occurs.) When it's close to zero, the relationship is close to random chance. Significance is a function both of how large your experimental sample size is and the range of values across the sample. The "threshold of significance" also varies from field to field—correlations tend to be lower in the social sciences. (Lightning very clearly causes thunder, but for anger and shouting, the most that can be said is that they generally occur together.) Galton uses these tools to argue that intelligence, basic virtue, and merit are trademarks of the white race and the male gender.

Among his other contributions, Galton may be credited as the first to suggest that measurements could be useful for evaluating schools' performance as well as monitoring the development of individuals. He envisioned a full anthropometric laboratory in every school and a system of tracking students after they left school to further correlate their life performance and successes with the measurements taken of them in youth. (The idea of long-term, multidimensional tracking is much more feasible in the era of big data and has champions today, as I'll get into in Chapter 4.) He proposed a system of "public examinations" and advocated that the highest scorers should be presented with large cash prizes if they elected to marry and breed.

In a 1905 lecture to the Royal Congress of London on Public Health, titled "Anthropometry in Schools," Galton defined anthropometry as "the art of measuring the physical and mental faculties of human beings." He asserts, "By recording the measurement of a small sample of his dimensions and qualities, . . . these will sufficiently define his bodily proportions, his massiveness, strength, agility, keenness of sense, energy, health, intellectual capacity, and mental character, and will substitute concise and exact numerical values for verbose and disputable estimates."

The lust for concise and exact numerical values and the desire to boil down the complexities of humans' "mental faculties" to an easy-to-manage set of measurements has never left us, no matter how unsatisfying the results.

AT THE WORLD'S FAIR

In 1893 Joseph Jastrow, a psychologist at the University of Wisconsin, opened an outpost of Galton's laboratory at the Chicago World's Fair, with a focus on the measurement of "the more elementary mental powers." Jastrow acknowledged some of the basic problems with all mental tests, which are still bugging us today: "Mental tests of this kind are burdened with difficulties from which physical measurement are comparatively free. Our mental powers are subject to many variations and fluctuations. The novelty of the test often distracts from the best exercise of the faculty tested, so that a very brief period of practice might produce a more constant and significant result. Fatigue and one's physical condition are also important causes of variation."

One point Jastrow didn't seem to worry about is whether his test items, as administered to fairgoers fresh from riding the world's first Ferris wheel and eating the first Cracker Jack, actually had "predictive validity"—that is, whether they told you anything worthwhile about the person being tested.

He provides detailed records on twenty-nine different tasks, including some memory tasks that might not be out of place on an intelligence test today, alongside some downright goofy stunts, like:

Equality of movements. The subject places the point of a lead pencil at the left end of a sheet of paper 15 inches long, and makes five movements by raising the pencil and bringing it down again, the attempt being to make the distances between the dots so recorded equal. The test is made with the eyes closed, the estimate of the distance moved depending upon the motor sensibility. The only limit of movement is that suggested by the length of the paper. The average distance between the dots and the average percentage of deviation are computed and recorded.

Around the same time, 1889, James McKeen Cattell at the University of Pennsylvania established a permanent lab for similar "mental tests," such as hand strength, rate of movement, pain threshold, reaction times, and perception of time elapsed. (Cattell was another student of Wundt at the University of Leipzig, where he became the first American to write a PhD dissertation, with the title *Psychometric Investigation*, underscoring the close relationship between the rise of intelligence testing, the science of psychology, and the history of American academia.)

In 1891 Cattell moved the lab to Columbia University, where he tested all entering freshmen, energetically promoting his program. Unfortunately, Clark Wissler, his graduate student, applied Galton's correlation coefficient to the results and found close to zero correlation between these "mental tests" and the students' actual class grades. In other words, the tests had no predictive validity whatsoever. Cattell's program was quickly scrapped, marking one of the only times that scientific evidence limited the spread of intelligence tests. Still, some vestiges of Cattell's notions persisted, as Ivy League freshmen were routinely photographed nude for "research" purposes through the 1960s and 1970s.

THE BINET SCALE

The quest for a usable test of intelligence, one that would both produce results matching the famous bell curve and actually have some power to predict real-world performance in school or life, continued into the twentieth century. In the 1880s the French government established free, mandatory, and secular education. With a much broader influx of the population into schools, they needed a way to predict which children would need early intervention in special classes. Asked to correlate test results with school performance, two French psychologists, Alfred Binet and Theodore Simon, abandoned most anthropometric-style measures in favor of trials of practical knowledge, abstract thinking, vocabulary, and problem solving, with a few memory tasks, mental arithmetic, and moral dilemmas thrown in.

After trying out his questions, first on his own two daughters and later on small groups of Paris schoolchildren, Binet developed the concept of mental age, adjusting test results to the norm of tasks that at least 75 percent of children could accomplish at a given age. Simon and Binet introduced the Binet Scale in 1905.

Because they set the age of full adult mental development at sixteen, contrary to current neurological findings that significant brain development continues through the age of twenty-five, the Simon-Binet test has a low ceiling. The shape of the scale makes it much easier to score high at age four than to do so at age twelve. In fact, I was one of those "geniuses" in diapers—my parents had me tested at age two.

Anthropometrics was giving way to psychometrics, a Sisyphean series of attempts by the discipline of psychology to establish itself as a science through the application of numbers and instrumentation to the study of the human mind. (The current generation of that effort would be neuroscience. Brain scans and the prefix "neuro-" are these days applied to every subject under the sun, creating such exotic new fields as "neuroeconomics," "neuromarketing," and "neurolaw.")

But it's worth emphasizing that psychometrics has a scholarly lineage entirely different from that of learning and teaching. Colleges of education teach theories of instruction based in part on developmental and behavioral psychology, but psychometrics as a discipline has more in common with statistics. That means tests may be able to show whether you know something, but even the best of traditional tests can't show how you learned it or what to do if you don't know it. "Among the last people I'd ask for instructional advice would be my psychometrician friends," said Joseph Ryan, a fellow of the American Educational Research Association and a professor emeritus at

Arizona State University. "Their training isn't in learning, cognitive or educational psychology."

Although the era of anthropometric measurements like "Strength of Pull and Squeeze" looks silly now, Binet's decision to include content-based questions on intelligence tests presented its own problems. Rather than aiming directly at abstract reasoning skills or the functioning of the brain, knowledge questions tie tests to a very specific context of time, place, culture, and schooling that makes it difficult to compare across time or even across populations within one society. A five-year-old French child at the turn of the century probably knew her way around a butter churn, whereas American children today may be more familiar with microwaves.

DINOSAUR BONES

Charles Spearman was a British psychologist. Like Galton and Cattell, he was a student of Wilhelm Wundt. He was obsessed with the idea of the fixed, unitary, and hereditary nature of intelligence, writing, "All branches of intellectual activity have in common one fundamental function (or group of functions)." He named this fundamental function the "g" factor, for general intelligence.

It blew my mind to discover that the first point of origin of intelligence testing could be found in eighteenth-century astronomy, one of the earliest moments in experimental science. It blew Harvard scholar Stephen Jay Gould's mind even more when he realized that something called factor analysis, the key mathematical tool he used every day as an evolutionary biologist connected to . . . well, I'll let him tell you: "There can be only a few such moments—the eurekas, the scales dropping from the eyes—in a scholar's life. My precious abstraction, the technique powering my own research at the time, had not been developed to analyze fossils, or to pursue the idealized pleasure of mathematics. Spearman had invented factor analysis to push a certain interpretation of mental tests—one that has plagued our century with its biodeterminist implications." Gould, an eminent paleontologist and one of the twentieth century's most beloved popular science writers, published an award-winning book about his eureka moment, *Mismeasure of Man*, in 1981. It's a blistering, page-turning critique of psychometrics and how racist ideology perverted science.

In an attempt to secure the scientific bona fides of their efforts, psychometricians felt pressure to prove that their tests were measuring some real thing—the g factor, for general intelligence. Throughout history the creators and champions of intelligence testing have insisted on what Gould called the "reification" of intelligence—arguing that it is not some artifact of the tests (like your time in a mile race) but instead that it is fixed, that it is unitary, and even that it is hereditary (as if the time on a particular mile you ran at age eight determined your lifetime athletic potential, health, and life expectancy and indicated that of your children's as well). The obsession with the inherited nature of intelligence, of course, is what defines so many prominent psychometricians—Galton, Spearman, Cattell, Lewis Terman, Cyril Burt, Arthur Jensen—as eugenicists and racists.

To Gould, as to many latter-day observers, the ideology is abhorrent, and the tools used to establish it are faulty. "The reification of IQ as a biological entity has depended on the conviction that Spearman's g measures a single, scalable, fundamental 'thing' residing in the human brain," Gould wrote. Factor analysis is the tool not only used but also invented, Gould argues, to argue for the thing-ness of intelligence. And the scientists who use it this way are misapplying it, running roughshod over the data.

But what is factor analysis?

Factor analysis is a statistical technique to simplify the correlations among separate measurements by drawing lines of best fit and then plotting them as vectors across various axes.

Let's translate with an example from Gould's field, paleontology: You have a bunch of stegosaurus skeletons. You measure eleven separate bones belonging to each skeleton. You can see that when the ribs get wider, the vertebrae get thicker—in other words, each separate measurement is correlated. By doing some calculations, you can simplify these correlations. The size of various bones in the skeleton correlates with the likely age of each stegosaurus at its death. You have *analyzed* your measurements and found that one underlying *factor* explains them all: age.

You can't observe the growth and development of the stegosaurus directly because all you have is fossils. There may be other contributing factors to the size of a particular creature, such as gender, nutrition, and genetic variation. It's possible that the factor analysis is incorrect, and what you're dealing with is in fact a bunch of different subspecies, one of which is sixteen inches tall at maturity whereas another one is fifteen feet.

But it's much more likely that this factor is meaningful, that there is such a "thing" as age. First of all, growth and development is observable in living organisms. Secondly, and more important, the correlations Gould found when doing exactly this type of calculation are very high—on the order of 1.0 to 0.91 between the width of a rib bone, say, and the corresponding length of a spine.

In his best-known paper, published in 1904 and titled "General Intelligence: Objectively Defined and Measured," Spearman took a set of tests given to a small group of students and applied factor analysis to argue that a single factor, "g," explained the correlation between a single student's performance in, say, Greek and English grammar. However, correlations between scores for the same person on different kinds of intelligence tests can be pretty low. Scores on different mental tests of the type given in Jastrow's laboratory to World's Fair attendees or by Cattell to college freshmen, for example, weren't meaningfully correlated at all either with each other or with other types of performance such as that in school. Numerous critics have accused Spearman of cherry-picking his data to get the results he wanted.

If you can't argue that intelligence is unitary, it becomes harder to say that it is fixed. If it's not fixed, it's harder to say that it is entirely genetic. At most, you can speak of a genetic predisposition to learn, made up of several different cognitive qualities and personality factors, like working memory and openness to experience.

Gould and many others have argued that the early psychometrician's faith in the g factor was motivated less by objective knowledge of intelligence and more by ideology about the nature of inequality. In the next chapter we'll get into the role that tests are playing in furthering inequality in America today.

TERMAN AND THE TERMITES

It would not be long before intelligence tests saw their first large-scale use by the US government. In 1917, soon after America's entry into World War I, Robert M. Yerkes, the president of the American Psychological Association, proposed that the field of psychology contribute to the war effort by examining military recruits; the process got underway in August of that year.

Lewis Terman, the chair of psychology at Stanford University, at the time was busy adapting the Binet intelligence test, renamed the Stanford-Binet. Terman was yet another eugenicist, an advocate of forced sterilization for the "feebleminded," who argued that the low Binet scores of "negroes," "Spanish-Indians," and Mexicans were racial characteristics. He created the intelligence quotient by dividing a subject's mental age by her actual age and multiplying by 100. An eight-year-old with a mental age of twelve has an IQ of 150—a genius.

"There is nothing about an individual as important as his IQ, except possibly his morals," Terman stated in 1922. He had a special interest in gifted children and conducted a longitudinal study of fifteen hundred children whom his test labeled "geniuses." The "Termites," as they were known, went on to mostly lead lives of accomplishment, although William Shockley and Luis Alvarez, winners respectively of the 1956 and 1968 Nobel Prizes in Physics, both missed the cutoff on the test. Terman was also an early proponent of the idea that a properly scientific and calibrated test could be smarter than a teacher, providing a "more reliable and more enlightening estimate of the child's intelligence than most teachers can offer after a year of daily contact in the schoolroom."

Terman and Yerkes's team threw together a test for the Army's recruits in just two weeks. There were two versions, known as "Army Alpha," for those who could speak and read English, and "Army Beta," for those who could not (this second test was full of mazes and hidden-picture puzzles). In 1917 and 1918 an astonishing 1.7 million men were examined and graded from A to E. Those scoring below C were deemed unfit for the officers corps and, below D, unfit for service.

The "Intelligence" rubric of the Alpha and Beta tests included a wide range of practical qualities, as follows: "Accuracy, ease in learning; ability to grasp quickly the point of view of commanding officer, to issue clear and intelligent orders, to estimate a new situation, and to arrive at a sensible decision in a crisis." The test also purported to cover leadership and character with paper and pencil questions such as opposites and "France is in (circle one): Europe Asia Africa Australia." This last item was an example of a recent invention: the multiple-choice question.

The multiple-choice question was an important technique for simplifying and mass-producing tests. Frederick Kelly completed his doctoral thesis in 1914 at Kansas State Teacher's College. He recognized that different teachers tend to give different judgments of student work. And Kelly saw this as a big problem in education. He proposed eliminating this variation through the use of standard tests with predetermined answers. His Kansas Silent Reading Test was a timed reading test that could be given to groups of students all at the same time, without requiring them to write a single sentence, and graded as easily as scanning one's eyes down a page.

As digital humanities scholar Cathy Davidson writes in her book *Now You See It*, "To make the tests both objective as measures and efficient administratively, Kelly insisted that questions had to be devised that admitted no ambiguity whatsoever. There had to be wholly right or wholly wrong answers, with no variable interpretations. The format will be familiar to any reader. . . . Here are the roots of today's standards-based education reform, solidly preparing youth for the machine age."

Throughout the twentieth century, innovations in efficiency made intelligence tests ever more beloved by bureaucracy. Of course, the most convenient, efficient, and cheap test design is rarely the best possible option for capturing the complex process of learning—which was not the business of psychometricians.

BIRDS BUILDING NESTS

According to Stephen Murdoch's history of intelligence testing, *I.Q.: A Smart History of a Failed Idea*, the Army didn't think much of

Army Alpha. Fewer than eight thousand recruits—half of 1 percent— were actually rejected based on the tests, and officers often found that low-scoring men turned out to be fine soldiers. The test administration was also racist, with blacks often being given the Beta version of the test for illiterates regardless of whether they actually could read and write. But Yerkes, Terman, and others nonetheless were able to parlay their war experience into a huge opportunity to advertise the idea of mass testing to schools.

Army Alpha was the first intelligence test designed to be administered to groups of people rather than one on one, as at the Anthropometric Laboratories in London and Chicago. Arthur S. Otis, who worked with Terman, became another father of the standardized mass test. His PhD dissertation proposed procedures that made it easier to score large groups of multiple-choice tests at the same time. This involved using tracing paper, the precursor of the Scantron sheet.

Otis's Group Intelligence Scale, modeled after Army Alpha, became the first commercially available standardized mental test, published by World Book, the encyclopedia makers, in 1918. Terman and Yerkes's National Intelligence Test was first used around 1920 to test school children and sold four hundred thousand copies within a year of publication. In 1923, while working at World Book, Otis published the Stanford Achievement Test (SAT), positioned as an objective way to test what children had learned in school.

The Otis tests are designed for students who can read and write and have had at least three years of school. The test items included pairs of opposites, simple pencil exercises like "drawing a tail on the kitty," and "commonsense" multiple-choice questions such as the following:

> Why do birds build nests? Correct answer: to make a place to lay their eggs; wrong answers: because they like to work, or to keep other birds away.
> If you hurt someone without meaning to, what should you do? Correct answer: beg his pardon. Wrong answers: say you didn't; run away.
> Why is it a good thing to brush our teeth? Correct answer: to keep our teeth clean and white. Wrong answer: so we can have a toothbrush; because toothpaste has a pleasant taste.

When you read items like these, it becomes clear that the quality early-twentieth-century tests labeled "intelligence" really had a lot to do with social conformity or, as Juan Huarte de San Juan put it, docility. At a minimum, doing well on a test like this assumes that a child wishes to do well in order to please authority figures. Getting the right answer requires knowing and obeying the rules of one's society. Originality, critical thinking (sometimes birds do build nests to keep other birds away), or even honesty ("run away") is likely to count against you.

RAISING THE STAKES

Right away standardized intelligence tests became high stakes for individuals. Binet's, Otis's, and Terman's tests were meant to determine how educational resources were used—who gets placed into a slow class and who into a gifted class, who becomes an engineer and who a car mechanic, who goes to college and who gets invited to leave school, just as Army Alpha and Beta were pressed into service as a way of weeding out the mentally inferior from commanding positions. Meanwhile, the SATs, first introduced in 1926, and the American College Testing programs(ACTs), introduced in 1939, gradually assumed more and more importance in college admissions. But the use of test results to reward and punish schools and teachers, rather than just students, didn't really take off until the end of the twentieth century.

Most deplorably, the Stanford-Binet test played a role in forced sterilization. According to Stephen Murdoch's review of these cases, at least sixty thousand Americans—and possibly more—were sterilized for eugenics purposes in the twentieth century. The 1927 Supreme Court case *Buck v. Bell*, which legalized eugenics-inspired sterilization, hinged on the IQ results of one Carrie Buck. At seventeen, Buck's foster parents sought to institutionalize her when she turned up pregnant, allegedly after their nephew raped her. They handed her over to Dr. Albert Priddy, the superintendent at Virginia's State Colony for Epileptics and Feeble-Minded, who had a longtime interest in asserting his right to sterilize people he saw as unfit to reproduce. He examined Buck and found her to have a mental age of nine, and her infant's intelligence was denigrated as well. "Three generations of imbeciles are enough," Supreme Court Chief Justice Oliver Wendell Holmes wrote in the famous decision approving her surgery. But Buck's school records indicated that she had actually been a fine student, and her daughter went on to make the honor roll.

NONSENSE!

In the twenties Otis and Terman's tests began to be marketed nationwide. By the mid-twenties there were over seventy-five different such tests on the market, administered to about 4 million school children annually.

The market for their work had grown because between 1880 and 1920 the United States experienced massive waves of immigration. Basic intelligence tests were among the first attempts to restrict immigration into the United States. A doctor looked over each new arrival at Ellis Island, screening for infectious diseases like tuberculosis or trachoma. An "X" was chalked on the coat of an arrival who was suspected of mental defect or insanity—these were examined in a separate room, perhaps by being asked to solve a puzzle or describe the action in a photograph. If they failed, they could be put in quarantine or turned back.

Due to immigration, urbanization, compulsory attendance laws, and the anti-child labor movement, overall school enrollment grew rapidly, from 12.7 million in 1890 to 19.7 million in 1915. The swelling and increasingly diverse tide entering classrooms raised concern over how best to maintain educational quality and allocate taxpayer resources.

More tests seemed like the answer. But not everyone agreed that they were a good idea.

An article titled "Credulity," published in the *Ohio Educational Journal* in January 1922, satirized the broad claims already being made for these tests: "I cavorted about like a glad dog and shouted 'Eureka! Eureka!!' For I just knew that no door could withstand the magic of a standardized test. Never! With it, I felt I could jimmy open the Pyramids, and I told people so."

In a series of withering essays published that year in the *New Re-public*, Walter Lippmann, one of America's most accomplished social critics, inveighed against the new phenomenon of mass intelligence testing and its noxious bedfellow, eugenics. Lippman took on the claim made by white supremacist Lothrop Stoddard, author of *The Rising Tide of Color*, that Army Alpha intelligence testing revealed the average mental age of American adults was just fourteen, a remark that made headlines coast to coast. "Nonsense," writes Lippman. "Mr. Stoddard's remark is precisely as silly as if he had written that the average mile was three quarters of a mile long." (Stoddard was probably referring to the Stanford-Binet, an IQ scale that, remember, topped out at age sixteen.)

"There are . . . two uncertain elements," in intelligence testing, Lippman also wrote. "The first is whether the tests really test intelligence." This is systematic error of the kind Hugh Burkhardt talks about (see Chapter 1). Lippman pointed out that no one really knows what intelligence is. "You know in a general way that intelligence is the capacity to deal successfully with the problems that confront human beings, but if you try to say what those problems are, or what you mean by 'dealing' with them or by 'success,' you will soon lose yourself in a fog of controversy."

The second problem, Lippman writes, is one of sample size. The scores for the tests are based on small, homogenous samples, and then the results are overgeneralized to large, more diverse populations. "Something to keep in mind is that all the talk about 'a mental age of fourteen' goes back to the performance of eighty-two California school children in 1913–14," Lippman wrote, referring to Terman's research. "Their success and failures on the days they happened to be tested have become embalmed and consecrated as the measure of human intelligence."

Finally, he wrote, numbers give off that deceptive aura of accuracy that lead to test results being trusted more than other forms of human judgment. "Because the results are expressed in numbers," he said, "it is easy to make the mistake of thinking that the intelligence test is a measure like a foot rule or a pair of scales. It is, of course, a quite different sort of measure."

In fact, as Lippman pointed out, it's the creators of the tests who have the power to define success and failure. By choosing 75 percent as the "normal" point, Binet decided to label at least one-fourth of all children backward. If he wanted to, he could have adjusted the rules so that 5 percent of children would be considered slow, or 50 percent would be.

In 1926 the Twenty-Sixth Yearbook of the National Society for the Study of Education presented official educator objections to testing: "This Committee condemns emphatically the evaluation of the product of educational effort solely by means of subject-matter types of examinations now prevalent in state and local school systems. We have reference specifically to the rigid control over the school curriculum exercised by those administrative examinations, which over-emphasize the memory of facts and principles and tend to neglect the more dynamic outcomes of instruction." By 1930 psychometrics had become sufficiently established that one observer decried an "orgy of testing" in the public schools. Critics of standardized testing are repeating themselves to this day.

HOPE FOR THE HOPELESS

Even as mental tests shifted from the anthropometrics of marking down sensory impressions toward more and more questions focusing on learned content, psychometrics stuck to the premise that the tests were measuring some fixed quantity in the human mind.

In his handbook Otis assured test givers: "The degree of brightness of an individual is expected to remain approximately constant. Were this not so, prognostication would be impossible. Intelligence testing would be of little value." Henry Goddard, who helped popularize the Binet scale in the United States by testing those of below-normal intelligence, put it more bluntly. "No amount of education or good environment can change a feebleminded individual into a normal one, any more than it can change a red-haired stock into a black-haired stock." The genetic metaphor, of course, was not accidental.

At the end of the 1930s, however, the science of psychometrics took a brief detour into proving the opposite, demonstrating a more hopeful, fluid, dynamic conception of human intelligence and potential. It happened by accident and was forgotten almost as quickly.

In the midst of the Great Depression two baby girls, who had been dismissed as "hopeless" cases, unadoptable because of their severe mental disability, were transferred out of an overcrowded orphanage to a ward for mentally disabled adult women. They were aged just thirteen and sixteen months, but their IQs had been estimated at between 46 and 44, in the "moderately to severely retarded" range. Harold Skeels and Harold Dye, two young psychologists charged with documenting and monitoring their cases, observed, "The youngsters were pitiful little creatures. They were tearful, had runny noses, and coarse, stringy, and colorless hair; they were emaciated, undersized, and lacked muscle tone or responsiveness. Sad and inactive, the two spent their days rocking and whining."

But a strange thing happened at their new institutional home. The babies became the pets of the women residents and attendants, who bought them toys and books. They were constantly held, talked to, and lavished with affection. Because of their unusual living situation, their intelligence tests were repeated, which wasn't normally done in the orphanage. After just six months their IQ scores had improved to 77 and 87, and a few months after that their scores had climbed into the mid-90s, near average levels.

Skeels and Dye convinced the state authorities to repeat the accidental experiment. This time, thirteen children between the ages of one and two whose intelligence scores were too low for them to be considered suitable for adoption were placed in the care of "foster mothers" at the adult women's institution, aged eighteen to fifty, whose mental ages were rated between five and twelve years. The foster mothers were instructed in proper infant care, and the babies also participated in an organized preschool program. A control group remained at the orphanage, only two of whom initially tested as well below average. According to an article discussing the case, the toddlers at the adult women's home had toys bought for them by the attendants and clothes made for them by the residents. Their "mothers" cheerfully competed over which ones could be made to walk and talk first.

The children remained on the ward for a mean of nineteen months. All but two of the eleven gained more than 15 IQ points during that time. Once they tested at average intelligence they were moved to regular foster homes. A year after the experiment ended, of the thirteen original children, none was still classified as "feeble-minded." At the first follow-up two and a half years later, in 1943, the mean IQ of the experimental group was exactly average, 101.4. Meanwhile the control group left at the orphanage had shown "marked deterioration" and now had an average IQ of 66.1, down from 86 at the beginning of the study.

When Skeels and Dye published their findings from this sad yet hopeful study of the power of love and human potential, they were met with general apathy and derision. Psychometric experts such as Terman asserted that IQ was fixed even in young children and that tests were reliable. If the test results varied over time, this was proof not of some miraculous transformation in the subjects but of slipshod science. The study was dubbed the "wandering IQ" study and placed on a shelf.

THE CENSUS OF ABILITIES

Throughout the history of psychometrics a debate has carried on between those who celebrate the diversity of human intelligences, including how they grow and change over time, and the prevailing interest in pinning intelligence down as fixed, inherited, and unitary. Some early intelligence testers were interested in what would later be called "multiple intelligence" theory. Take Louis Leon Thurstone, creator of the American Council on Education's psychological examination for high school graduates and college freshmen, introduced in 1924. Thurstone claimed in a 1938 paper that his experiments actually indicated the existence of seven distinct factors of intelligence: numerical, reasoning, spatial, perceptual, memory, verbal fluency, and verbal comprehension.

When resources were unrestricted, the resulting test designs could be remarkable for the range of qualities tested. In 1941, President Roosevelt issued an order for the creation of the Office of Coordinator of Information, later the Office of Strategic Services. Although the United States had not yet officially entered World War II, the OSS was charged with espionage, intelligence gathering, propaganda, subversion, aiding resistance movements, and even "psychological warfare" in service of the Allied cause. But undercover agents, men and women with diverse backgrounds and skills, started to suffer nervous breakdowns under the constant threat of being found out. In order to identify the best candidates for this demanding job, the OSS created a major psychological assessment program, screening over five thousand people in a year and a half.

The OSS tests went far beyond Army Alpha. They sought to test general intelligence, especially practical smarts under stress, alongside qualities like motivation, energy, initiative, social skills, and emotional stability as well as propaganda skills (i.e., persuasiveness in writing and speaking), observational ability, and the ability to keep a secret—in short, "the whole man," a concept borrowed from the contemporary theory of Gestalt psychology. Furthermore, their results were correlated with later performance on the job, at least for a certain percentage of recruits. Doing this kind of follow-up is an important way of establishing a test's predictive validity, which illuminates whether it's worth giving at all—just as Bissell's follow-up work discredited Cattell's assessments of Columbia freshmen.

The OSS test included paper and pencil questions. But there was also a full life story interview plus performance and situational exercises in teams of four. For a full three and a half days the recruits were asked to prepare a cover story and keep it up at all times, even under different styles of interrogation.

One unique trial was called the Construction Test. In it a candidate was given ten minutes to construct a five-foot square box with an assortment of materials. He was assigned two "helpers." In fact, both were stooges. One acted incompetent and the other behaved like a jerk. This task was never completed within the time limit and was a tremendous test of not just leadership and social skills but also emotional stability. Several of the candidates actually physically attacked the helpers during the test.

When money and time are no object, as was the case in these examples, it's possible to get very creative in testing and arrive at very different factors of intelligence beyond IQ or g. But when money and time are objects, as they usually are, the default is multiple-choice bubble tests.

As Nicholas Lemann describes in his wonderful history of the SAT, *The Big Test*, Henry Chauncey, founder of the Educational Testing Service, originally dreamed of conducting a grandiose-sounding

Census of Abilities that would "categorize, sort, and route the entire population." In the first decades of developing the SATs he experimented with psychological measures, such as the Myers-Briggs personality scale and the Thematic Apperception Test, to incorporate a fuller picture of human capability. But these posed logistical, cost, and sometimes ethical problems.

Despite Thurstone's interest in multiple intelligences, the ACE test, which he produced with his wife, Thelma, ended up with just two scores: an L (linguistic) and a Q (quantitative) score. By the same token, by the end of the 1950s the College Board had definitely settled on the IQ-style items that still dominate the SAT today, with, again, a system of two scores: math and reading.

And that's where we have left it today, with most high-stakes tests still testing just these two areas.

#2 PENCILS

Mass testing grew throughout the twentieth century alongside other forms of industrial mass production, with American innovations spreading throughout the world. In 1937 IBM filed patents for the 805 test-scoring machine, which read the electrically conductive marks of a graphite pencil with a pair of wire brushes scanning the page. The story is that the inventor, Reynold B. Johnson, then a high school science teacher in Michigan, remembered pranking his older sister's dates by drawing pencil marks on the outside of a car engine: the spark from the spark plug traveled toward the marks and refused to ignite. Johnson came on board at IBM and went on to develop the first commercial computer disk drive and contribute to the videocassette tape.

Everett Franklin Lindquist, a member of the College of Education at the University of Iowa, then started the Iowa Academic Meet for high school students, known as the Brain Derby. This led him to develop the Iowa Tests of Basic Skills (ITBS), debuting in 1935 for grades six through eight, followed in 1940 by the Iowa Tests of Educational Development for high school students.

The Iowa Tests covered reading comprehension, spelling, and mathematics. By 1940 school districts throughout the nation were purchasing and administering the Iowa Tests along with others like the National Assessment for Educational Progress (NAEP, or the Nation's Report Card), the California Achievement Tests, the Comprehensive Tests of Basic Skills, the Metropolitan Achievement Tests, and the Stanford Achievement Tests (SATs). Schools, districts, and states adopted these tests voluntarily to help them classify students and allocate resources as well as a means of quality control. Lindquist would go on to cofound the American College Testing program, or ACT, in 1959 and also had a key role in the development of the General Educational Development (GED) and National Merit Scholarship tests. All of these, plus the Advance Placement (AP) exams and the SATs, constituted the primary menu of standardized tests right through the 1980s.

Then, in 1962, Lindquist received a patent for an optical scanner that could grade up to one hundred thousand answer sheets per hour: the cotton gin of standardized testing. Because of this, Lindquist has been called "arguably the person most responsible for fostering the development and use of standardized tests in the United States."

TESTING LEARNING VS. TESTING SMARTS

The distinction between intelligence testing (how smart are you?) and achievement testing (what do you know?) is often murky to the general public and even to test makers themselves. Throughout their history, for example, the SAT's "A" has stood for "aptitude," "assessment," and "achievement," and today SAT, like KFC, stands only for itself.

Still, the achievement tests that began to be introduced midcentury and are emphasized today differ in their design from the intelligence tests of the 1910s and 1920s. The scores on the SATs, ACTs, and Iowa Tests are meant to correlate with grades in school. Accordingly, these tests contain more questions covering specific areas of knowledge.

Another important distinction between intelligence and achievement tests is that intelligence tests are designed to be "norm-referenced." That is, they are meant to compare individuals to the norms found across a population. That means, for one thing, that the results tend to conform to a bell curve. A predetermined percentage of students will score at the bottom or top end of the scale. This is what it means to "grade on a curve." Norm-referenced tests are normed on a particular sample population at a particular place and time—Lippmann's "eighty-two California school children in 1913–14." If the population taking the test differs in important ways from the sample population, the results may be extremely misleading.

Achievement tests, however, are supposed to be "criterion referenced." They are not graded on a curve. They're meant to measure the acquisition of knowledge according to fixed criteria. Think of a driving test. If absolutely everyone passes the driving test on the first go, it's probably too easy. But 87 percent of American adults are licensed to drive, some of whom took the test multiple times, and few people have a problem with that.

Statewide accountability tests should, in theory, be criterion referenced. The goal is for everyone to meet a certain baseline of knowledge. But because achievement tests evolved from intelligence tests and many of the same psychometric procedures are used to develop and test the tests, in practice the distinction between the two is often muddied.

In reality there is no objective definition of what it means to be a proficient third grader; the standard can be set only by referencing previous third graders' performance. The size and makeup of the sample population matters a lot. Then again, if you create a test and project in advance, based on field tests, as psychometricians often do, that 80 percent of students will get one block of questions right and 60 percent will get another block right, are you unfairly predetermining the outcomes?

When you claim to test achievement and test children at the end of school rather than on entry, you are in part evaluating the work done by the schools themselves, with consequences that would reach their fullest expression nearly sixty years later.

SKEELS AND DYE REVISITED

In the 1960s a University of Chicago researcher dug up Skeels and Dye's paper and was excited enough to find the researchers and persuade them to follow up with the original experimental groups. The results were published in 1966. Of the thirteen girls who had been adopted, first informally by developmentally disabled women in the institution and then by families in the outside world, all of them were self-supporting. Eleven of them were married. They had a mean of 11.68 years of education. They earned an average wage of $4,224, which was in the range of average annual earnings for men in Iowa, their home state—not bad for a group of women from an institutional background in the 1960s.

Of the twelve girls in the control group, only four of them had jobs, all of them working in the institutions where they lived. Only three had been married. On average they had less than four years of schooling. The cost savings to the state for rescuing the girls who went on to live healthy, productive lives was approximately $200 million in today's dollars.

Skeels's lifetime of research testing the effects of nurturing on children's intellectual development influenced Head Start, the federal preschool program, as well as the field of special education. But to this day his name and his discoveries about the malleability of IQ are far less well known than those of Alfred Binet, Francis Galton, or even Lewis Terman.

Maybe that's because his research pointed to something that the creators and promoters of tests didn't want to acknowledge: at best, intelligence tests can only be an indicator of someone's situation at a given point in time and can serve only as a benchmark for the real work of educators and caregivers in cultivating a child.

Skeels concluded his 1966 follow-up study with these urgent words: "It seems obvious that under present-day conditions there are still countless infants with sound biological constitutions and potentialities for development well within the normal range who will become retarded and noncontributing members of society unless appropriate intervention occurs . . . sufficient knowledge is available to design programs of intervention to counteract the devastating effects of poverty, sociocultural, and maternal deprivation."

The same problem is just as apparent today, and the need for comprehensive "programs of intervention," if anything, even more so.

RACISM, DIFFERENCE, AND TESTS

In the Jim Crow era a rogue variant of high-stakes standardized test emerged: the so-called literacy test, employed to systematically restrict the voting rights of African Americans. Oral, written, or multiple choice, these were all buried in bureaucratic verbiage familiar to any subject of Terman or Otis.

Louisiana, my home state, crafted a special breed of pencil-and-paper test featuring nonsense worthy of an evil Lewis Carroll.

Sample questions on the 1964 Louisiana Voter Literacy Test:

"1. Draw a line around the number or letter of this sentence."

"20. Spell backwards, forwards."

The Voting Rights Act of 1965 specifically prohibited tests like these, and any jurisdiction that had employed them in the past became subject to federal oversight.

As I went through the lively history of standardized testing I had to face again and again the awkward question: Why so many racists in psychometrics? My intention is not to throw a rhetorical Molotov cocktail at today's state-mandated testing programs. I'm not saying anyone involved in testing today is, de facto, racist. But it's hard to ignore the shadow of history. The majority of the foundational intellectual figures in this relatively small scientific field were directly associated with eugenics, discrimination, or both. Why? And what, if anything, does it mean for today's test-obsessed school system?

What is the commonality between Galton's anthropometric laboratory, the Army Alpha and Beta tests of World War I, the intelligence tests given at Ellis Island, and the logic-defying Jim Crow literacy test? How do these all relate to the achievement gaps of today?

One common theme is that the people in power create the tests, and disempowered people have to pass them. Another is that tests represent the urge to sort and stratify, to catalog, correct for, normalize, and, ultimately, erase difference.

(A) RACE, (B) CLASS, (C) TESTS

Are standardized tests biased against minorities, or do they reveal an unpleasant ground truth about groups' fixed abilities, as would be argued by generations of "scientific" racists, from Galton to Charles Murray, author of the 1994 book *The Bell Curve*? The achievement gap, or the tendency of poor people and minority groups to score lower on standardized tests, is really at the heart of the testing controversy. Researchers have looked at the problem from all angles.

There are cultural arguments, such as that African Americans develop an "oppositional" attitude toward academic achievement because of racism. Research has shown that tests, written largely by privileged, educated white people and normed on similar populations, are likely to assume prior knowledge common to their own group, which depresses the scores of the nondominant groups. My mother-in-law, a therapist and university instructor, told me about a possibly apocryphal example of class-based assumptions embedded in an intelligence test for young children in the 1970s. One question has three pictures: a man in overalls, a man in a tuxedo, and a man in a pinstriped suit. The question was, "Which one is a picture of Daddy going to work?" Whether or not this item actually appeared on tests, it's a great illustration of what bias looks like on a test.

Here's a more anodyne example from my own childhood. In third grade I was enrolled in public school in Cambridge, Massachusetts, while my parents were on sabbatical from Louisiana State University. While there I remember vividly taking some kind of multiple-choice test that included the question: Which of the following fruits do we eat fresh, and which are dried? One of the options was "fig." Back in subtropical Baton Rouge, Louisiana, we had a fig tree growing in our backyard. So I got that one wrong.

The cultural bias arguments are provocative but gild the lily a bit. The "achievement gap" is a tautology masquerading as a problem: all it really means is that students with disadvantages, on average, are at a disadvantage.

Of the 50 million students in American public schools, 51 percent receive free and reduced-price lunches. Their families earn less than 185 percent of the federal poverty level—less than $50,000 for a family of four. That means that nearly half of public school students struggle economically to some extent. Economic struggle in turn affects academic achievement in multiple ways. Poor kids may not get the same quality sleep because they share a bed or sleep on a couch. They may come to school without breakfast. Their vision goes uncorrected. They are likely to have less educated parents who own fewer books and talk to them less from the time they are infants—a gap that's been estimated at 30 million words by the time they start kindergarten. They are more likely to suffer from "toxic stress"—a parent in jail, abuse, trauma, or risk of homelessness—that interferes with their ability to concentrate day to day and can distort their brain development over time.

In 2013 Dr. Michael Freemark, a professor of pediatrics at Duke University took a look at state test results for students in Raleigh-Durham and Chapel Hill, North Carolina, and found that "85 percent of variability in school performance is explained by the economic well-being of a child's family, as measured by eligibility for subsidized lunches." No other single factor comes close in its correlation with test scores.

The great American project is how to have a broadly successful, competitive, vital, dynamic society with the full participation of people of varying backgrounds and abilities. The provisional answer we've come up with is meritocracy. This means providing opportunities to all to participate and then rewarding talent combined with effort.

But meritocracy relies on accurate sorting so that the cream rises to the top. Intelligence and aptitude testing offer a fantasy of objectively identifying fixed quantities of merit and awarding opportunities based on those quantities: a spot in a gifted kindergarten, a spot in Harvard's freshman class.

But what if the tests are not objective? And what if merit is not fixed? The converse, the possibility that Skeels and Dye's "wandering IQ" study puts in front of us, is a huge moral challenge. Their study, laughed out of the hall, suggests that disparities in human flourishing are partly circumstantial, that they can be mitigated with a mixture of hard effort and love. A diversity of achievement and talents would naturally persist even if our society did the utmost to promote the advancement of each person. But nonetheless, the idea that tests represent only a snapshot, a moment in time, puts a huge responsibility in the hands of everyone tasked with bringing up children.

TESTS AND CIVIL RIGHTS

In the 1960s psychometric tests pivoted from being a frank instrument of racism to being marketed as a tool used to diagnose racist wrongs. Richard Halverson at Wisconsin-Madison, quoted in Chapter 1, traces the latest wave of obsession with high-stakes testing to school desegregation policies, beginning with *Brown v. Board of Education* in 1954. "That's the historical root of the interest in assessment," he said. "With the civil rights movement we made huge public investments in our schools and said, schools, remediate the results of Jim Crow and civil rights abuses. By the '70s and '80s it was pretty clear those effects had not been remediated by our schools. So the question became, what are we putting all this money into schools for?" Some conservatives used that question as a bludgeon to try to reduce educational spending. Some progressives asked it in order to spur more spending and intervention. In either case, there was an increasing interest in methods of evaluating program outcomes, and this often meant tests.

At roughly the same time, in the 1970s, the quest for educational access as a civil right resulted in a wave of antitesting activism, media coverage, and federal court cases. A central figure in this movement was none other than Ralph Nader. In 1980 he published Allan Nairn's five hundred–page magnum opus investigative report on the practices of the Educational Testing Service (ETS), creator of the SATs and GREs. The paper, titled "The Reign of ETS: The Corporation that Makes Up Minds," questioned the validity of the tests as well as the powerful position of ETS, a private nonprofit that takes in millions in revenue while deciding who will pass through the gates of America's colleges and on to economic opportunity. The accompanying campaign led to the passage of "truth in testing" laws in New York and California, requiring that companies publish tests after they were administered along with the answers and any accompanying background reports so individual items could be publicly examined for racial and class bias.

In January 1980 Nader appeared on the *Tonight Show*. Illustrating how little the terms of debate have changed, according to a contemporary account by Walt Haney, "After condemning the 'reign' of ETS, Nader gave an impassioned plea for wider consideration of traits like perseverance, wisdom, idealism and creativity. . . . The *Tonight Show* audience broke into spontaneous applause." Once again, as with Walter Lippman in the 1920s, a major cultural critic had mounted a popular critique of intelligence testing on intellectual and moral grounds. But the reign of standardized tests was not to be ended so quickly.

THE RAINBOW CONNECTION

The racists in the center of this history focused on consistent scoring differences between racial and ethnic groups. The current obsession with narrowing the "achievement gap" is based on those same stubborn trends. The implication is that poor students and minorities must constantly labor to catch up on systematic and persistent weaknesses. Small wonder that even being reminded of one's race can, research says, be enough to depress math scores, a condition known as "stereotype threat."

Poverty and racism are very real and distinct disadvantages. But certainly it would be more useful if tests could somehow filter out the background noise that arises from the accident of birth and instead highlight the individual strengths that can help determine success in life as well as people's capacity to grow and develop these strengths. That would especially improve the quality of gatekeeper tests such as the SATs.

Dr. Robert Sternberg knows from smart. He's a psychologist and psychometrician with degrees from Stanford and Yale. He knows from successful. He's been the president of both the American Psychological Association and the University of Wyoming. And he knows from complex. At the age of sixty-four he has two grown children plus toddler triplets with his current wife, a former student. And he resigned the University of Wyoming presidency after four months, having lost the confidence of the board of trustees.

For the past thirty-odd years Dr. Sternberg has been developing and perfecting a new, more complex theory of intelligence, called successful intelligence, measured by tests useful in high-stakes contexts. "There's more to people than SAT and ACT scores," he said. "You need to be creative, because the world changes so fast that if you can't adapt to novelty and respond to new social and emotional challenges, you just fall behind." Sternberg's characterization of intelligence, which he emphasizes is just a working definition, focuses on the broadest possible range of qualities that allow people to achieve what they set out to in life—hence, successful intelligence. In his scheme traditional academic abilities, including math and language, are just one of three legs of a stool. These are called "analytic intelligence." The other two legs are practical and creative intelligence.

The idea that intelligence includes emotional, creative, and practical ability is common sense across cultures and is enjoying a bit of a renaissance these days. But without reliable, easy-to-use tests to measure the full range of human strengths, it's proving quite difficult to incorporate these into our reckoning of what makes people successful, much less the systems by which we judge the success and failure of students and schools. As documented throughout this book, our schools then end up concentrating on analytic intelligence, especially memorized information, the easiest kind to test. It's like the old vaudeville routine in which a comedian comes out onstage hunting for his spectacles.

"Did you lose them out here?" asks the emcee.

"No, I lost them backstage."

"So why are you looking out here?"

"Because the light is better out here!"

Our comedian is committing a systematic error.

Being the rare learning psychologist who is also a psychometrician, Sternberg has developed a solution to this conundrum. He has designed a series of tests to shine a light on his broader definition of intelligence, with the evocative names of "Rainbow," "Kaleidoscope," and "Panorama."

The College Board funded the development of the Rainbow test. Sternberg tested almost seven hundred undergraduates from diverse backgrounds. He used the SATs to measure analytic intelligence and devised a multiple-choice test to get at practical and creative intelligence. The Rainbow test also included free-response items reminiscent of personality testing or the old OSS tests in the 1940s. The creative portion, among other tasks, asked students to come up with captions for *New Yorker* cartoons and write short stories after being given only a title. The practical portion asked them to recommend a solution to common interpersonal dilemmas people face in the workplace or at school.

The results, published in 2006, were impressive. Testing all three kinds of intelligence predicted the GPAs of college freshmen far better than the SAT alone. And even more interesting, testing for all three kinds of intelligence greatly reduced the gaps among racial and ethnic groups. Groups who scored lower on analytic intelligence had correspondingly higher scores on the creative and practical tests.

The results of Sternberg's Rainbow study was published as a lead article in the journal *Intelligence* and featured in the media. But despite its success, the College Board stopped funding it. "There are differing interpretations of why," Sternberg said. "I can only say what they said, which is that they had reservations about whether this could be scaled up." In particular, the multiple-choice items Sternberg had designed ended up correlating only with analytic skills, regardless of what they were intended to measure. It was just the open-ended tasks, which had to be graded by humans, that produced separate scores for creative and practical intelligence. Sternberg said he learned that "if you want to test something other than analytic intelligence, don't go with multiple choice."

However, Sternberg disagreed that his tests couldn't scale. He was impatient to put his ideas into practice, so he moved to a position as a dean at Tufts University in Boston. This time he'd be working with the admissions office. "I spent thirty years as a professor at Yale and eventually concluded that as a professor I couldn't change squat. So I said, the hell with it, at least as an administrator I can do something."

Sternberg's next phase, dubbed the Kaleidoscope Project, gave Tufts applicants the option of doing an essay or submitting a project that demonstrated successful intelligence. To the creative, analytical, and practical legs of his model he'd added a fourth component:

wisdom. He defines this as the ability to apply knowledge and skills toward a common good by balancing your interests with those of others and the greater good over both the long and short term. The entire Tufts application was scored using rubrics, with admissions officials trained in criteria to evaluate the students' successful intelligence.

Over the course of five years and thousands of students, systematically measuring all of these factors increased the university's ability to predict incoming students' academic success, leadership, and extracurricular involvement. They did all this while nearly eliminating ethnic-group differences in admissions consideration—a significant achievement considering the Supreme Court cases that have greeted attempts to do the same at universities across the country. Tufts applicants reacted positively to the idea that the university was emphasizing a full range of strengths. As a result, both the diversity of applicants and their SAT scores went up. At Sternberg's next stop, Oklahoma State University, he achieved similar results with a very different student body. "The purpose of college education is to produce active citizens, ethical leaders, who will make the world a better place," Sternberg said. "You're not going to do that only by looking at their SAT scores. If you believe in that, your admissions process should reflect what you are trying to optimize for."

Like Skeels and Dye's "wandering IQ" study, Sternberg, whose research continues at Cornell University, asks us to consider a dynamic definition of intelligence, one that incorporates students' relationships with others and, above all, their ability to learn. "Learning from experience is the most important skill," he said. "We should be looking at kids' growth potential."

In the next chapter we'll see the consequences when, in the twenty-first century, the federal government decrees that every student in the nation must achieve a single standard on a test.

THE POLITICS
OF TESTS

What is the most important lesson the young bird learns in this story?
  (A) Stay close to your nest.
  (B) Be careful where you land.
  (C) Swimming is easier than flying.
  (D) The marsh is safer than the pond.

—Florida Comprehensive Assessment Test (FCAT) 2.0,
third grade reading test sample question

On the lawn of a single-story apartment complex in south Orlando, on a sunny afternoon in October 2013, a gaggle of kids were shooting squirt guns and slurping homemade Hawaiian Punch popsicles, killing time before football and cheerleading practice. One of them was Laela Gray, a petite, blond-haired, blue-eyed nine-year-old who resembled Stephanie from the nineties sitcom *Full House*. She and her twin brother, Caleb, were the middle children of five, and their mother, Ali Gray-Crist, thirty, said, "Out of all five she is the one that loves school the most. She loves to read. She was always good about doing her homework and got really good grades."

In third grade, however, there was a break in the straight As. Laela started bringing home Cs in reading. Her mother says this was largely due to the teacher's introduction of short passages with comprehension questions in preparation for the annual Florida Comprehensive Assessment Test (FCAT) state tests. Laela was no good at answering these kinds of questions. "A lot of the passages were really difficult for her because the questions were tricky. It says 'pick the best one,' but there's two best answers."

In Florida the third- through tenth-grade tests aren't just used to grade the performance of schools and of teachers; they're also used in a third way they were never designed for: to determine whether individual students should be promoted from one grade to the next.

When Laela got her FCAT scores back in the spring of 2013 there was bad news. "I failed," she tells me shyly, sitting on her couch and staring straight ahead at her brother's video game. She had failed the reading portion of the test by 1 point: 181, when the cutoff score was 182. Caleb would be going on to the fourth grade without her.

How did our nation arrive at a system that gives one point on a standardized test more weight than four years of a little girl's performance in school?

Step by confusing, largely well-intentioned step.

A NATION AT RISK . . . THANKS TO FAULTY MATH

The origins of the latest era of high-stakes testing are usually traced to the publication in 1983 of a now-infamous report titled *A Nation at Risk: The Imperative for Educational Reform.* "The educational foundations of our society are presently being eroded by a rising tide of mediocrity that threatens our very future as a Nation and a people" is probably its most quoted line.

A Nation at Risk marked the establishment of an enduring bipartisan consensus that schools were failing and that tests could tell us how and why. The authors were largely educational authorities—commissioners of education, university presidents. Their findings were reported as fact. But they weren't pursuing a dispassionate inquiry. *A Nation at Risk* was produced by a group already alarmed by what they saw as the decline of America's educational standards.

As Yvonne Larsen, the vice chair of the commission that authored the report, described it, "I was called by the President's office. They told us that we were going to have a commission of about 18 people and meet for a year and a half to two years to address the challenge that we faced in trying to upgrade America's education to the rigorous education that we had in the past. . . . We felt the rigor in our schools had diminished. We were concerned. There was a strong feeling that if we continued how we were going, we wouldn't continue to improve."

The case for decline—again, something the authors agreed upon before starting their study—is made with scary statistics like, "The average achievement of high school students on most standardized tests is now lower than 26 years ago when Sputnik was launched" and "The College Board's Scholastic Aptitude Tests (SAT) demonstrate a virtually unbroken decline from 1963 to 1980. Average verbal scores fell over 50 points and average mathematics scores dropped nearly 40 points."

The reference to Sputnik was no accident. *A Nation at Risk* made rescuing our failing schools a matter of Cold War–era national security as well as global economic competitiveness. They could have said "the average achievement of high school students on standardized tests is lower now than 26 years ago, when Jimmy Hoffa was caught" or "when Jack Kerouac wrote *On the Road*." But that would have been off-message.

The report was scary. How accurate was it?

"THE BAD NEWS IS RIGHT"

The apparent "risk" in *A Nation at Risk* was a basic manipulation of statistics, one that is actually acknowledged briefly in the report itself: "It is important, of course, to recognize that the average citizen today is better educated and more knowledgeable than the average citizen of a generation ago—more literate, and exposed to more mathematics, literature, and science."

If citizens are more educated and knowledgeable, how can you fear a "rising tide of mediocrity"? The average decline in performance on standardized tests between the 1960s and the 1980s was real, but it was easily predictable, and in fact entirely explained by the fact that larger numbers and more diverse groups of students were taking the tests in the 1980s than in the 1960s.

A follow-up analysis of historical test score data commissioned by the Department of Energy in 1990 showed the opposite of what *A Nation at Risk* claimed. When broken down by population subgroup, "To our surprise, on nearly every measure, we found steady or slightly improving trends," wrote the authors of the Sandia Report, who weren't educators or partisans with an ideological stake but rather engineers taking an objective look at the data for economic planning purposes.

"Steady or slightly improving trends" means that student test scores between the 1960s and the 1980s didn't get worse—they stayed the same or got better. The aggregate downward trend on the SATs was produced by a statistical effect known as "Simpson's paradox." Although each subgroup—boys, girls, whites, blacks, Hispanics, low-income students, high-income students—was improving or holding steady from year to year, the mix of students was changing. In the 1960s schools were in the process of racial integration. Men dominated in higher education. Only top students took standardized tests or applied to college. By the eighties, however, society was more open, and college was more important. More kids of all backgrounds were taking the tests—more women, more racial minorities, more working-class students. The lower average scores of less advantaged groups pulled down the overall average.

A Nation at Risk was covered on radio and TV. There was a series of public hearings attended by hundreds around the country. President Reagan mentioned it in several speeches. The Sandia Report, which brought good news, had no such public profile; instead, it was the target of suppression efforts by Department of Education officials, including Diane Ravitch, who wrote an op-ed headlined, "U.S. Schools: The Bad News Is Right," and Deputy Secretary of Education David Kearns, who allegedly told the authors, "You bury this or I'll bury you."

The narrative of educational system failure based on either low or declining test scores was just too compelling for its own good and too useful for those in power. It sounds truer every decade that it's repeated. Over the years of political jockeying, tests have taken their place as, first, the measure of our school system's performance and, then, the solution to the problems they inevitably diagnose.

1980s: THE ACHIEVEMENT GAP

Throughout the 1980s, partly in response to *A Nation at Risk*, more schools gave more tests more often: the Iowa Basic Skills Test, the California Achievement Test, the Stanford Achievement Test, and more. States and district bureaucracies grew to administer and collect the results of these tests. And states began attaching the tests to consequences for districts, schools, and individual students, such as grade promotion and high school graduation.

Immediately a disproportionate impact was felt on historically disadvantaged groups, including the poor, African Americans, English learners, recent immigrants, rural, and Native American students. True to their historical origins, standardized exit tests ended up denying certain groups their high school diplomas at higher rates than if the diplomas were based on class grades alone.

FairTest, a coalition of education reformers and civil rights activists, formed in 1985 to respond to the new tests, released a paper in 1987 titled, "Fallout from the Testing Explosion: How America's 100 Million Standardized Tests Undermine Excellence and Equity." The paper argued, "Standardized tests often produce results that are inaccurate, inconsistent, and biased against minority, female, and low-income students. Such tests shift control and authority into the hands of the unregulated testing industry and can undermine school achievement by narrowing the curriculum, frustrating teachers, and driving students out of school."

A litany of complaints arose about testing from the point of view of equity, pedagogy, and influence on teachers, complaints that were just emerging then yet still sound current thirty years later.

CLEAR NATIONAL STANDARDS: 1980s AND 1990s

The eighties and early nineties were not a time when it was fashionable to address racism or child poverty directly; rather, it was the era of "ending welfare as we know it." Arguments about cultural bias in testing were dismissed as cultural relativism. Educational tests were positioned again and again as a means of diagnosing the perpetual crisis in education and, at the same time, a cure.

"The first President Bush had proposals for national testing," Bob Schaeffer of FairTest recounts. "That was defeated by a strange-bedfellows coalition of progressive educators, civil rights activists, and [archconservative 1960s antifeminist] Phyllis Schlafly. Then Bill Clinton pushed for some form of national testing. The political alignment changed, with more mainstream Democrats supporting those kinds of proposals, but for partisan reasons many more Republicans opposing it."

Bill Clinton claimed to represent a "Third Way" in politics—smarter government, not bigger government. More tests, more data, fit into that technocratic vision. On the occasion of Clinton's first term in 1992, Marc Tucker, an influential reformer and president of the National Center on Education and the Economy, wrote a letter to the new First Lady, Hillary Clinton, laying out an ambitious four-part plan reimagining the education system as "a seamless web of opportunities to develop one's skills that literally extends from cradle to grave and is the same system for everyone—young and old, poor and rich, worker and full-time student."

Entered into the Congressional Record in 1998, what became known as the "Dear Hillary" letter mostly focused on Tucker's longstanding interest in workplace preparedness and a national apprenticeship system modeled on Germany's. But Part 4 laid out an ambitious program of elementary and secondary education reform that is fully recognizable two decades later. Tucker called for an "aggressive" move toward school choice, for freeing school administrators from union rules, and making school professionals "fully accountable." Most of all, he wanted uniformly high, unyielding performance standards, stating, "Clear national standards of performance in general education . . . set to the level of the best achieving nations in the world for students of 16, and public schools are expected to bring all but the most severely handicapped up to that standard. . . . A national system of education in which curriculum, pedagogy, *examinations*, and teacher education and licensure systems are all linked to the national standards" (emphasis mine).

Marion Brady, an education reformer who began his career in 1952, says the impact of "Dear Hillary" grew in tandem with another notable sally that appeared around the same time. This one came from the right: a 1995 *Washington Post* editorial by Milton Friedman, mandarin of the conservative movement and winner of the 1976 Nobel Prize in Economics. In the piece, titled, "Public Schools: Make Them Private," Friedman called for a voucher system enabling students to use taxpayer money to attend independent schools. Like Tucker, he focused on innovation and choice, with the underlying justification of reducing class stratification.

Vouchers would eventually prove politically radioactive in most places. But marketization—in the form of charter schools, homeschooling, and a growing role for various for-profit technology and service providers—remains the goal of a significant faction of the education reform movement. Testing assumes an important role as the basis of decision making within that marketplace.

HOW THEY DO IT IN OTHER COUNTRIES

Though reformers like Tucker and the authors of *A Nation at Risk* invoked the specter of our foreign rivals, it was actually in the nineties that the United States began to diverge from most other countries in its use of tests. Three-fourths of students in developed countries attend a school that administers a standardized test of some sort, but no country in the world administers as many standardized tests as the United States or uses them for the same purposes—particularly, to grade and punish teachers and schools. "The US is extraordinary," said Dylan Wiliam, the British curriculum expert. "In basically every country apart from the US, there's a tradition of examining kids at the end of learning. In the US [tests are] used for teachers."

As Wiliam notes, the most common type of high-stakes standardized test, found throughout Europe, Asia, Africa, and South America, is the high school exit/college entrance exam. In the UK it's the General Certificate of Education Advanced Levels, also known as the A-levels. In Central and Eastern Europe it's known as the Maturitat, or Matura. Even Finland, which is held up in US ed-reform conversations as the most laid-back yet highest-performing school system in the world, gives a national matriculation exam (*ylioppilas-tutkinto*) for entrance into college. In countries like Germany and France tracking exams are also given at the beginning of high school to determine students' paths either to university or technical schools and apprenticeships.

Wiliam said evidence shows limiting testing to a single occasion can spur deeper learning and higher achievement. Because students won't be tested at the end of each year, teachers adapt their teaching styles for long-term memory and deep mastery of their subjects. Also, a system that administers just one or only a few big tests can afford to spend the big bucks to design and grade tests with lots of free-form long answers, including complex, multistep math problems and essays that require research and referral to documents. One equivalent in the United States would be the AP exams, which are written and graded by subject-matter experts and require students to demonstrate critical thinking as well as memorized knowledge through long written responses. They also charge a fee, currently $91 per student.

Countries with high-performing students, including Singapore, Finland, Denmark, and Australia, are marked by diverse national assessment systems that consider exams alongside real student work, like research projects, science experiments, and presentations.

Even when used sparingly, high-stakes, single-occasion tests around the world bring with them all the familiar ills of severe anxiety, cheating, and gaming. This is especially true in the many nations where seats in public university systems are rationed according to the results of these tests. In China, where high-stakes tests were more or less invented with the Imperial civil service exam around the year 600, students take tests for competitive admission into middle school, high school, and, finally, university. "The *gaokao* (college entrance exam) robs Chinese students of their curiosity, creativity, and childhood," as Jiang Xueqin, deputy principal of one of Beijing's most prestigious high schools, wrote in 2011.

South Korea is another paradigmatic case. It is among the top five highest-performing countries in the world on the PISA exam and boasts the most highly educated population in the world, a feat reached in a sprint from very low levels post–World War II. The Korean education system is dominated by the tests that determine competitive entrance into middle school, high school, and college. From the earliest elementary school years Korean students commonly spend forty or more hours a week studying in private "cram schools"—over and above regular school hours. Despite repeated crackdowns on the practice, parents spend more than $19 billion a year on private tutoring, more than half what the government spends on public education.

Yet for all their achievement, Korean students are also, according to surveys that are part of the PISA exam, the unhappiest in the world. Between one in eight to one in four students reportedly considered suicide in 2012, and the nation had the second highest rate of youth suicide in the Organisation for Economic Co-operation and Development (OECD). They commonly refer to the senior year of high school as the "year of hell."

GOALS 2000

Where US education most differs from other industrialized nations is in the high degree of local school control. The Elementary and Secondary Education Act (ESEA), first passed as part of the War on Poverty in 1965, is the federal government's most significant intervention in K–12 education policy. It awarded what is now billions of dollars in aid to "Title 1" schools with high-poverty populations. This sum, though large, has never been more than 3 to 7 percent of total public education spending. So education policymaking on the federal level has historically been a matter of *Carrots, Sticks, and the Bully Pulpit*, as the title of a 2012 edited volume by American Enterprise Institute's (AEI) Frederick Hess and Andrew P. Kelly put it.

In the 1990s, in a highly polarized political environment, the full "Dear Hillary" agenda faltered. Both the right and the left fought apprenticeships and vocational "tracking" as un-American. Further, the fight over healthcare reform exhausted Bill Clinton's domestic policy momentum.

The education reform package that did make it through, known as Goals 2000, consisted of school choice and tests. Clinton's 1994 reauthorization of the ESEA introduced for the first time a set of universal, voluntary content and performance standards to be aligned with the first federally mandated tests: one each in the grade spans three through five, six through nine, and ten through twelve. An accountability system would identify schools whose students could not achieve the necessary test scores and target them for sanctions. During the period from 1994 to 2000 most states responded to the law by adopting content and performance standards, collecting longitudinal data, and administering more and more tests.

"Clinton's connections in Arkansas sold to the business community a plan to increase school revenues through taxation in exchange for more testing," explains Schaeffer of FairTest. Testing was like a form of 10K reporting for schools: the regular collecting and publishing of data would tell the "shareholders" exactly what they were getting for their money. "More money in exchange for more test-based accountability: that's exactly how it was done."

Tests serve multiple purposes in this approach to reform. They are the means of enforcing standards and the basis of informed choice for families. Test scores provide the data for a data-driven education policy that sends resources to winning schools and shuts down losers. And some argue that tests are employed as a political weapon to undermine the power of teachers' unions and push forward market-based reform.

Most states published their test results and began to attach a broad range of consequences, rattling behind them like tin cans on a bumper. For students it was diagnosis of learning disabilities, tracking, grade promotion, and high school graduation. Schools could be designated for takeover, reorganization, closing, extra help, or more resources for low-performing schools and rewards for high-performing schools. Districts could be subject to similar interventions from the state level.

BONANZA!

Thanks to the new laws, the testing industry, which was still controlled by a few tradition-bound companies with nineteenth-century roots, experienced an unexpected bonanza that dwarfed its previous expansion in the 1920s. Test sales grew from $7 million in 1955 to $263 million in 1997—a 3000 percent increase in constant dollars. As late as October 2011 just three companies—Harcourt, CTB/McGraw-Hill, and Riverside Publishing—still wrote 96 percent of the statewide tests, while Pearson, one of the largest publishers in the world, was a leading scorer.

NO EXCUSES

A central justification for this bipartisan shift toward testing was set forth in the 2000 book *No Excuses: Lessons from 21 High-Performing, High-Poverty Schools*, published by the conservative Heritage Foundation. The author was Samuel Casey Carter, a thirty-four-year-old fellow of the foundation who had attended Catholic schools, joined a Benedictine order, and briefly studied to be a priest. He told the stories of schools from small towns like Portland, Arkansas, to cities like Detroit, Michigan, that were succeeding with dedicated leadership, an emphasis on basic skills, parental outreach, and, above all, standards and tests.

Carter listed seven common traits of these schools. Number 4, he wrote, was "Rigorous and regular testing leads to continuous student achievement." He explained, "High expectations without a means of measurement are hollow." The racist origins of standardized testing, however, were not part of this framing. "Diagnosis is not discrimination," Carter wrote. Carter became one of the strongest voices to inculcate this powerful and seductive idea: improve test scores and you will erase poverty.

The book, like *A Nation at Risk* before it, had some math problems. Carter chose a set of schools that were, by definition, outliers. Then he simply asserted, without evidence, that if every high-poverty school had talented enough leaders and worked hard enough, they too could become high performers.

You might compare the overwhelming influence of poverty on test scores to the influence of height on someone's chance of playing in the NBA. The average height of an NBA player in 2013 was six feet seven inches tall. But there were eight guys who were under six feet tall. Does the existence of those eight players prove that if you are under six feet, you have "no excuse" for not making the NBA?

When I asked Carter how he came by the conviction that poverty could be "no excuse" for student performance, his answer was a mishmash of anecdotal evidence and conservative faith. "My mother was very proud to tell us that she was an Irish ditch-digger's daughter," he said. "My great-aunt Kathleen Craig only had a high school education but she was a total polymath. . . . It was never my personal experience that demographics had anything to do with destiny."

I asked: What *would* help change the destiny of poor kids? "I was really convinced that the system to produce the greatest good for the greatest number of people was a free market," Carter said. For public schools that means competition and executive-style leadership. "*No Excuses* is an application of basic well-understood management principles," Carter said. "If you can't measure it, you can't manage it. And you've got to measure like you mean it and monitor what you want to improve."

Today "no excuses" is ed-reform dogma, upheld by charter school chains such as KIPP and Uncommon Schools, big-city superintendents, right-wing think tanks like Heritage and social advocacy groups such as the Education Trust and Michelle Rhee's StudentsFirst. The common refrain is that erasing the achievement gap is the "civil rights movement of our time." Test scores are the linchpin of this movement.

Wendy Kopp, the founder of Teach for America (TFA), which sends graduates of elite colleges into high-poverty schools with minimal training for two-year commitments, repeated this philosophy to me in a 2012 interview:

A few years ago there was a Gallup poll asking, Why do you believe we have low educational outcomes in low-income

communities? The top three answers were student motivation, parental involvement, and home-life issues.

We asked our [Teach for America] corps members and
alumni, and their top three answers were teacher quality,
principal quality, and expectations at the school level.

Once you've taught successfully in low-income communities you realize, wait, this is not about kids not having the
motivation to do well or parents not caring. This is about
us—teachers and school leaders working hard. We can do
more to provide kids with the opportunities they deserve.

This is a laudable moral attitude for TFA corps members to
maintain. It's an example of a psychologically healthy internal locus of
control: the belief that one's own efforts determine the outcome of a
situation. But it's possible to be too rigid in writing such an attitude
into the law. Dr. Michael McGill is superintendent of Scarsdale Public
Schools, one of the best-regarded districts in the nation. "I've been
doing this work for about two hundred years," he said, tongue in
cheek. "I began as a school superintendent in 1973. And so for me the
story goes back before NCLB to the early 1980s and *A Nation at Risk.*"

Within the "no excuses" movement he sees an unholy cross-
pollination, "a misinterpretation of a premise or several premises that
were liberal premises in the sixties and seventies. Back then, when I
was in grad school, there were studies coming out pointing up the
disparities in performance between rich and poor, white and black
students," he said. The research made these disparities more explicit
and harder to ignore. This challenged a prevailing complacence
among some educators.

"Up until that time the problem is seen as not a school problem.
You know: 'these kids come without breakfast, whadyagonna do?' At
the time liberal educators say we can't take that point of view—we
have to assume every child is capable of learning. If we as educators
start out from the assumption that they can't, then they won't. We
have to give our best effort and *act as if.*" This "acting as if" is exactly
the attitude expressed by TFA corps members.

"The big mistake that NCLB makes," said McGill, "is it takes
that theoretical or philosophical stance toward student achievement

as literally true. Every child is capable of learning at a high level. And if you don't do that as a teacher, that's your problem and we're going to hold you accountable." It's a fine thing for teachers and school leaders to believe wholeheartedly that every child has an equal opportunity to learn. It's another thing to penalize teachers and schools for children failing to perform. Imagine that a gym teacher could be fired unless he could get every student in his class to run a seven-minute mile.

THE TEXAS MIRACLE

The most important no-excuses reform of the 1990s happened in Texas. In 1993 Sandy Kress, a Dallas lawyer and school board member—and, incidentally, a Democrat—oversaw the publication of a policy report on accountability. Like Samuel Casey Carter, Kress argued that because some schools do a better job than others educating low-income children, "schools and the people running them can and should be held responsible for student results."

So that year the state legislature passed rules creating a new assessment system. Schools would have to break out the test results of minority, low-income, and disabled students and would be ranked based on test scores and graduation rates.

As Bill Ratliff, who was a state senator at the time and later lieutenant governor, sees it, the reforms were actually meant to give more autonomy to local schools, not less.

> We had a public education code that was a thousand pages or more long. Any time a particular school wanted to do something with respect to teaching methods or curriculum or lesson plans, they had to look in the code to see whether or not they were authorized, and if they were not specifically authorized they took the position that they couldn't make any changes at the local level. In the early nineties we tried to change that paradigm. I sat down and took the public education code and stripped out the vast majority of those mandates. . . . We said, all right, the state of Texas will stop talking about methodology and look at outcomes.

Outcomes measured, of course, by tests.

In Texas the new focus on outcomes produced immediate results. Dozens of high schools suddenly reported zero dropout rates. Reading and math scores went up while achievement gaps shrank. When George W. Bush ran for president, with no foreign policy experience and little executive experience, he leaned heavily on the "Texas Miracle" in education as a policy win from his time as governor. Houston's superintendent of schools, Rod Paige, who oversaw a plunge in dropouts in that city, came to Washington with him as secretary of education. Sandy Kress became a Bush presidential policy adviser and, simultaneously, a lobbyist for Pearson, the largest company involved in creating tests. Kress would go on to be the key architect of No Child Left Behind.

THE BLUEPRINT

The legislative blueprint for No Child Left Behind was released just three days after George W. Bush's inauguration and was initially well received on both sides of the Hill. Different versions passed the Senate and House in early 2001 and went to conference committee over the summer of 2001.

The law more than doubled the number of federally required standardized tests. It declared that all states must test at least 95 percent of children annually in grades three through eight in reading and mathematics and report test scores by race, ethnicity, low-income status, disability status, and limited English proficiency. On top of their own tests, states would be required to participate in NAEP, the Nation's Report Card, previously a voluntary benchmark test.

Schools that failed to report "adequate yearly progress" toward proficiency for each and every subgroup of students would be publicly designated "in need of improvement." If they continued to miss targets, they would be subject to various policy incentives year after year—both carrots, such as funding for outside tutoring services, and sticks, such as "exit vouchers" allowing students to leave public for private schools, restructuring and replacement of staff, or closing the school. By 2014 all students, in all subgroups, were supposed to achieve 100 percent proficiency on state tests. No exceptions. No excuses.

COMMON SENSE ALMOST PREVAILS

Late-breaking information about NCLB's procrustean design came close to killing the bill. State leaders raised concerns that under NCLB, sooner or later, every school in the country would be declared a failure. Indeed, by 2011, before a majority of states had received waivers from the consequences of the law, about half of the nation's public schools were "failing" under NCLB.

Other observers raised questions about attaching such high stakes to tests, given the unreliability of the tests themselves. The law didn't put money toward developing new, better tests; as ever, it would be up to the highly concentrated assessment industry to produce and market them.

In May 2001 the *New York Times* ran a series of front-page exposés about screw-ups in that industry. In the three years prior to NCLB, their investigation showed, test companies had the highest level of recorded errors of any period in history, affecting millions of students in twenty states, not surprising for an industry expanding so quickly. Worse, companies lied and stonewalled to cover up errors— not a confidence booster for the future.

NOT SO MIRACULOUS

As for the Texas Miracle itself, it, like *A Nation at Risk* before it, would be discredited, again to deaf ears. In 1999 Julian Vasquez Heilig was a freshly minted master's graduate from the University of Michigan interviewing for a position with the Houston Independent School District. "I sat down with the assistant superintendent, and she told me they'd closed the achievement gap and had 0 percent dropout rates. This was 1999. Rod Paige was superintendent. I started working in the research and accountability department and was able to see behind the scenes what was happening. I was really troubled."

Eventually, for his PhD dissertation at the University of Texas, Heilig tracked forty-five thousand Houston students and found results very different from what his and other school districts were reporting. Heilig and other researchers found that 40 to 45 percent of African American and Latino students—those who failed any core course—were being held back in the ninth grade in Houston. They could take sophomore classes, but they were officially reclassified as freshmen, meaning the lowest performers would sit out the tenth grade accountability test. Larger numbers of students were classified as English-language learners and/or special ed, exempting them from the tests as well. When it came to eleventh grade, the tactics got more insidious. The state of Texas eventually changed their reporting rules in response to evidence that these students were being "pushed out," advised to leave and take the GED, then counted as transfer students rather than dropouts. (Heilig continues to document similar practices in Texas schools today.)

The majority of high schools in the city, Heilig found, had falsified their dropout rates. The effect was not small. At the same time that the US Department of Education was listing Houston's high school dropout rate above 30 percent, Houston itself was reporting to the state a rate below 2 percent. Heilig's dissertation would not appear until 2006. But he was not the only researcher on the case.

Walt Haney, now retired, was a senior research associate in Boston College's Center for the Study of Testing, Evaluation and Educational Policy. He started his career in education as a conscientious objector to the Vietnam War, teaching in impoverished Laos. He did his graduate work at Harvard. For over twenty years he's served as an expert witness in a series of lawsuits by civil rights groups against states over the misuse of standardized tests.

Haney was among the first to publicly debunk the Texas Miracle, publishing his initial findings in 2000. He's a dogged researcher, stacking his office with boxes full of paper as he combs through state records and correlates the results of tests with other demographic data, such as immigration, incarceration, GEDs, and college enrollment rates. "The claims were that achievement had improved, test score gaps had decreased, and the dropout rate had decreased," he told me. "I concluded that the evidence on all three points was not sound, that in fact the dropout stats were bogus. When I analyzed the twenty-year enrollment data by grade, race, and number of grads, the actual dropout rate was four times worse than the reported rate."

Education officials in Texas applied a wide range of techniques to "juke the stats." They aggressively flunked ninth graders before they could get to tenth grade. They overtly or covertly encouraged kids to drop out of school, then claimed that they had repatriated to Mexico or had left to study for the GED. They used the wrong student ID numbers so students would get lost in the state system. Sometimes, after holding students back, they would assign them to catch-up "supersemesters," where they earned multiple credits for completing easy work on a computer over a couple of days. (Lorenzo Garcia, superintendent of the El Paso Independent School District, went to prison for pulling these kinds of dirty tricks in the late 2000s, as discussed in Chapter 1.)

Heilig found that even as students' scores on the state tests rose, the scores on a non-high-stakes college readiness test were flat. Far more students took the GED rather than graduated from high school. And the numbers of students taking the tenth-grade tests who were classified as special education and hence not counted in schools' accountability ratings nearly doubled between 1994 and 1998. Since NCLB passed, Haney has documented at least three states where these kinds of behaviors have spread in reaction to high-stakes policies.

SOFT BIGOTRIES

September 11, 2001, brought a moment of renewed national unity. Congressional leaders, including Democrat Ted Kennedy and Republican John Boehner, rallied behind Bush's education legislation as a policy that all Americans could feel good about. No Child Left Behind, conceived on shaky evidence and trailing unintended consequences, became law in early 2002.

Bush highlighted the law in a long section of his second-term acceptance speech at the 2004 Republican National Convention in New York City. While record numbers of protestors were being arrested in the nearby streets of Times Square, he intoned a favorite phrase from speechwriter Michael Gerson, the ace wordsmith behind phrases like "axis of evil" and "we don't want the smoking gun to be a mushroom cloud." This was one Bush had often trotted out on the campaign trail—"the soft bigotry of low expectations."

BUSH: I believe every child can learn and every school must teach, so we passed the most important federal education reform in history. Because we acted, children are making sustained progress in reading and math, America's schools are getting better, and nothing will hold us back.

To build a more hopeful America, we must help our children reach as far as their vision and character can take them.

Tonight, I remind every parent and every teacher, I say to every child: no matter what your circumstance, no matter where you live, your school will be the path to the promise of America.

[APPLAUSE]

We are transforming our schools by raising standards and focusing on results. We are insisting on accountability, empowering parents and teachers, and making sure that local people are in charge of their schools.

[APPLAUSE]

By testing every child, we are identifying those who need help, and we're providing a record level of funding to get them that help.

BUSH: In northeast Georgia, Gainesville Elementary School is mostly Hispanic and 90 percent poor. And this year 90 percent of its students passed state tests in reading and math.

[APPLAUSE]

The principal—the principal expresses the philosophy of his school this way: "We don't focus on what we can't

do at this school; we focus on what we can do. And we do
whatever it takes to get kids across the finish line."

See, this principal is challenging the soft bigotry of low
expectations.

[APPLAUSE]

And that is the spirit of our education reform and the
commitment of our country: No dejaremos a ningún niño
atrás. We will leave no child behind.

THE WANDERING CUT SCORES

In the 2000s test-based accountability became the hammer, and
everything in education looked like a nail. "Data-driven decision
making" became a watchword, with tests as the data.

Standardized tests had many useful properties for politicians.
They produced authoritative-sounding numbers, as Walter Lippmann
had observed in the 1920s. Yet unlike other statistics that politicians
have to contend with, such as unemployment or air-quality figures,
test scores are more easily manipulated to produce any desired outcome. That's handy in case leaders want to trumpet a victory before
an election or drive a hard bargain with teachers' unions.

A testing company's brief is to design a test that validly and reliably assesses a given set of standards, providing predictable results,
and to score it correctly. It's up to educators in each state to decide
who passes or fails the test. Just as Alfred Binet set the norm for his
intelligence tests at 75 percent, states have the prerogative to set the
cut score—higher if they want to declare a crisis in education, close
down schools, fire teachers, and shift resources to charter schools,
and lower if they want to say that everything is going great.

To take just one example, in New York State in the 2000s the
tested proficiency level of students rose steadily. Mayor Bloomberg
ran for reelection in part on those improved test scores. But in 2009
the cutoff scores, which had drifted lower and lower over the years,
were readjusted. The city's pass rate in reading for grades three
through eight then immediately fell from 68.8 to 42.4 percent, and in
math it fell from 81.8 to 54 percent.

OBAMA, RACE TO THE TOP, AND COMMON CORE

When President Obama was elected in 2008 some hoped he might slow the relentless march of testing in favor of dealing with educational resources. Instead, he beat the drum even faster and louder.

In June of Obama's first year a task force of progressive advocates and scholars released the "Broader, Bolder Approach to Education" manifesto, calling for school funding to be equalized and for supplementing the education system with high-quality preschool, afterschool, health care, and mental health services for children and other supports for parents. Elaine Weiss—whose Economic Policy Institute convened the original Broader, Bolder task force—told me that, "a smart accountability system would look at all the inputs for schools. . . . In a country in which we have so much child poverty and inequity, we need to ensure that all children have the basics—that kids are not getting to school hungry, going to sleep in shelters, and going to school with so many barriers in the way." At the same time, a rival group issued a manifesto calling for redoubling the test-driven agenda: tougher standards and pushing school leaders harder to raise achievement. Arne Duncan, who Obama brought along from Chicago's public school system to lead the Department of Education, was the only big-city school leader to sign both manifestoes.

The country was in the throes of a financial and economic crisis after the collapse of the mortgage market and banking industry. When Obama came into office, there was a brief political window to introduce new federal spending as a means of arresting economic decline. But rather than create and fund new social programs aimed at schools or children, in July 2009 Duncan announced Race to the Top. This was a $4 billion package of competitive education grants, paid for with the stimulus package passed earlier in the year. States could apply by introducing reform plans that met a set of core principles.

Duncan outlined the four principles of Race to the Top in a series of speeches. As specified in a White House press release, these were:

- adopting internationally benchmarked standards and assessments that prepare students for success in college and the workplace;

- recruiting, developing, rewarding, and retaining effective teachers and principals;
- building data systems that measured student success and inform teachers and principals how they can improve their practices; and
- turning around the nation's lowest-performing schools.

The first principle, college-ready standards and assessments, referred to what became the Common Core State Standards initiative. This was officially a state, not a federal, initiative led by the National Governors Association and a nonprofit called Achieve.org. It was bigger than any previous attempt to establish US goals for what children should actually be learning in school. The watchword of the Common Core was "fewer, higher, deeper"—promoting deeper learning by focusing on what was truly important, which meant reading, writing, and math. Although the federal government, for political reasons, didn't want to mandate the Common Core from above, the prospect of Race to the Top money incentivized forty-eight states initially to adopt the standards. And Obama's Department of Education awarded a total of $350 million to two multistate coalitions, PARCC (representing 22 million students), and Smarter Balanced (19 million students), to develop a set of new tests aligned with the Common Core to be unveiled in the 2014–2015 school year. This was the first time federal money had gone to actually create educational assessments.

With two sets of policies, NCLB/Race to the Top and the Common Core, traveling at varying speeds on parallel tracks, an uncomfortable gap would appear and begin to widen: The Department of Education was rewarding states for attaching more and more stakes to existing tests even as it advertised that new, much better tests were coming to replace them.

"World-class standards are the foundation on which you will build your reforms," Duncan said in a speech at the 2009 Governors Education Symposium. But the real foundation was not standards. It was tests. As had become clear from decades of state-level experience by then, tests are greedy. They are the yardstick of success by which everything else is measured, so they become the focus:

"Adopting internationally benchmarked standards and assessments"—new and harder tests.

"Building data systems that measured student success" using test scores.

"Turning around the nation's lowest-performing schools," performance defined by test scores.

The only place where the connection with tests was not immediately clear was in the second item on the list: recruiting, developing, rewarding, and retaining effective teachers and principals.

In his speech to the governors Duncan called "our method of evaluating teachers . . . basically broken." The numbers bore that out. Across the country 99 percent of teachers were rated "effective," by subjective and varying means. Duncan and others in the administration were convinced that the way to rigorously and objectively rate teachers was to incorporate "achievement data," which is to say, test scores. "How can you possibly talk about teacher quality without factoring in student achievement?" Duncan asked.

This became the most prescriptive piece of Race to the Top. In at least three states, laws restricted evaluating teachers or awarding tenure based on test scores. Race to the Top did not dictate that states adopt the Common Core or establish a specific proportion of charter schools, but it did demand that any state wanting the money get rid of this prohibition.

A major reason Race to the Top–related reforms went wrong was that states were in a rush for the money. These were dire economic times. There were historic deficits at the state level—a cumulative shortfall of $113.2 billion for fiscal year 2009, and $142.6 billion in fiscal year 2010.

Compared to other measures of student achievement, tests were cheap. States didn't have the luxury of time to carefully design, pilot, and vet value-added measurement systems or other new reforms. They created the plans and put them into place, and the federal government funded them in eighteen states and DC.

THE BILLIONAIRE BOYS' CLUB

The political science term of art is that policy in the United States is created by an "iron triangle" of Congress, the bureaucracy, and interest groups. This is nothing new. Still, it is worth noting the very special relationship between the Department of Education under President Obama and the nation's wealthiest people, particularly through the nonprofit, philanthropic Bill and Melinda Gates Foundation.

Bill Gates, the founder of Microsoft and the country's richest man, began his philanthropic adventures with international health in the nineties. But his wife, Melinda French Gates, had always had education nearest to her heart. In 1999 her Gates Learning Foundation merged with the William H. Gates Foundation, which Bill Gates had set up for his father upon his retirement, to form the Bill and Melinda Gates Foundation. In 2006 Warren Buffett, the second-richest man in the country, pledged most of his fortune to the Gates Foundation as well; today its endowment is valued at $41 billion.

The Gates Foundation is the largest private foundation in the world and, proportionately, the largest private funder that the US education system has ever seen. Its influence has often been compared to that of the Carnegie and Rockefeller foundations in the nineteenth and early twentieth centuries. But whereas those Gilded Age millionaires set up their own institutions, from libraries to universities, Gates has chosen to site its programs within existing public schools and fund a wide variety of organizations to carry out its research and other initiatives. Its influence is felt everywhere, from politics to research to media to afterschool programs. (Disclosure, and for example: the Gates Foundation funded me to write an ebook in 2011, it funded the nonprofit education news service where I had a blog in 2013, and it funds education coverage, among other areas, at NPR, where I now work.) "Our role in philanthropy in general is as a catalyst," Vicki Phillips, the director of the US education program, told me in an interview. "We never look at our accomplishments as being *us*. Our proverbial 'we' is all of our partners across the country—states, districts, and groups like the Council of Chief State School Officers."

That said, from the start the personal interests and convictions of its founding family have driven the foundation's agenda, the more so when Bill Gates stepped down from Microsoft in 2008 to chair it full time. The emphasis in their grant making on data and metrics has permeated the entire philanthropic world. "We are big fans of the potential of data and tracking," as Phillips puts it. In the international programs they track metrics like how many wells dug and how many doses of malarial medication administered. In the domestic education program the metrics of choice have been test scores.

Arne Duncan recruited both his chief of staff, Margot Rogers, and one of his assistant deputy secretaries, Jim Shelton, from the Gates Foundation. The administration waived ethics rules, allowing Shelton, Rogers, and others in the Department to consult more freely with their former colleagues at the foundation. Gates funded the initial development of the Common Core State Standards through the nonprofit Achieve, supported charter schools, and in 2009 pledged $335 million to raise student achievement—measured through test scores—and promote teacher evaluation systems tied to student performance—also measured through test scores.

Even the competitive structure of Race to the Top itself, a grant process in which applications could win "points" based on a system of priorities set by the Department, is reminiscent of today's philanthropic grant making. At the time civil rights groups led by the National Association for the Advancement of Colored People (NAACP) protested that this conditional method of funding left states full of poorer students at a disadvantage because of their inability to dedicate resources to the grant application process. They objected to what looked like a never-ending pileup of unfunded and underfunded mandates descending on poverty-stricken schools.

Diane Ravitch, a conservative education official under the first George Bush, has reinvented herself in the last decade as perhaps the single-most prominent and controversial critic of no-excuses-style school reform. Her 2010 bestseller *The Death and Life of the Great American School System* has a chapter titled, "The Billionaire Boys Club," characterizing the influence of three foundations that are top donors to public schools: Gates, the Eli and Edythe Broad Foundation, and the Walton Family Foundation. The full roster of the "Billionaire Boys Club" promoting a similar ed-reform agenda would include former mayor of New York City Michael Bloomberg, the

Koch brothers, the education task force of the American Legislative Exchange Council (ALEC), the members of a group of wealthy financiers known as the Democrats for Education Reform, and Laurene Powell Jobs, the widow of Apple founder Steve Jobs.

This influx of private wealthy interests has upset the apple cart of school reform, challenging old alliances. Although teachers' unions remain a powerful force in both local and national politics, for example, many mainline Democrats and progressives, notably within the Obama administration, have "defected" to the ed-reform agenda that includes charters, standards, and metrics.

The Common Core, meanwhile, has split the right side of the political aisle, with the Republican National Committee opposing it on states' rights grounds while ALEC, the powerful corporate-dominated lobbying group, supports it. Major past ALEC contributor Exxon Mobil has even run national TV commercials in favor of the Common Core.

Many of the strongest ed-tech advocates, too, are on the conservative side of the political spectrum, like Jeb Bush, former Florida governor, 2016 Republican presidential hopeful, and leader of the Foundation for Excellence in Education.

The Common Core, together with ed-tech, creates a massive business opportunity. Gates spoke about this in a keynote address to the 2013 South by Southwest Education conference, an offshoot of the music and technology industry conferences focused entirely on the growing convergence between education, entrepreneurship, and technology. "Because of the Common Core, developers no longer have to cater to dozens or even hundreds of varying standards," he told the crowd. "Instead, they can focus on creating the best applications that align with the core." This idea about the power of standards is borrowed from the web. Online, interoperability rules allow developers to create pages and applications that are viewable and usable by anyone with a browser or mobile operating system.

Clayton Christensen, the Harvard Business School professor and management business guru who coined the term "disruptive innovation," has been increasingly focusing on education for the past decade. In the same speech Gates borrowed Christensen's lens to talk about the massive opportunity that technology poses for schools, not only to radically improve the quality of learning and make it more accessible, but also to grow businesses and make lots of money. Because of broadband, computers, and the Common Core, formerly separate and fragmented markets in textbooks, materials, and tests can now be served by integrated products. "When you add textbooks, supplements, and assessments together, you're talking about a $9 billion market that's wide open for innovation," Gates said.

Rupert Murdoch, the CEO of News Corp, went even farther in a 2010 press release, when announcing the purchase of what became his education technology brand Amplify, which produces both tablets and software for the K–12 market. "When it comes to K through 12 education," he wrote, "we see a $500 billion sector in the U.S. alone that is waiting desperately to be transformed by big breakthroughs that extend the reach of great teaching." Casting an acquisitive eye on every public dollar spent on education, he seemed to envision a future when handheld devices and multimedia content largely replace school as we know it.

GATES ON GATES

When I interviewed Gates in March 2013 he defended the tests. "We can make massive strides doing measurement even with imperfect measurement systems," he said. "No Child Left Behind let us know that we weren't doing very well. It was fairly minor in terms of particular ways of solving it, but it did have a wonderful thing that it showed on an absolute and relative basis—for inner-city schools, low-income groups—what a poor job we're doing."

When I asked about the danger of teaching to the test or overemphasizing the basics, he pushed back: "Where they go and create a test in, say, art or music that can distort what you're teaching, just because they want to have a teacher measure, we don't think that's a good thing. But in general the idea that you are tested on your ability to multiply and divide, there's not a problem. It's kind of like, should you teach phonics or just let the kid 'creatively' not ever learn phonics?" he said, warming to his subject. "The whole-language debate. That was wrong."

When Gates was a high school student himself, he spent hour upon hour outside of class learning to use computers and even took a semester off to do an independent study. His own children attend an exclusive private school, Lakeside, that does not administer state standardized tests, and he described using online resources to help feed his son's curiosity about any possible subject.

I asked whether there was room for that kind of exploratory, immersive learning in a testing-driven environment. He dismissed this concern: "You're not going to hurt a highly curious, self-motivated student. Unfortunately that is a small percentage of the kids. Now, you might try to figure out how you get more people into that mode or keep them in that mode. But the fact that we insist people understand math, I don't see the downside of that."

I wanted to ask Gates more about the critics who attest that his education philanthropy is really in the service of Microsoft's business interests and that wealthy donors like himself exercise outsized and undemocratic influence over education policy in ways that serve their own interests more than those of the nation's children, but our time was up after twenty minutes.

LAELA MEETS RICK ROACH

When Laela got her test scores back in the summer of 2013 the school sent her to a "summer reading camp," which was billed as a second chance to raise her scores and let her move on to the fourth grade. But it had the opposite effect, says her mother. "She took a pretest and scored a 76 on the first day. At the end of it she took a post-test and scored a 67—her score actually went down. Then on the last day of summer camp she took the real test and scored a 48, 2 points shy of what she needed."

Laela was "sad" about repeating the third grade, she tells me. "She was completely devastated, confused, embarrassed," elaborates her mother. "Any time anybody would talk about it she would put her head down and start crying or go sit somewhere and sulk. The week before school started we went to meet the teacher, the same she had the previous year. Her teacher was fabulous—I loved her—but when all the other kids were going into their classrooms all excited to see where they would sit, she just walked in with her head down and tears rolling down her face."

Laela's mother started doing research, sitting at the computer in the living room amidst piles of folded laundry. "I sent letters all over the place, and Rick Roach was the one that was right there with us. He really felt for us and wanted to do something to help. He told us he'd been fighting all this for three years now, that these standardized tests do not really measure a kid's ability to read."

Roach, a lifelong teacher, counselor, and coach with brown hair and a graying mustache, served four terms on the school board of Orange County, Florida, which includes Orlando, starting in November 1998, three years before the start of NCLB. He has seven children and two grandchildren, and he's spoken out nationally as a voice for sanity when it comes to poorly designed and inflexibly applied standardized tests. In the summer of 2014 he left the school board to prepare for a State Senate run in order to get closer to changing "the bad decisions made about testing."

One day Roach was attending a speech by his school board chair. "He announced four or five goals that he wanted the schools to adopt and one knocked me off my chair—in two years he wanted 50% of our 10th graders reading at grade level," he said. "I thought, 61% are failing now? That can't be true." Roach's suspicions lay with the test design, not with the performance of Florida children. So he decided to take the test himself. He scored just 10 out of 60 on the math section of the tenth-grade state test, which he says were all guesses, and 62 percent on the reading section. "It seems to me something is seriously wrong," Roach wrote at the time.

> I have a bachelor of science degree, two masters degrees, and 15 credit hours toward a doctorate. I help oversee an organization with 22,000 employees and a $3 billion operations and capital budget, and am able to make sense of complex data related to those responsibilities. . . .
>
> It might be argued that I've been out of school too long, that if I'd actually been in the 10th grade prior to taking the test, the material would have been fresh. But doesn't that miss the point?

A test that can determine a student's future life chances should surely relate in some practical way to the requirements of life. I can't see how that could possibly be true of the test I took.

Roach started digging into the extensive literature of test criticism—Jim Popham, Diane Ravitch, Alfie Kohn—and the nuts and bolts of psychometrics. "I kept getting madder and madder," he said. He found the commonly used practice of predictive score rates—the test writers' best guess as to how many questions a child will get right, which helps calibrate the difficulty of the test—to be tantamount to rigging the tests in advance.

"There are three types of questions on the FCAT: easy, average, and challenging," he said. "The easy ones are designed for 70% to get them right, the average questions are designed for 40–70% to get it right, and the challenging questions are meant for no more than 40%," he explained. "Now on the test I took, 85% of the questions were average or challenging. The failure rate was in it before they put the first pencil mark in a bubble." I didn't independently confirm those numbers. It's true that on a test designed along those lines, a 50 percent pass rate should surprise no one—it's more or less exactly what the test makers predicted. But that pass rate becomes a problem when you have a 100 percent proficiency target.

LAELA MEETS THE WIZARD

Roach decided that the best way to undermine the tests in his state long term while also helping individuals like Laela in the short term was to pull back the curtain. For that he needed a wizard. "I found a former test writer in Kissimmee, bought him breakfast, and got him teaching me how to beat the test," he said.

Bob Alexander has an egg-bald pate and a pair of rimless glasses suiting his nickname, the Wizard. In 1991 he was one of the last people personally hired by Stanley Kaplan, the original founder of the Kaplan SAT prep company. But he grew disillusioned with the marketing tactics of "Big Prep." By the mid-nineties he had moved to Florida and was working as a successful private SAT and ACT tutor, giving workshops for teachers as well, and running a nonprofit to offer his services on a sliding scale to students with financial need. "I have a reputation as the guy you call if you need someone to meet NCAA requirements," he said, referring to promising student-athletes who need to get their scores up in order to qualify for college sports scholarships. "Nine of my guys have made it to the NBA—of course, I can't tell you their names."

In 1998, when Florida began phasing in its state standardized test, the FCAT, he met with a local high school principal who asked him to create an FCAT test-prep course. "I said, I'm not interested—the SAT and ACT are keeping me plenty busy. He said, 'Well, we're not going to care about SATs and ACTs anymore. We'll only care about FCATs. So I won't hire you next year to help with our SAT, but I certainly would hire you for the FCAT and pay you a lot more money.'"

"At the time I was living in Celebration, Florida," a high-end planned community built by the Walt Disney Company. "He told me, if you get into the FCAT business, you will own the biggest house in Celebration. Well, I left Celebration a few years later and built a 3,300-square-foot lake home. And did I have the FCAT to thank for it? Absolutely."

Even though—or especially because—his livelihood springs from standardized tests, Alexander delights in debunking their mysteries for people of all ages. "I tell kids I'm going to teach you to think like a test writer. The more you think like your opponent, the easier it will be to win. And that's the very skill that I taught Laela."

Ali took Laela for just two ninety-minute tutoring sessions with Alexander. Before the first session she gave her daughter a set of eighteen practice questions from Florida's Department of Education website. The girl got just two of the eighteen right. Immediately after the session Ali gave her the questions again and this time she got just two of the eighteen wrong. "It was amazing—night and day. I could not believe it," she said. "She did not learn in an hour and a half how to read better. He taught her how to take a test, basically."

With Roach's backing, Ali's tireless lobbying, and Alexander's coaching, Laela got a second chance about a month into the new school year to take the third-grade exam for promotion. For good measure, they wanted her to take the fourth-grade benchmark as well. She scored 70 on the third-grade test, which had a cutoff of 33. She also scored 63 on the fourth-grade test, which had a cutoff of 35. "The day they found out the scores, the principal called me," says Ali. "She was very monotone. You would think she would be celebrating. They told me she'd be starting Monday, September 30, into the fourth grade—'unless you want to keep her in the third grade, because we weren't expecting this and we didn't order any textbooks for her.' I'm thinking in my head, did this lady really say that?! I said, no, she will be going on to the fourth grade."

Alexander, who's worked as a test writer as well as a coach, sees tests being both overprescribed and misused. "What it boils down to is, we realize that what's happened here in Florida and in many other states where they have a home-brewed test, it was never designed for individual assessment, yet the politicians have turned it into an individual assessment and attached high stakes to it." The FCAT, like many state tests, has both norm-referenced and criterion-referenced sections. "This test was designed to measure a population of students, not whether Laela should go to the fourth grade."

Walt Haney, the professional expert witness, concurs that norm-referenced test design was incorrectly used for the Florida FCAT, as it is in other states. "I've basically concluded that public education in Florida is about the worst in the country" in part because of the misuse of tests, he said, echoing Roach. Florida is transitioning to Common Core–aligned tests and away from the FCAT, but they'll still be part of a high-stakes system. "Professional standards regarding educational psychological tests clearly state that test results should not be used in isolation to make decisions because they're so highly fallible," Haney said. "To use them to make decisions mechanically about individual schools, teachers, or students is a clear violation of these professional standards. It's not just wrong, it's idiotic." Tests, like any human creation, are imperfect. It's when they are used as a sole decisive point of evidence that they become truly harmful.

THINGS FALL APART

A dozen years of carelessly applied high-stakes testing has done little to improve students' thinking or learning as far as tests themselves can tell: small gains on the NAEP, the Nation's Report Card, and no relative gains on PISA, the international achievement test given every other year in sixty-five countries. Between 2002 and 2006, according to the independent nonprofit organization Center on Education Policy, state test scores themselves went up in most states, while achievement gaps narrowed slightly. A second independent study found evidence of improvement in math but not in reading.

By 2010–2011 half of all public schools in the nation stood to miss their 100 percent proficiency targets under No Child Left Behind, which were due to kick in during the 2014–2015 school year. The Department of Education wanted to forestall the political firestorm that would come when so many schools were declared "failing."

Up through the midterm elections in 2010 the Obama administration held out hope to make the reauthorization of the Elementary and Secondary Education Act a bipartisan cause. The ascent of the Tea Party, whose members, like Ronald Reagan before them, opposed the very idea of a Department of Education, drove the nail in the coffin of that plan. Instead, the Education Department took advantage of its regulatory power to grant waivers to states—that is, flexibility on NCLB's rules.

Forty-two states now have waivers specifying their own individual accountability standards. Most have abandoned the inflexible 100 percent proficiency rule in favor of incremental targets. For example, Ohio has pledged to raise the proficiency level in reading for the general population of students from 81.9 percent in 2010–2011 to 86.4 percent in 2014–2015. Though they no longer have ironclad proficiency targets, states are still giving NCLB tests; almost two thousand schools a year are still being closed, and teachers are evaluated based on the scores.

Because of the waivers, however, "NCLB as a common state accountability metric has fallen apart," said Diane Stark Rentner, author of the Center on Education Policy report on NCLB scores. "The data is old now. I can't tell you whether scores are up or down." As long as ESEA isn't reauthorized and with the waivers in place, "accountability" loses any coherence it might once have had.

LONELY DEFENDERS

I had trouble finding anyone who would defend No Child Left Behind as a piece of legislation in 2014.

Frederick Hess, a longtime scholar and advocate of school reform with the conservative American Enterprise Institute, told me, "Back before NCLB, it's important to remember the vast majority of states couldn't even tell you how well kids were doing at reading and math. Each and every state could point to its assessment results and tell you it's performing above the 'national mean.' Prior to NCLB—as mixed as I am on NCLB—school systems found it very easy to excuse poor performance." Of course, they found it nearly as easy to do the same after NCLB, with the help of a little mathematical manipulation.

I ask Hess to refer me to the staunchest defenders NCLB has left. "That would be the Education Trust," he said, a nonprofit advocacy group in DC. But they are cagey about interviewing, agreeing at first to speak only on background.

When I get Daria Hall, the director of K–12 policy development for the Education Trust, on the phone, she said of course poverty is a big part of the problem with education. "We know the achievement gap starts before students enter school. . . . We let far too many kids grow up facing the worst that poverty has to offer." The problem, she said, is that "we give them less inside school too: weak, watered-down, boring curricula. Less money, less access to the strongest teachers. The reality was that some students were getting taught at a high level, but on the other side of town they were filling out worksheets, watching movies, drawing pictures. So we have long advocated for rigorous standards for what students should know and be able to do. A body of work reaching back for decades indicates that all students, if given the appropriate support, can achieve at high levels."

This is the best fundamental argument I have heard for giving the same test to all children in all schools: to equalize expectations for all students regardless of background.

I heard it from my best friend too, in a conversation that galvanized my decision to write this book. Linda is earthy and hilarious, the youngest daughter of a large, prosperous family of midwestern-ers. She rides her bike all over Brooklyn, plays the violin, and used to sing in a church choir. Her entire career has been spent in the New York City public schools under No Child Left Behind. She graduated from Yale in 2002 and went directly into the New York City Teaching Fellows program, which trained her and placed her in a classroom within a few months. Then she was fast-tracked to principal, starting out at a high-poverty public middle school in the Bronx at the age of twenty-eight.

She keeps a critical perspective on the system, even as she works tirelessly within it for the benefit of her students. So I was surprised to hear her defend the state tests. "Before we had them, entire popu-lations of students would be written off" by their teachers, the very people who were supposed to be helping them, she said. "Before the tests, that was the norm," echoing Michael McGill of Scarsdale Public Schools. "It was like, oh, the kids are doing all right, they're coming to school, they have tough lives, I make sure they get a good break-fast. At least the teachers are now paying attention." Test scores, she said, also serve as ammunition to convince reluctant or disconnected parents that their kids need extra help. They trigger consequences: parent conferences, summer school, tutoring, increased scrutiny for teachers whose students fail year after year.

I pointed out that over the dozen years that tests have been in place, achievement gaps haven't shrunk; that she has found it ex-tremely difficult to remove demonstrably ineffective teachers; that the tests don't show the kind of progress her kids are actually mak-ing, such as when a sixth grader moves from a third- to a fourth-grade reading level; that tests take precious time and resources and impose stress and anxiety on her kids, her staff, and herself; that the requirements change year after year; their diagnoses aren't al-ways accurate; that they put her entire school at risk of closure; that they address no part of the pathologies that stand in the way of her students' success, from homelessness to horrifying trauma and abuse.

"I think it's a process, and we're at the first stages," she replied.

Okay, so what are the next stages?

RESOURCE ACCOUNTABILITY

"All students, if given the appropriate support, can achieve at high levels," said Daria Hall.

Let's break that down for a second.

What does "high levels" mean? If it represents some kind of personal best, it's subjective enough to be meaningless. If it means some arbitrary, middle-of-the-road proficiency on a standardized test, it's patently false for a second-percentile special needs child like Jackson Ellis, and almost as useless for a high-achieving original thinker like Laela Gray or, for that matter, Bill Gates.

And what about "given the appropriate support"?

That's never been tried. Imagine for a second what kind of school system we'd have if the "broader, bolder" agenda had been put in place. What if the mandate was to provide the most disadvantaged kids with the best-funded schools, the most advanced curricula, the highest-qualified teachers, and all of the wraparound services they need?

Resource accountability is the name given to the idea of holding states responsible for equalizing educational inputs rather than or in addition to outcomes. The idea has never gained traction at a federal level. At one education conference a weary think tank policy expert at a Gates Foundation–sponsored cocktail party warned me against even bringing it up. It is too hard to enforce or too politically inconvenient or just too expensive.

The bulk of public school funding comes from local property taxes, meaning that the schools of the rich continue to be better funded than the schools of the poor. According to the 2014 edition of a "National Report Card" on school-funding fairness, only fourteen states in 2011 even attempted progressive funding, giving more money to high-poverty districts than to more affluent districts to address the greater needs of high-poverty districts' students. In every other state either the funding is flat across districts or rich districts get more.

THE BACKLASH

No Child Left Behind had critics from the beginning: teachers' unions, scholars, activist groups like FairTest, and parents. But 2011 marked the beginning of a full-blown backlash. Waivers weakened NCLB. The Common Core stirred up controversy. And discontent with test-dominated education grew.

The rumbling started where NCLB was born—in Texas.

In 2011 Texas House Bill 3 passed, levying the heaviest, most draconian testing requirements in the nation. High school students would have to take a total of fifteen state tests in four years. Not only would these tests be a requirement for high school graduation, but they would also make up 15 percent of the final grade in each tested subject. Plus, students would be required to hit a certain score on the English II and Algebra III exams in order to be eligible for admission to a four-year state university. "I mean, these were ridiculously high stakes," said Theresa Treviño, a mother of two high school students and who founded Texans Advocating for Meaningful Student Assessment (TAMSA) with other parents in response to the new rules. "It was a drastic change."

In a series of public remarks in January 2012, Robert Scott, the state's education commissioner, condemned the new law as a "perversion of its original intent," stating,

> The assessment and accountability regime has become not only a cottage industry but a military-industrial complex. And the reason that you're seeing this move toward the "Common Core" is there's a big business sentiment out there that if you're going to spend $600–$700 billion a year in public education, why shouldn't there be one big [defense-style] Boeing, or Lockheed-Grumman contract where one company can get it all and provide all these services to schools across the country. . . .
>
> What we've done in the past decade, is we've doubled down on the test every couple of years, and used it for more and more things, to make it the end-all, be-all. . . . You've reached a point now of having this one thing that the entire

system is dependent upon. It is the heart of the vampire, so to speak.

All you have to do is kill that, and you've killed a whole lot of things.

In the spring of 2012 the Texas School Board introduced an antitesting resolution inspired by Scott. The first line of the resolution reads, "The overreliance on standardized, high stakes testing as the only assessment of learning that really matters in the state and federal accountability systems is strangling our public schools." By the end of the year districts representing 91 percent of the state's school children had adopted the resolution. By 2013, in response to a public outcry organized by TAMSA and other groups, with some hearings lasting until 3 a.m., Governor Rick Perry signed two bills cutting the number of "end of course tests" for high school students, from fifteen down to five, and exempting students who scored high enough on tests in third or fifth grade from future state tests.

Resistance to testing ignited elsewhere around the country. In January 2013 teachers at Garfield High School in Seattle voted unanimously not to administer the state Measures of Academic Progress (MAP) test for high school graduation. The boycott spread to nine high schools and ended in victory when the district made the test optional. The wave of opt-out protests spread across the country in the 2013 and 2014 testing season, making news in Illinois, Colorado, New York, and other states.

ACCOUNTABILITY FLUX

The twelve-year anniversary of No Child Left Behind, which was supposed to be the deadline for every single public school in the country to achieve 100 percent proficiency, passed in January 2014. The Department of Education didn't even bother issuing a press release.

By the spring of 2014 over a dozen states had already vowed to scale back on tests. In a single week in February Missouri's state board of education cut back on tests, Virginia's Senate voted to delay test-based rating of schools, Alaska's state board of education voted to rescind the high school graduation exam, and New York State announced they would delay implementation of the Common Core and take steps to limit testing. And both California and Washington State walked into showdowns with the federal government over testing in the spring of 2014.

Washington State risked about $40 million in federal funds when it refused to approve the linkage of teacher evaluations to test scores. California decided to suspend high-stakes testing during the transition to the Common Core. The plan was that students would take a sampling of the Smarter Balanced consortium tests in spring 2014 for the purpose of field-testing the tests; the results would not be published and would not be used to evaluate teachers, and California would avoid double-testing students by giving both the old and new tests at the same time. Arne Duncan threatened the state with the loss of their NCLB waiver and $3.5 billion in cash.

Michael Kirst, president of California's State Board of Education, says everyone knows that the old tests aren't good enough, and the state needs time to give the new tests a chance. "I think every state that's been doing value-added measurements off of cheap closed-end multiple-choice tests is going to have trouble maintaining the validity of their testing systems for use in teacher evaluation," Kirst said. "Teachers have never felt those assessments were true measures of what they were trying to teach."

In February 2014 the president of the National Education Association (NEA), the nation's largest teachers' union, issued an open letter calling for a "course correction" on Common Core. The NEA had previously backed the standards, but President Dennis Van Roekel called the implementation "botched." "Old tests are being given, but new and different standards are being taught," he wrote. "This is not 'accountability'—it's malpractice." By June 2014 three states, Indiana, South Carolina, and Oklahoma, had dropped the Common Core. The number of states that planned to use the consortium-produced tests from PARCC and Smarter Balanced had dropped even further, from forty-five to twenty-seven, with the rest either purchasing Common Core tests from vendors like Pearson or still undecided.

Even Vicki Phillips at the Gates Foundation, which had played such a strong role in driving the shift toward tests and the rapid adoption of the Common Core, said in an open statement in June 2014, "Assessment results should not be taken into account in high-stakes decisions on teacher evaluation or student promotion for the next two years," to ease the transition to the Common Core. An interesting opinion, especially as it appeared to call for changes to state law and/or federal waivers.

Then, in the spring of 2014, the College Board announced a major overhaul to perhaps the most feared and iconic standardized test of all: the SAT. The news made the cover of the *New York Times* magazine. The changes to the test mirrored many of the concerns raised in this book. For years critics have pointed out that the SAT is a weak predictor of college performance and that scores are highly correlated with family income. David Coleman, the head of the College Board, was also a major architect of the Common Core State Standards. He announced his intention to better align the SAT with the Core and to make the test harder to game through costly tutoring. But rather than placate critics, the SAT overhaul kicked off more attacks on its relevance and fairness as well as new calls to eliminate the test altogether.

THE BACKLASH HEARD 'ROUND THE WORLD

The current wave of resistance to high-stakes testing is global. In China there is a growing interest in alternative forms of education, from Western-style liberal arts colleges to a small movement of Montessori, Waldorf, and other progressive education styles. Singapore, widely praised and emulated here in the United States for its math teaching especially, is debating its reliance on standardized testing. And a few provinces in Canada are phasing out traditional standardized tests or considering doing so.

Over the last decade Mexico has come closer than any other country to adopting the US model, particularly in using test scores to judge teachers. Here, test-based accountability has been deployed as a political weapon against the national teachers union, one of the largest labor unions in the world and derided as a bastion of patronage and corruption.

In the mid-2000s the government introduced national tests, the EXCALE and ENLACE, with cash bonuses to teachers for good results. Half of teacher evaluations were based on test scores. In September 2013 the right-wing government of Enrique Peña Nieto voted to tie the hiring and firing of teachers to mandatory standardized testing for both teachers and students as a means to take personnel decisions out of the hands of the union. These reforms have repeatedly drawn tens of thousands of teachers into the streets of Mexico City in protest. The ENLACE test was suspended in February 2014 amid widespread allegations of coaching, cheating, and erasing parties, where teachers get together to change answers.

Israel is another site of testing controversy. It introduced a national standardized test known as the Meitzav in 2002–2003. It's given every two years in elementary and middle schools, rotating among four core subjects: math, English, science, and Hebrew language. But when the country started publishing the results of these tests, the education minister, Shai Piron, told the press that it bred a familiar list of unintended consequences. They found schools shifting teaching hours to spend time on test prep and spending scarce money on prep materials. Students and teachers felt "undue pressure." The integrity of the tests was questioned. Schools that served the poor and Israel's large immigrant populations felt the strongest urge to close the achievement gap on tests. The published results made the schools feel like sports teams pitted against one another. Piron said, "An atmosphere of bad culture and league tables arose, which harmed schools, especially those which integrate students from lower socio-economic status, and do God's work to close gaps. . . . The message is we've gone crazy, confused. This thing turned into something that drives us from learning to measuring." Piron made the controversial decision to cancel the country's tests for the 2013–2014 school year while a new means for reporting student achievement and school quality could be developed.

TEETERING ON THE EDGE

After this book first came out in 2015, the Senate introduced a bill to reauthorize ESEA with bipartisan sponsorship. This bill, The Every Child Achieves Act, would still mandate annual testing, but remove most of the the high stakes. In the spring of 2014, Chicago public school parents, the Chicago Teachers Union and the AFT staged one of the most politically charged opt-out protests to date. And in the spring of 2015, the action intensified. The *New York Times* reported 165,000 students opted out of testing in New York, the state most affected. Major media carried the story for months. Something's in the wind. The edifice of high-stakes standardized testing may be more fragile than it appears.

There are three possible responses now to the testing madness.

We can *not take the tests*. Just opt out. Opting out can be a surprisingly effective protest, and sometimes it's the best thing for kids developmentally. On a national basis cutting back on standardized testing, lowering the stakes, and getting rid of value-added teacher measures can all be positive changes.

We can *build better tests* that measure more important things, more accurately, and better accountability systems to go with them. Better tests merge learning with assessment. They move beyond the known pitfalls of standardization. They aim at measuring thinking rather than memorized information, motivate and reward better teaching and deeper learning, and address the full range of factors that are key to success. They form the foundation for true, two-way accountability, providing the information needed so students, families, educators, and lawmakers can work together to improve schools. I was surprised to learn just how close this future of better tests and real accountability might be.

In the meantime, and as individuals, we can try to pursue positive strategies as parents and educators that help our children *beat the tests*. The best of these strategies, it turns out, can help kids do better in the rest of school and even in life, thus rendering the flawed tests we have less than a total waste of time.

The rest of this book will take on these three options one by one.

PART II
THE SOLUTIONS

○ ● ○

4

OPTING OUT

In the United States, parents, teachers, and other concerned citizens have been protesting testing at least since the 1840s. In his 2013 book *Testing Wars in the Public Schools: A Forgotten History*, historian William J. Reese tells the story of what happened in 1845 in Boston when reformers led by Horace Mann gave a surprise test to public high school students. At the time, most schools demonstrated their achievements to the public through "examinations" that were more like pageants, full of recitations, plays, performances, and perhaps the answering of a few questions posed by a village elder. The method was far from rigorous. The Mann test, by contrast, was a series of free-response and essay questions covering patriotism, history, geography, natural history, and other subjects. Some items were nearly impossible, whereas others were nonsensical ("On which bank of the Ohio is the Cincinnati River, on the right or left?")

In Reese's telling, the reformers used the Mann test as a weapon to enforce top-down control of schools by creating anxiety around failure. Local leaders and parents resisted, arguing, as they do today, that the tests narrowed the curriculum and deprofessionalized teaching. But "once written tests entered the schools, they were never going to leave." The contrast between performances that emphasize students' strengths and standardized tests that reveal their weaknesses is a tension still very much in play in the assessment world today.

○ ● ○

Still, large numbers of students sitting out state-administered tests is a relatively new phenomenon, a response to the age of universal high-stakes testing. After No Child Left Behind passed in 2001, Scarsdale Public Schools, in the affluent suburbs of New York, and among the best-regarded districts in the country, became the site of the first major test boycott. "A lot of parents got very upset," said Scarsdale Superintendent Michael McGill. "They saw that good curricula was being thrown out in favor of stuff that was necessary for kids to perform well [on the tests]. Time was spent just prepping kids, and teachers' time was lost out of class, either getting trained to give the test or correcting the tests."

"Fundamentally, we feel the tests are not a good measure of what a child learns," Deborah S. Rapaport, whose daughter was then in the eighth grade at Scarsdale Middle School, told the *New York Times* during the boycott. "Many students do not perform well on standardized tests. These kinds of tests reduce content, they reduce imagination, they limit complex curriculum, they add stress and cost money."

The Scarsdale boycotts began with the eighth-grade science tests in May 2001. As the *Times* reported, two-thirds of the class opted out of the first round of tests. A dozen parents organized a minivan caravan to shuttle them away from school for the two-hour test period, which they spent doing homework at nearby houses.

"It was very weird for the district," McGill recalled. "As a board and as educational leaders, we completely agreed with the parents' objections. On the other hand, as public school officials, we were responsible for upholding state laws and regulations." The district had their wrists slapped in an official report by the state commissioner of education. Then the Scarsdale Board of Education issued a response making clear their position. McGill paraphrased, "We may be required to give the tests, but we want our teachers and schools to provide kids with a deep, rich education and let the test scores take care of themselves. And we understand this may depress the results, but that's okay with us."

Of course, an affluent district like Scarsdale doesn't really need to worry about demonstrating bare-minimum proficiency. Fourteen years later, with annual tests imposed every year from third grade up,

McGill sees them as little more than a distraction. "Our approach to state mandates on assessment is largely to drink a lot of radiator fluid," he said, tongue in cheek. "What we try to do is ignore it as much as we can. . . . The main drawback for us is more and more time spent on activities that don't really have a lot to do with better teaching or better learning, taking time and energy away from more important activities."

In the spring of 2014, after forty-one years as superintendent, McGill stepped down. He wrote in *Education Week* that "for almost a quarter of a century now, Scarsdale educators and parents have tried to help state officials understand that high-stakes testing and related reforms make it harder to provide a quality education. . . . In a more hopeful future, there's a place for standardized tests, but they're used judiciously, and they're not high-stakes." Like the Florida teacher who quit over YouTube and Manhattan math teacher Carolyn Abbott, high-stakes testing had driven another seasoned educator out of the schools.

THE NEW OPTION: OPTING OUT

Starting in 2013 the reforms that began with Race to the Top and continued with the Common Core triggered a new wave of opt-out protests and boycotts initiated by parent groups and teachers' unions, a wave that Bob Schaeffer of FairTest told me was "unprecedented." "The closer you get to classrooms, the stronger the opposition is to high-stakes tests," he says, citing opinion polls of parents and teachers.

That opposition is rising in response to the transition to the Common Core. Many states are administering the old NCLB tests while beginning to teach Common Core–aligned lessons or giving both sets of tests at once. Meanwhile millions of students in the spring of 2014 took the Smarter Balanced and PARCC Common Core–aligned assessments for "field test" purposes, which helps the test creators but not the students. All of the upheaval has made tests a focal point of resistance, within a larger movement by teachers' unions and parent groups in favor of local control and better resources for schools and against aggressive choice policies, school closures, standards, and cutbacks.

The present-day opt-out movement has supporters on the right, left, and in between. It's cropped up across the country, from cities to rural areas. Middle-class districts, though, have tended to dominate—affluent Scarsdale notwithstanding. "The higher-income districts are all about their test scores," said Jeanette Deutermann, who has organized against the tests across Long Island. "And the low-income districts, they're struggling to survive, trying to keep their schools open. It's too much for them to think about bucking the system."

In 2013 an antitesting rally initiated by Deutermann's group Long Island Opt Out drew sixteen hundred people. About half the families at a Tulsa, Oklahoma, middle school opted out of a ninety-minute "pilot" reading test. In Providence, Rhode Island, forty students staged a sit-in at the office of the state education commissioner. More than 80 percent of the parents at Castle Bridge Elementary in New York City opted out of spring tests. Students staged walkouts in Portland, Oregon, and Denver, Colorado. On December 9 a union-backed organization called United Opt Out National declared a National Day of Action in support of public education, calling for the "Elimination of all high stakes standardized testing." The organization announced coordinated events in Massachusetts, New York, New Jersey, Maine, Pennsylvania, Washington, DC, Florida, Illinois, Ohio, Iowa, Kansas, Texas, Minnesota, Idaho, New Mexico, and California.

In the spring of 2014 the action intensified. A reported twenty-one thousand students opted out in dozens of districts across Long Island. Chicago public school parents, the Chicago Teachers Union, and the American Federation of Teachers (AFT) staged one of the most politically charged opt-out protests to date. Groups of teachers at two elementary schools, Maria Saucedo Scholastic Academy and Thomas Drummond Montessori, voted to sit out the ISAT state test. And in all, parents at more than seventy Chicago-area schools submitted letters requesting that their children sit out the test. A Chicago teacher described the protests to me as an evolution of the energy from the 2012 teachers' strike. Colorado and the rest of New

York State also saw significant opt-out organizing in the 2014 testing season, and protests made news in Kansas, Oklahoma, Maryland, Massachusetts, New Jersey, New Mexico, and Pennsylvania.

THE TEACHER

Jesse Hagopian is a tall, charismatic, goateed teacher and union leader at Garfield High School in Seattle, making him a national figure in the opt-out movement. I met him when he spoke to a small group of parents and teachers at Earth School, a progressive elementary school in New York City's East Village, in spring 2013. Manhattan schools were organizing their own opt-out protest with the help of a progressive caucus within the New York City teachers' union, and Hagopian came to tell his success story and cheer them on.

Hagopian's career tracks the era of high-stakes testing. He started out at as a Teach for America recruit after just five weeks of training at a 100 percent poor and black elementary school in Washington, DC. "My first year teaching was the beginning of NCLB," he said. "My school was one of those that was reconstituted with a new principal, and I was one of the fresh-faced new teachers who was going to fix everything."

He is African American like his students were, but the urban dysfunction they faced was unlike anything he'd grown up with in Seattle. "I had a hole in the ceiling in my classroom, and the first assignment I ever gave the kids, they turned it in on a Friday and when we got back to school on a Monday they were all destroyed because it had rained," he remembers. "It was the test scores that had labeled this school a failure to be reconstituted. And it was total chaos in that school, from the new principal and the new teachers like me. I saw from the beginning that test scores were being used to punish our schools rather than support them with the resources they needed."

As a high school history teacher back in Seattle, Hagopian didn't like the effects of testing, especially graduation exams, on his fellow teachers or his students. "I had students who don't pass the end-of-course exams in high school and aren't allowed to graduate. And I find that problematic on several levels. It completely disrespects the profession of teaching, saying that the educators can't decide whether this person has met the requirements for graduation. We know where the kid started from and where he ended up. We know the effort and the commitment that student has put in. And we can assess and make our own judgment based on that intimate knowledge," he said. "Whereas someone a few thousand miles away who has developed this test and administered it on a certain day—they don't know if the kid's parents have split up, or they're sleeping on the street that night." Garfield High is 62 percent racial minority and 38 percent poor. Students from urban public schools like these who don't make the cut on graduation tests are likely to continue the cycle of poverty and face a greater risk of going to prison. Teachers felt that the mandated MAP test did not align with state standards, that it singled out and demoralized English-language learners and those with disabilities, and that it led to lost instructional time.

Among other subjects, Hagopian teaches the nation's history of direct action in support of civil rights and other causes. His conversations with colleagues about the detriments of testing came to a head in January 2013, when the school's union voted unanimously not to administer the MAP tests in math and reading. The PTA voted its support of the boycott. Hundreds of students brought official opt-out letters to school. Many who didn't have notes from their parents sat out the tests by hitting "A" repeatedly until their results were invalidated. After the media picked up the story, Hagopian's group received messages of solidarity from Florida, Australia, British Columbia, Japan, and the UK.

"Really, this has been the most incredible year of my life," Hagopian said. "My son was born just a few days after we launched the boycott. And this boycott has turned into not just a citywide struggle but a national and international inspiration for people who are struggling for authentic assessment." A total of nine schools in Seattle eventually joined the boycott. Although the superintendent initially threatened the Garfield teachers with insubordination and ten days' suspension, ultimately the school district fully backed down, announcing that the MAP test is now optional for high schools and no longer a graduation requirement.

THE STUDENT

Alex Kacsh was a senior at Jefferson County Open School, a progressive public school in the suburbs of Denver, Colorado, when he organized a test walkout in the spring of 2013. His school, which is lauded across the city, has projects and portfolios instead of grades and promotes student leadership. The entire freshman class goes on an annual camping trip with teachers. Once a week students leave campus to pursue a personal passion, like cooking at a restaurant or writing and performing plays. But under a law Colorado passed in 2006, the school, like every other, had to be evaluated solely on standardized test results.

"We didn't take the tests seriously because they had no relationship to our curriculum," said Kacsh. "So our school was labeled a turnaround school, in the bottom 5 percent. There was a three-year plan to shut us down." The state's threat took a toll on the school's progressive philosophy. Classes reverted to the textbook. Students spent time taking practice tests. "We were hearing the phrase 'this will be on the state test' a lot." Kacsh's walkouts led to networking with fellow student organizers in Portland, Oregon, New York City, Philadelphia, Newark, Providence, Chicago, and Florida.

THE PARENT

Until the fall of 2012 Jeanette Deutermann led a "calm, normal" existence in the close-knit community of Bellmore, Nassau County, New York. Her husband commuted to a job in finance in Manhattan, arriving home around nine o'clock each night. After she quit teaching to stay at home with her two sports-obsessed boys, she sometimes helped out with her mother's decorating business. She saw or spoke with her parents and two sisters almost daily. Her kids spent summers camping with their cousins on Cape Cod.

That all changed when her older son, then in third grade, started crying and begging not to go to school. He developed a nightly stomachache. The doctor said it was probably stress-related.

Deutermann, a charismatic, athletic blonde, was mystified. She was plugged into the school community, knew all the parents and most of the teachers, so she could rule out bullying or similar problems. "All the usual suspects of why your child might not like school weren't there," she said. "In kindergarten, first, second grade, he wasn't a kid who was like, please let me go to school, but he didn't have issues."

The one change she could pinpoint was the advent of high-stakes standardized testing, particularly in combination with the new Common Core–aligned curriculum. Her son's homework became a four-hour nightly ordeal as he struggled under the Common Core's increased emphasis on writing, which turned even math into a series of word problems.

Teachers constantly told him that this or that would be on the test. Deutermann saw the curriculum narrowing. "I started asking the teachers, why aren't they doing science? We haven't studied for even one social studies test. And teachers are saying, we don't have a lot of time for it. The testing's coming up, we can't afford to spend a lot of time doing the other subjects. It shifts the entire focus of the classroom."

For Deutermann the last straw came in February 2013, when her son brought home a notice that he'd been "selected" for something called "Sunrise Academy." Based on their scores on a different benchmark test, the NWEA, a portion of the fourth grade—gifted as well as struggling kids—were asked to come in at 7:30 two mornings a week for state test prep.

"For me it was a total red flag," Jeannette said. "I didn't do this kind of work for the SATs. How is it my fourth grader is going to do this? Then I start asking, what happens if he doesn't do well? Will he be put on a lower track? What is the consequence? And they say, well, it has none for him but it's for the teacher and school." As Deutermann gets madder, her Long Island accent gets thicker. "I said, wait a minute, he's going to get up an hour early on Tuesdays and Thursdays and do all this work only so that it can be an improvement for the teacher and the principal? Are we kidding here? I was literally twitching."

Deutermann founded the Facebook group Long Island Opt Out in February 2013. By the end of the 2013 testing season it had about four thousand members; by the next year it had over fifteen thousand. Deutermann spent the summer and fall movement building. She built a network of volunteer liaisons representing 80 of Long Island's 124 districts. She connected with teacher and other parent groups across the state. They organized protests at the capital in Albany and cofounded a statewide group, the New York State Allies for Public Education. With the help of this ward-captain model, the spring 2015 Long Island test boycott stretched across 80,000 students in almost every district. The noise was heard at a political level as well: out of 75 local school board races in May 2015, Long Island Opt-Out endorsed candidates won 57. And seven of those were activists who had worked directly with Deutermann.

Like many parent activists, Deutermann has faced down the irony that the cause she adopted on her kids' behalf is also taking her away from her kids. She drives up and down the Long Island Expressway attending public forums two or three nights a week while her kids are with her relatives or babysitters. Her husband has to pick them up when he gets back from his long commute. "It's a gigantic sacrifice," she said. "I'm not home making dinner." At the same time, she said, the boys respect what she's doing. Her older son's school anxiety has gone away because he knows he won't have to take the tests anymore. The other day her boys were watching 42, the Jackie Robinson biopic, and it led to a conversation about civil rights and standing up for what you believe in. "That's like you, Mommy!" said her younger son.

SHOULD YOU OPT OUT?

If you believe that standardized tests are the wrong way to hold our students and schools accountable, the most direct means to register that opinion is to stay home.

If you have a high-anxiety child whose fear of testing is warping his experience of school, a break from that testing may be, literally, just what the doctor ordered.

Under NCLB, in order to demonstrate adequate yearly progress, 95 percent of a school's enrollment in each subgroup is supposed to participate in annual statewide tests. So the magic threshold for organizing a protest that will force action at an NCLB school thus becomes 5 percent of any group, such as English-language learners, special education students, African Americans, or Hispanics.

As a majority of states now have NCLB waivers and the transition to the Common Core–aligned assessments is producing its own upheaval, the accountability system is currently in flux. Local politics will vary. But schools or districts in danger of missing their progress goals are likely to take a harder line against students and parents who opt out.

Sitting out a benchmark, diagnostic, or practice test is less risky than skipping spring statewide tests. The potential consequences for students are greatest for those tests that are used to determine promotion, competitive admission to middle school (fourth-grade tests) and high school (seventh-grade tests), and for high school graduation.

Surprisingly, it's even possible to opt out of college admissions tests. Eight hundred of the country's three thousand colleges make the SATs and ACTs optional for admission. That number has grown by nearly one hundred in the last decade and includes institutions of all kinds. For-profit colleges and community colleges are common on the list, but there are high-quality, selective, and prestigious schools that don't require the tests: Arizona State University, Bard, Bowdoin, Pitzer, Mount Holyoke, Smith, Wake Forest, Worcester Polytechnic, American, and George Mason, among others.

A 2014 study of over 123,000 students and alumni from score-optional schools showed "few significant differences" in college GPAs and graduation rates for students at the same schools who submitted test scores versus those who did not. This was true even though the students who did not submit test scores for admission were more demographically diverse, more likely to be racial minorities, and more often the first in their families to go to college.

THE RIGHT TO OPT OUT

The parental right to opt children out of testing is still in question but may itself be tested soon in the courts. State law generally requires schools to administer accountability tests to all students who have been in the country for at least a year, with accommodations for those with learning disabilities. According to the advocacy group United Opt Out National, only three states—California, Pennsylvania, and Wisconsin—have statutes protecting parents' rights to keep students out of state assessments. In addition, the Kansas State Department of Education explicitly permitted opt-outs in a 2013 letter. However, successful opt-out protests have taken place in several states where no such protection exists—New York, Washington, Colorado, and Illinois, to name a few.

Though there are no documented reports of this, in theory parents who deliberately kept children home from school in violation of state law could be prosecuted under truancy laws or for contributing to the delinquency of a minor. There also haven't been any cases yet that I've seen of students being kept back a grade or suffering other consequences for opting out of state tests, as opposed to students whose academic careers were derailed by administrators rigging test results, as Lorenzo Garcia did in El Paso.

Still, students and families who threaten to opt out are often pressured to conform. Actions have included repeated—sometimes automated—calls home, suspensions, and detention. In some schools parents are asked to pick students up or keep them home for the duration of the tests. In others students have been required to "sit and stare," without books or other diversions, for hour upon hour while their peers take the test.

There have also been reports of petty intimidation: eight-year-olds being forced to verbally refuse in Long Island, asked to call home and ask their parents for permission to take the tests in Colorado, or a nine-year-old girl in Chicago being forced to watch the test takers rewarded with ice cream and candy.

THE CONSTITUTIONAL RIGHT TO PARENT

Regardless of the current statute, parents who choose to keep their children out of state tests have a strong legal argument in their favor. The Supreme Court has repeatedly recognized the constitutional right of parents to "direct the upbringing and education of their children." In one 1923 case, *Meyer v. Nebraska*, a teacher taught German to a student in violation of a state law prohibiting the teaching of foreign languages before the eighth grade. This law had been passed to enforce the assimilation and English learning of first-generation students. The court found that in arresting the teacher, the state was violating the parents' liberty under the Fourteenth Amendment, which guarantees equal protection under the law.

In another oft-cited precedent, *Pierce v. the Society of Sisters* (1925), two private schools, one parochial and one military, challenged an Oregon state law requiring all students to attend public school. The court found in favor of the schools, agreeing with *Meyer v. Nebraska* that the Fourteenth Amendment protects parents' right to decide how best to educate their children. The decision begins with words that serve well for the purposes of would-be opt-outers: "The fundamental theory of liberty upon which all governments of this Union rest excludes any general power of the State to standardize its children."

More recently some states have passed "opt-out" statutes that affirm parents' rights under the First Amendment's freedom of religion or freedom of speech clauses to keep their students out of sex ed or evolution classes. The First Amendment, then, is another potential defense if parents want to make a case that the use of high-stakes standardized tests violates their personal beliefs about, say, human potential, equal opportunity, or self-determination. With regard to standardized testing, parents in both Chicago and Colorado have submitted complaints to the American Civil Liberties Union (ACLU) that school leaders' responses to opt-out protests violate parents' Fourteenth Amendment right to guide their children's education.

The organization United Opt Out National publishes state-by-state opt-out guides on their website.

HOW TO OPT OUT: STEP BY STEP

1. Write a letter or e-mail to your principal, and if you wish, copy the district superintendent, explaining the reasons for

your decision. Templates may be found on United Opt Out National's or FairTest's website.

2. If the test has personal consequences for your child, you'll need to make plans for an alternative evaluation. Most states and districts have existing provisions for placement of students without state test scores, for example, homeschooled students, students coming from out of state or from private schools, or those with disabilities. They are little known and not much talked about, but in New York City, for instance, students have the right to request a portfolio evaluation, including classroom work and special projects, or the results of a different test for admission into middle or high school.

3. Make a plan for your child during test days and confirm with school leaders whether your child should stay home, will be allowed to work in the library, or should stay in the test administration room with a book.

4. Make sure your child is on board with opting out and able to state the reasons in her own words. She might be asked to verbally refuse the test or pressured to change her mind.

5. Consider joining forces with other families and teachers via the PTA or a Facebook group. Depending on the size of your school, even a few families can make a big impact. Solidarity makes a big difference in how positive or negative the experience will be for your child. You don't have to picket the school or hold a rally; opting out is an action that speaks for itself.

Opting out is a rejection of the status quo. To find out how we can build a better future for students, read on.

5

THE FOUR TEAMS

There are elements worth salvaging from the current assessment and accountability regime. One is the focus on the success of all students. Another is the idea of measuring school performance in a way that is transparent to everyone who holds a stake in that success—that is, everyone. Attaching consequences to the results of these measurements would be defensible too, under two conditions: one, if we had great confidence in the tests or other indicators, and two, if those consequences emphasized giving schools, teachers, and students the support they need to succeed, not just punishing them for failing.

To meet those two conditions, the rest of the mess needs a do-over. Let's go back to our ten arguments against testing to figure out where the remedies lie.

1. We're testing the wrong things.
2. Tests waste time and money.
3. They are making students hate school and turning parents into preppers.
4. They are making teachers hate teaching.
5. They penalize diversity.
6. They cause teaching to the test.

7. The high stakes tempt cheating.
8. They are gamed by states until they become meaningless.
9. They are full of errors.
10. The next generation of tests will make things even worse.

The time wasted on testing and test prep (argument #2), the anxiety and demoralization felt by students, teachers, and parents (arguments #3 and #4), and the gaming and cheating (arguments #7 and #8) stem largely from a single cause. It's the way the tests are being *used*: as a high-stakes, high-frequency, stand-alone measure of the performance of teachers, students, schools, and districts.

High stakes means the use of any academic assessment, in any form, as a single determinant of student, school, teacher, or administrator performance. You could lower the stakes if you evaluated students using multiple measures rather than just one all-or-nothing test. "The notion of a multiple-measures system," Linda Darling Hammond told me, "is that at every level of decision making—student, teacher, school—you should assemble evidence from multiple sources. A decision should never be made mechanically on the basis of a single score."

Accountability reform comes before assessment reform. Lowering the stakes should be the fundamental principle of test reform.

Getting rid of impossible 100 percent proficiency goals, as NCLB waivers do, can and will make things better. So can cutting back on tests, as some states and districts are taking steps to do. There have been proposals to limit all standardized testing to a single exit exam at the end of high school, as many countries do—though this act, in isolation, would merely raise the stakes of that one test to apocalyptic, *Hunger Games* levels. Or we could achieve accountability at the school level by testing samples of kids rather than every kid every year, with a single national measure such as the NAEP, NWEA, or PISA exam.

All these ideas will help. But they're not enough.

Testing the wrong things (argument #1), penalizing diversity (argument #5), teaching to the test (argument #6), and the infuriating errors all through the tests (argument #9)—these problems come from the *nature* of standardized testing itself. Psychometrically valid and reliable, standardized, machine-gradable tests are sadly limited in what and how they can test—they always have been. They conceptualize proficiency as a fixed quantity in a world where what's important is your capacity to learn and grow. They are a twentieth-century technology in a twenty-first-century world. Which brings us back to argument #10: it's only going to get worse as we attempt to upgrade our academic standards while administering the same kinds of outdated tests. Unless we rethink the way we do things.

To solve these problems we don't just need to use the tests we have differently; we need new approaches to assessment.

And in order to design a better system of tests we have to go back to the beginning and ask: What do our kids need to be happy? What does our society need to thrive? Tests' greatest crime is that they have derailed the education reform conversation from addressing these essential questions.

The last few decades have brought a wave of new research that is changing the way we think about learning and intelligence—and reminding us of what we all learned in preschool.

AI VS. IQ

It turns out that the integration of cognitive, social, and emotional development, the cultivation of creativity, the emphasis on growth and process rather than outcome are all highly relevant to kids' success today, and not just from ages zero to five.

There are many definitions out there of what are called twenty-first-century skills, depending on whether you're talking to employers, educators, or economists, but the emerging consensus is that our society is placing new demands on people at an increasing rate. And new approaches to education are required to best prepare young people to meet those demands.

For the employers' view, consider remarks made by Lazslo Bock, the head of hiring at Google, to the *New York Times* in 2013 and 2014. After hiring tens of thousands of people over the past decade and tracking their performance within the company, Google found, he said, "G.P.A.'s are worthless as a criteria for hiring, and test scores are worthless. . . . We found that they don't predict anything."

What is a big, technologically advanced, extremely successful company looking for instead of GPAs and test scores? Technical ability counts, of course, especially for the half of Google jobs that require coding. But "the number one thing we look for is general cognitive ability, and it's not I.Q. It's learning ability. It's the ability to process on the fly. It's the ability to pull together disparate bits of information."

The second thing they look for, Bock added, "is leadership—in particular emergent leadership as opposed to traditional leadership. Traditional leadership is, were you president of the chess club? Were you vice president of sales? How quickly did you get there? We don't care. What we care about is, when faced with a problem and you're a member of a team, do you, at the appropriate time, step in and lead."

The third related factor is collaboration skills, including a necessary dose of humility. "Do you step back and stop leading, do you let someone else [lead]? Because what's critical to be an effective leader in this environment is you have to be willing to relinquish power. What can we do together to problem-solve?" Bock asked, in the words of a successful candidate. "I've contributed my piece, and then I step back."

Google has created its own form of qualitative assessment to screen applicants for these essential qualities, what Bock described as, "Structured behavioral interviews that we validate to make sure they're predictive." It's a technique reminiscent of OSS recruiting practices back in the 1940s, including following up to see whether the test results actually correlate with later performance. Partly as a result of the company's changing hiring criteria, the proportion of people without college degrees at Google has grown.

A 2012 research paper by Patrick Kyllonen, a senior research director at Educational Testing Service (ETS), reviewed several taxonomies of twenty-first-century skills and came to the following summary that sounds fairly similar to Bock's version:

- Cognitive skills—critical thinking, problem solving, creativity (defined here as divergent thinking, or the ability to come up with multiple approaches to a problem)
- Interpersonal skills—communication skills, social skills, teamwork, cultural sensitivity
- Intrapersonal skills—self-management, self-regulation, self-development (a propensity for lifelong learning), adaptability

Being cooperative, creative, and adaptable has come in handy in pretty much every time and place in human history. So what makes these skills particularly twenty-first century? Well, for one thing, computers are lousy at them.

See, we, and even more so our kids, are in a race with robots. Ever-more-complex analytic tasks requiring literacy and numeracy, the kind that formal schooling used to emphasize, are now being outsourced to silicon. Computers no longer just play chess or even win at Jeopardy; a study published by Oxford University economists in the fall of 2013 estimated that up to 47 percent of current US jobs are at risk of automation within a decade or two. Workers living under this uncertainty include telemarketers, tax preparers, radiology technicians, tailors, librarians, insurance underwriters, and mortgage clerks, to name a few.

But there are still three domains that artificial intelligence is unequal to. The first area is complex physical tasks requiring integration of sensory information and manipulation of the environment, like preparing food, driving a truck, or cleaning a house. This territory, requiring electronics integrated with delicate mechanical parts, is shrinking: robots can already assemble a car, and they're getting better and better at driving one.

The second domain is social intelligence like empathy, collaboration, values-based decision making, persuasion, and motivation. These are important for the caring and service professions, but equally for managers. A computer program might read a CAT scan, but humans are preferred for breaking the news of a life-threatening diagnosis and discussing treatment options. Software can generate the year's sales numbers, but it takes a flesh-and-blood leader to get the staff fired up to do better next time.

The third domain is creative intelligence—unstructured problem solving, posing new questions, picking out what is most relevant in a flood of data. Human minds are uniquely suited to identify new problems and create new solutions where the rules do not currently exist.

Exercising creative intelligence often requires collaborating deftly with technology. This might include a lawyer crafting a novel argument, a musician writing a song, a designer creating a web application, or an architect drawing up plans for a house.

MATTERS OF THE HEART

Try your hardest. Keep going. Be kind. Bounce back. Paul Tough, in his 2012 book *How Children Succeed*, summarized these qualities as "character"—perseverance, integrity, empathy, resilience. These aren't just nice to have; their relationship to important life outcomes is at least as strong as and, in some cases, stronger than academic indicators like test scores or GPA.

Emotional and social intelligence, both internal and external, can be viewed as a subdomain of the twenty-first-century curriculum. But it's equally valid to look at these qualities, sometimes called noncognitive skills, as necessary prerequisites for success in any field. In the past decade research from psychology and economics has strongly reinforced this view.

The history of research on noncognitive skills starts with a piece of candy. Walter Mischel, a Columbia psychologist, is known for his famous marshmallow test. This was a series of experiments beginning in the 1960s in which four-year-olds were offered a marshmallow, cookie, or pretzel. The children were told that if they waited fifteen minutes before eating the treat, they could have two. Variations on this experiment over decades have shown that the ability to delay gratification at a very young age is correlated with eventual educational attainment, healthy weight, and other positive outcomes.

This longitudinal data was impressive. In the 1970s and 1980s economists took up the question of whether the impact of certain character traits showed up across large populations as well. For example, Christopher Jencks, a Harvard professor and major scholar of human capital and inequality, found in a 1979 study that qualities such as industriousness, perseverance, and leadership, measured in young people, later influenced wages just as much as years of education, IQ, and parental socioeconomic status. And James Heckman, a Nobel Prize–winning University of Chicago economist, analyzed data on tens of thousands of people beginning at ages fourteen to twenty-one in 1979 up through the present. In one particular survey he looked at the results of two questionnaires designed to record self-esteem and the degree to which someone believes she controls her own life. Heckman found these noncognitive factors had an influence, independent of demographics, on whether people finish high school and college, whether young men go to jail and whether young women become pregnant as teens, and whether people smoke.

So both psychologists and economists had found proof that noncognitive skills and attitudes could be important. But they didn't know exactly which ones or how they could be cultivated. Carol Dweck, a Stanford psychologist, has a longstanding interest in the role of motivation in learning. In the 1990s she coined the term *mindset* to refer to beliefs about the mind itself. "In my work growth mindset is the idea that you can become smarter through good strategies, hard work, and help from others," she told me. Fixed mindset, however, describes the more common view, held by centuries of intelligence theory, that people are born with a certain IQ and can't change it any more than they can turn their brown eyes blue.

Experiments by Dweck and others have found that a growth mindset is a powerful self-fulfilling prophecy. When people act under a growth mindset, they indeed work harder and achieve more. And, furthermore, a growth mindset can be induced in young people simply by instructing them about it. In a 2007 study one group of seventh graders were taught that the brain is like a muscle that grows stronger with use and forms new connections. The control group received instructions in basic study skills. The seventh graders who had had the neuroscience lesson showed a marked improvement in their math grades.

Following on from both Dweck's and Mischel's research, the field of noncognitive skills is currently focused on one particular quality. Angela Duckworth, a former classroom teacher, a Penn psychologist, and a 2013 MacArthur genius grant recipient, popularized the term *grit*. This might be described as perseverance, or the willingness and ability to apply a growth mindset to overcome obstacles. Duckworth created a twelve-item questionnaire to measure both grit and self-control. Respondents rate themselves on a series of statements, including "I have overcome setbacks to conquer an important challenge" and "My interests change from year to year." Using variations on this survey, she has established that grit and self-control together predict success better than and independently of talent alone. Grittier people get more education on average and are less likely to divorce. Self-control predicts report card grades better than intelligence. Grit and self-control also predict success among West Point trainees, Special Forces recruits, National Spelling Bee finalists, and graduation from tough urban public high schools. For all these groups initial grittiness is more predictive than indexes of relevant ability, such as SAT scores or physical fitness.

THE M&M EFFECT

Evidence about the importance of attitude and effort undermines tests that purport to measure any kind of fixed g factor. Duckworth and her team have analyzed the effects of attitude and effort on tested IQ, which pop up in many studies. For example, one experimenter was able to get an average 10-point increase in tested IQ simply by offering young children an M&M for each right answer, a quick and dirty goosing of motivation. In another study observers coded videotapes of test-takers, rating them on how hard they were trying. An outsider's perception of test-takers' effort predicted about a third of the variation in scores.

It may be neither useful nor accurate to think of intelligence as fixed or isolated. But subjecting our kids to year after year of standardized tests perversely reinforces this view. "We did some informal research on this," said Dweck. "Many kids believe these tests measure how smart they are and how smart they'll be when they grow up, that the tests can really predict their futures." Think of eleven-year-old Lucas at the Leaf School telling me the tests are "life or death."

As Dylan Wiliam, the British assessment expert, put it, "Feedback is one of the mechanisms by which kids form mindset." On a baseball team kids hear about trying hard and teamwork. At piano lessons they get reminded to practice. In school class grinds to a halt while they sit in anxious silence for hours at a time, then are labeled year after year with a 1, 2, 3, or 4. Somehow they come out with the idea that athletic and musical ability are amenable to hard work, but math and reading ability are fixed. According to mindset theory, low-scoring kids may get discouraged and give up, whereas high-scoring kids fear taking on new challenges lest they violate their self-image of being smart.

To combat fixed mindset, we need to try harder to design good tests.

BETTER TESTS

If we want to shift our education system toward twenty-first-century skills, we desperately need to measure them in ways that everyone can trust—and in ways that themselves promote those skills. There's no scenario in which we meaningfully change our schools without changing the tests.

The world really needs people who come up with new solutions to problems, who know how to behave with others, who are internally motivated, and who are equipped to adapt to new situations and to act effectively. Schools are currently being held accountable for students' solo, static, one-dimensional demonstrations of proficiency over limited areas of just two subjects. The mismatch is painful.

David Williamson Shaffer is a professor at the University of Wisconsin-Madison in the Department of Educational Psychology and a game scientist at the Wisconsin Center for Education Research. He is one of the researchers at the forefront of new approaches to assessment. Shaffer gives me some great examples of how, exactly, values like empathy and collaboration—what Robert Sternberg, the creator of the Rainbow Assessments to measure a broader definition of intelligence, calls wisdom—contribute to life success. And it has everything to do with why these qualities are so tough to measure. "Much of what we do as adults is learn how to solve problems and answer questions that aren't just about what *we* want," Shaffer said. "Take an urban planner: the job is not to make the city look how they want it to look; it's to understand what's best for the city. Or even a plastic surgeon: their job is to make the nose look the way a patient wants it to look. A huge part of becoming an adult and thinking about problems in the real world is decentering, stepping outside of what you want."

The problem is that the ability to decenter, like other emotional qualities, is just not very amenable to traditional psychometric testing, which tries to tie each question back to a single construct. If you want to measure whether a doctor cares about her patients, "it's not as simple as yes they do or no they don't," said Shaffer. "That only shows up in a decision that is evidence of caring, knowledge, and skills," and the interactions among those three factors.

If we want to cultivate wisdom, we need to qualify, if not quantify, it. "We can only value what we can measure," Shaffer told me. "If we can't measure it, we can't make policy. We can talk till we're blue in the face about twenty-first-century skills, but unless you can measure them they don't have much meaning." Leaders may pay lip service to higher-order skills and values, but they defer to test scores—what Sternberg has called the "pseudo-quantitative precision heuristic."

ROBOTS, MONKEYS, BUTTERFLIES, AND UNICORNS

Some attempts to test twenty-first-century skills are in use now, with hundreds of thousands of students at schools all over the country. Others are just over the horizon. Some are high-tech, quantitative solutions, and some are entirely personal and subjective.

Ideally we want tests that don't just get at what students know but also how they learn and think. In order to fully understand this, we need to examine their mental attitudes, their emotional health, and even their values. It's not so relevant whether every kid can hit the same standard on an arbitrary day in April; we want to know more about what makes each student unique—his interests and passions, her strengths and weaknesses. The measurement tools and techniques you end up with might not resemble traditional tests at all.

For the rest of this chapter and the next, I'll be outlining the future of testing, with examples from the frontiers of research. In some ways this chapter connects back to Chapter 2, the wild-eyed dreams of those who sought to "categorize, sort, and route the entire population," like Henry Chauncey with his Census of Abilities. Our era is seeing a reinvention of the science of measurement of the human mind, but this time with an appreciation for the beauty of difference, complexity, and growth.

As a memory aid, I've separated the current frontiers of alternative testing into four "teams."

Team Robot is the technologists, using software to reduce the inefficiencies of standardized testing and produce detailed feedback that emphasizes growth over achievement.

Team Monkey is the psychologists, using surveys to assess noncognitive qualities: social and emotional well-being, happiness, motivation, grit, and self-control.

Team Butterfly is the educators, using performance-based assessment. They believe that each child's unique transformation can only be captured in authentic settings, through a fully qualitative, anecdotal process.

And finally, **Team Unicorn** represents a perhaps mythical future. These researchers are experimenting with technologically enhanced testing of twenty-first-century higher-order skills and values. Like the best performance assessment, it's open-ended, authentic, and engaging for students. Yet like the best standardized assessment, it's data-rich, automated, and can be validated and compared across large populations.

In the remainder of this chapter we'll take a look at the first two approaches, Team Robot and Team Monkey, and see what they bring to the table.

TEAM ROBOT: BETTER TESTING THROUGH SCIENCE

Technologies in use by over a third of US K–12 students today have the potential, say their creators, to relieve some of the worst toll taken by standardized testing—the anxiety, coaching, and cheating, to give a few examples. These technologies belong to the world of learning analytics, also known as adaptive-learning software.

In 2009, at the first-ever Venture Capital in Education Summit at Stanford University, I met a brash dot-commer named Jose Ferreira. He painted his learning analytics company, Knewton, as nothing less than an educational messiah. "Look at what other industries the Internet has transformed," he told me then. "Print, digital, video, music, travel, hotels, restaurants, retail—anything with a big information component. But for whatever reason, people don't see it with education. It is blindingly obvious to me that it will happen with education." As he elaborated in a later interview, "All the content behind education is going to move online in the next ten years. It's one giant Oklahoma land grab—one big tectonic shift. And that is what Knewton is going to power."

As a reporter for five years for the technology and business magazine *Fast Company*, I've heard those kinds of claims quite a few times. But Ferreira was one bigmouth who put his money where his mouth was. By the fall of 2013 Knewton's software platform was available to the vast majority of the nation's colleges and K–12 school districts through partnerships with three of the five major textbook publishers, Pearson, MacMillan, and Houghton Mifflin Harcourt.

TEACHING MACHINES

The dream of automated learning is even older than computers themselves. In 1924 an educational psychology professor named

Sidney Pressey built a mechanical teaching machine that supplied questions, along with the correct answers, when a button was pressed. B. F. Skinner, the famous behaviorist, also introduced a teaching machine in 1954, a clunky thing that looked somewhat like a typewriter. He claimed some of the very same benefits for it that you hear from ed-tech entrepreneurs to this day: allowing every student to move at his own pace, supplying immediate feedback, improving motivation.

Computer programmers have been working on so-called intelligent tutoring systems since the 1970s, and they've gotten quite good for certain jobs. In a 2011 review of research that carefully compared software-based tutoring to one-on-one tutoring with a human, the resulting improvement in student performance was almost exactly the same in both cases—0.76, or three-quarters of a standard deviation, for the computers, and 0.79 for the humans.

Today, besides the Knewton-powered products, other adaptive software is sold by Dreambox, Scholastic, Khan Academy, Cengage Learning, Cerego, and more. Most of the products work similarly: they introduce concepts with text, video, or animations; ask students to respond in the form of quick short-answer or multiple-choice questions; give them increasingly broad hints when they get stuck; and choose what concept to bring in next based on the student's responses. What the "adaptive" part means is that the specific selection of questions and order of content presented to each student will vary according to the students' responses. You take a quick diagnostic test or start off with a medium-hard question. If you get it right, you proceed to harder questions; flub it and you get easier questions. As a result, each student's path and pace through the material is slightly different.

These platforms log and analyze lots of data on each student— not just each right or wrong answer but every mouse click, every hover, every hesitation or deletion. Most come with dashboards showing at a glance how many math problems a student has solved, how many concepts within a lesson plan they've covered, how many times they logged in, how much time they've spent, and similar indicators.

Math and English mechanics (grammar, vocabulary, spelling) are the subjects most commonly taught with the help of such programs. But software engines can be used to help present any set of facts and concepts. Since 2002 research group at Carnegie Mellon has created a set of free and openly licensed adaptive college courses that teach French, biology, statistics, logic, and more.

As I reported in *Newsweek*, Ferreira has long been a mortal enemy of standardized testing. A former professional poker player with a Harvard MBA, he started out in education working for Kaplan. At one point he discovered a flaw that turned a very technical math question on the GREs into child's play. As a result, ETS had to suspend testing for some time, deleted an entire section from the test, and referred to him privately as "the Antichrist." Kaplan turned the hack into the centerpiece of an international marketing campaign.

So it's not surprising that Ferreira believes his platform and those like it could reduce the need for high-stakes tests. "Knewton allows for much more gentle, passive data collection via ongoing formative assessment in homework/classwork," he told me in an online chat. "We can predict your score on a bunch of these high-stakes tests anyway, lessening the need for so many of them."

"Formative assessment" refers to the feedback that is part of nearly any teaching and learning scenario, such as when a teacher calls on the class during the lecture or when a student is studying vocabulary with flash cards and flips the card over to see the right answer. It's opposed to summative assessment, which "sums up" learning at the end of a period of time, ranging from a unit test to a graduation exam.

THE ANGRY BIRD MODEL

Most kids have experience getting ongoing formative assessment while playing video games. They can see at a glance how many Angry Birds they've already launched at the pigs, how many levels they have to go, their rankings compared to other players, and their all-time personal best. Because this feedback is ongoing, it's inherently more fluid. Games always offer the chance to try again and do better next time. Failure is part of the process.

I observed a seventh-grade remedial math class in Los Altos, California, using Khan Academy software in the fall of 2012 that seemed to operate on these principles. Students could earn badges, little sun and moon graphics, for solving ten similar problems in a row, solving problems quickly, attempting harder material, or for helping each other.

With a glance at her "dashboard," the teacher, Courtney Cadwell, could easily pinpoint where students were struggling. She pulled these students out for intensive work in groups of one or two while still making sure everyone else was on task. The program supplied the students much more practice time than in years past. They progressed quickly—gaining an astonishing two and a half to three and a half grade levels in the first twelve weeks. At one point, while I was watching, the teacher had the whole class racing to solve as many fraction multiplication problems as possible as they watched their collective progress zoom upward on a screen at the front of the room. It was exciting and even fun. Cadwell, a former NASA recruit, took advantage of the time the Khan Academy system saved the class to introduce more demos and experiments that brought math concepts to life. She saw her remedial students, at an age when they were statistically likely to give up on math altogether, instead discover a love for the subject. It's "kind of like a game," John Martinez, thirteen, told me. "It's kind of an addiction—you want a ton of badges."

Software-mediated learning can be powerful. For example, when Knewton first produced a remedial math course for college freshmen at the University of Arizona, half the students mastered the material four weeks or more ahead of schedule. Ferreira says this is because the course was presented to them at the exact pace they could handle it and in the order that made the most sense to them instead of as a predetermined chunk of the syllabus each week. (These great results haven't always been repeated as ASU started using the technology in more courses.) Most software platforms use the "mastery-based learning model," which means you don't move on to a new concept until you can demonstrate a good grasp of an underlying basic concept. Seems like a no-brainer for solid learning, except that's not at all what happens in a typical class, where the teacher dictates the pace for the group. Even for the Arizona students who couldn't pass the final exam, the system was able to identify who was making progress and would pass given, say, half a semester more. Compared to, "You failed, now start over," that's the kind of feedback that can really reinforce a growth mindset.

AIMING AT TARGET

Valerie Shute, a professor at Florida State University and former principal research scientist at ETS, coined the term "stealth assessment" to describe what Ferreira calls "passive data collection." "In 1974 businesses had to close down once or twice a year to take stock," she said. "Barcodes and automated checkout instead allowed for collection of a continuous stream of information. Business owners can aggregate data and examine the trends. It's very, very powerful and allows for all sorts of just-in-time decision making." In the business world this is dubbed predictive analytics. Marketers use it heavily. For example, by looking at patterns of purchasing for items like body lotion and vitamin supplements, Target was able to create a "pregnancy score" that guesses whether a particular customer is pregnant in order to start showering her with coupons for baby products and diapers.

Although the flow of interactions in a classroom is far richer than the flow of transactions in a Target, this doesn't mean similar tools can't yield important insights, Shute said. "If business can collect and use a continuous stream of information, why the hell can't we in education do that too? Wouldn't it be great to aggregate this information and make inferences about developing competencies at any point in time and at any grain size?"

Right now we bring school to a halt to take high-stakes tests. Maybe a student is nervous or had a bad night's sleep. Or she may be a good crammer but will have forgotten it all in three weeks. With stealth assessment there is no "taking stock." Testing is simultaneous with learning. And the cost of testing is folded into the cost of teaching.

All that is lacking right now is the large-scale studies to validate the results of "stealth assessment" by comparing them to students' actual performance in school as well as their scores on traditional tests. Kimberly O'Malley is the senior vice president of school research at Pearson Education. Pearson officially put together her research group in 2012 to get academics in the fields of learning, assessment, and educational technology working more closely together. "Invisible, integrated assessment, to me, is the future," she said. "We can monitor students' learning day to day in a digital scenario. Ultimately, if we're successful, the need for and the activity of stopping and testing will go away in many cases." The big test companies agree: software—of their design and manufacture, of course—could replace standardized tests very soon.

ROBOT ENGLISH TEACHERS

On a parallel track with embedded assessment, Team Robot is also working on automated scoring of writing and free-form math equations. "Automated scoring is in action now," said O'Malley. "It allows students to write and get very rich feedback in real time." Pearson's WriteToLearn and CTB/McGraw-Hill's Writing Roadmap are used in K–12 classrooms. PARCC began testing auto-scoring in the spring of 2014 for Common Core–aligned state assessments. Automated essay scoring has been used in high-stakes tests since 2004, including the new Pearson GED exam, the Compass placement test for community college students, and West Virginia's statewide English Language Arts exam.

Anyone who saw Spike Jonze's sci-fi fantasy *Her*, about a man who falls in love with his operating system, can guess how far computers are from really understanding human language. They can't parse the nuances of individual style or tone nor can they model the logic of an argument. They don't get jokes. They can't yet map what a student knows by reading what she writes, meaning that robo-graded research papers can't yet replace multiple-choice questions.

Essay grading is a natural-language processing problem, at the frontier of current computer science. It primarily uses what is called the "bag of words" approach. As crude as it sounds, this refers to classifying writing samples based on statistical features, including the frequency of certain words and how close together they occur. Given thousands of essays produced from the same handful of prompts, these systems can reliably identify characteristics common to high and low scorers, such as length, spelling errors, or the use of certain words and phrases. In many cases they assign scores at least as well as a human grader. Of course, that result becomes less impressive when you realize that human graders on most mass tests are low-wage contract workers moving at breakneck speed.

On the upside, these systems, when used in a classroom setting with human oversight, can enable teachers to assign much more writing without the drudgery of grading every little thing by hand. Like a souped-up version of spell-checker, they can save time for both students and teachers by instantly flagging misspellings, punctuation errors, and run-on sentences. And they can check for plagiarism, if the copied text is found somewhere on the web.

But there's a clear downside to incentivizing students to write to please an algorithm instead of a human, and this is particularly true on a high-stakes test. A series of experiments with various types of essay-grading software by Les Perelman, formerly at MIT, has shown that nonsensical essays can get high scores from computers if they use the right vocabulary, length, and quotes, even if incorrectly attributed. "In today's society, college is ambiguous. We need it to live, but we also need it to love. Moreover, without college most of the world's learning would be egregious," began a nonsensical Perelman-produced essay that received the highest possible score of six from ETS's e-Rater software. Perelman's work publicly discrediting robo-grading was influential in getting the SAT to make the essay optional in 2014.

DRILL AND KILL OR GROW AND EVOLVE?

Clearly Team Robot doesn't have all the answers. Learning-analytics platforms are, so far, largely customized for teaching times tables and "i before e except after c." That makes them a complement, not a replacement, for a twenty-first-century curriculum. They don't handle truly creative or collaborative work. In the hands of a less-skilled teacher than Courtney Cadwell in Los Altos, they have the potential to increase emphasis on drill and kill. And cheating could become as easy as hacking a computer.

The politics of software-centered testing are complicated too. The big textbook and test incumbents, alongside a raft of new start-ups like Knewton and large technology companies like Apple, are seizing on this stuff for a reason. The integration of assessment with textbooks and materials, all delivered on an electronic device, is a huge sales opportunity. More technology tends to mean a greater role for private business in schools, as vendors and partners, for good and for ill. Most troubling would be if computer-centered teaching and assessment were implemented as a means to improve the "efficiency" of education—that is, by hiring fewer teachers. There's something a bit, well, bloodless about a vision that puts software in the driver's seat in this way.

If education's purpose in the twenty-first century is to prepare students to excel at the very tasks that computers can't master, it would follow that any task gradable by a computer is probably less than central to that mission. The optimal role of software is as an aid to human teaching, not a replacement for it. The difference between what a piece of technology can accomplish in the hands of a skilled and creative human practitioner and what machines can do alone is like the difference between an espresso crafted by a master barista operating a $24,000 LaMarzocco and a cup of coffee from a vending machine.

Although overhauling our accountability system may not be as simple as a software upgrade, there are things to love about Team Robot—primarily, the way that it encourages a focus on how learning evolves over time. "The snapshot in time has driven the accountability system in the past, and that has served its purpose for a while," said O'Malley of Pearson. "We've really recommended looking at models of growth: not just where students are today, but where they've come from and where they need to go." The Scantron score sheets of the past focused on static "achievement" or, even worse, "aptitude"; today's technology, in theory, could enable schools to focus on growth. The snapshot is replaced with a video.

TEAM MONKEY

Team Robot offers new assessments for traditional subjects. School leaders are also using traditional psychological assessments to measure new skills and attitudes: social and emotional learning, motivation, well-being. I'm calling them Team Monkey because of their focus on our warm-and-fuzzy mammalian nature and because of the connection to experimental psychology.

Joshua Starr was the superintendent of Montgomery County Public Schools (MCPS) in suburban Maryland as well as a national figure in innovative school leadership, with fifteen thousand–plus followers on Twitter and a healthy grasp of MBA-speak. Starr leads a consortium of big county and suburban school districts that are lobbying the federal government to create a new approach to accountability. Among other ideas, they want to reduce the overall number of tests and to use higher-quality tests that address skills like critical thinking, problem solving, and communication, combined with low-stakes measures to inform decision making at a school level. "The tragedy of the last twelve to fifteen years is that I have not heard or seen in policy a clarity around what kids need to know and be able to do," he told me. "The conversation is based on structures: tests, charters, merit pay. I want to talk to parents about, what are the skills we want kids to have?"

Starr has three priorities for his students: traditional academics, creative problem solving, and social/emotional competencies. He summarizes the third area as "Grit, hope, the ability to resolve conflict, set goals, and understand diversity in the world around them." To his knowledge, his is the first large district to make social and emotional skills a priority on par with the other two areas.

In his schools state-mandated standardized assessments are used for academic achievement. Teacher-created assessments try to get at creative problem solving. To tackle noncognitive skills, in the

2012–2013 school year MCPS began partnering with Gallup to survey fifth- through twelfth-grade students and staff alike on their levels of hope, engagement, and well-being.

The twenty-question Gallup student survey asks students to register how much they agree or disagree with statements like "There is an adult in my life who cares about my future" (hope) and "At this school, I have the opportunity to do what I do best every day" (engagement). To make room both in the school year and in the budget for the Gallup surveys, Starr cut back on other conventional tests and eliminated one diagnostic test. "There's no need to test all kids every year," he said, as long as you focus on a few "critical" milestones, like reading in third grade.

The effect of using the hope survey, Starr said, is felt throughout his schools. He experiences its impact as a parent as well. "I've got an eleven-, ten-, and five-year-old," Starr said. "I want them to be straight-A students and great people, and if had to choose, I would rather they be average students and great people." Most parents would say the same thing, but typically our kids' report cards and their test scores reflect only the former.

THE WEAVING OF MESH

A survey may seem like a lightweight tool compared to a psychometrically verified test, but the use of surveys to track social and emotional skills and values in schools is catching on. In the fall of 2014, over 800,000 students completed the free Gallup Student Poll. According to independently reviewed research by Gallup's chief scientist, entering college freshmen's responses to the "hope" survey do a better job of predicting college persistence and GPA than students' high school GPAs, SATs, or ACT scores.

YouthTruth is a twenty-minute online survey for grades three through twelve that about 275,000 students have taken. "The schools that use it want to know across their student body—how engaged are they? How does it feel to be on this campus? Is this school respectful and fair? Are we really preparing kids for college and career?"

said Marny Sumrall, one of the directors. Schools are using Youth-Truth to gather feedback both on the schools as a whole and on individual teachers.

Starting in 1998 the State of California's Department of Education has administered the largest statewide survey program in the nation looking at "resiliency, protective factors, and risk behaviors," made up of the Healthy Kids Survey, the School Climate Survey, and a parent survey. The questions ask about sex, drugs, and other risky business. In 2013–2014 the state updated the survey to track learning engagement, student's connectedness to school, and a new optional social-emotional health section covering empathy, self-efficacy, self-awareness, persistence, emotion regulation, gratitude, "zest" (a measurement of enthusiasm and energy), and optimism. The social-emotional health section for middle school students asks them to identify with statements like "Each day I look forward to having a lot of fun" and "I can do most things if I try."

The OECD gives the Program in International Assessment, or PISA, to about half a million students around the world. It's best known for its "league tables" ranking countries on math and language achievement. But in addition to the two hours of word problems or essay questions, given in alternate years, PISA students also complete a thirty-minute questionnaire asking about things like self-efficacy, self-esteem, student-teacher relationships, the school climate, and the level of math anxiety, making it one of the largest attempts to measure MESH in the world. An infographic published on the website Buzzfeed based on PISA data sorted countries about evenly into four quadrants: happiest and least happy kids and high and low test scores. Korea stands out for its miserable kids and tip-top scores, Singapore has the happiest kids with the highest scores, Qatar and Argentina have sad, low-scoring kids, and Peru and Indonesia are whistling away with their weak scores. (The United States falls toward the center, in the slightly glum, mediocre bottom-left quadrant.)

School leaders around the world are using PISA findings on the emotional health of their students. In Korea, in February 2013, the new president, Park Geun-hye, announced that the happiness of citizens would become a national priority, and the Ministry of Education has taken this up as a goal.

Christopher Gabrieli is an entrepreneur and venture capitalist turned education reformer in Massachusetts. Although he started as a test-score hawk, in recent years he's become a believer in noncognitive skills and values. "It's totally clear when you look at the data— even hardcore pro-academic test score people believe it," he said. "In adult life test scores are only around half the story in terms of important life outcomes." He summarizes the other half of the story as "Mindsets and Essential Skills and Habits," or MESH. Gabrieli's group Transforming Education is dedicated to advancing MESH and developing new ways to measure it.

Transforming Education is advising the California Office to Reform Education, a group of eight school districts in California, including Los Angeles and San Francisco, that has obtained its own separate exception from No Child Left Behind. They are setting up what Gabrieli calls "the first large-scale accountability system we know of that places MESH measures as peers to test scores." Schools within these districts will be evaluated on 60 percent conventional test scores, 20 percent school culture/climate measures such as suspensions, expulsions, and bullying, and 20 percent social-emotional scores.

THE MONKEY TEST MAKER

There are monkey adherents deep inside the traditional testing world. According to Todd Balf, who wrote for the *New York Times* about the spring 2014 relaunch of the SATs, the College Board has been looking at noncognitive measures for at least a decade (not counting the early days, when personality tests such as the Myers-Briggs were considered). They considered including them in this relaunch, though they ultimately decided against it.

Patrick Kyllonen, the chief research scientist at ETS, is working primarily on developing instruments to measure noncognitive skills, from K–12 through the workforce. "I think everyone recognizes that there's more we learn in school than your ability to solve math problems or spell words or read paragraphs—that you learn a lot of other skills and a lot of other skills are important for success," he said. "But people are very unsure about how to measure those in a way that would be treated as seriously as a math test."

In a high-stakes context simple surveys of MESH present problems. "Surveys aren't always good as assessments," said Carol Dweck. "Once people learn what the right answer is, they know how to give it." It's as if, instead of asking people to solve math problems, we simply asked them whether they were good at math and then reported the answers as fact. And, said Dweck, the reference group really matters. For example, on the PISA exam East Asian students in general express lower opinions of themselves, whereas Americans tend to have inflated self-confidence. "There's some technical challenges with it being more vulnerable to faking and coaching and cheating than typical tests," Kyllonen said. "The measurement problem is pretty serious here," said Gabrieli.

Kyllonen's group has developed several machine-scorable alternatives that he says are proving harder to game than simple agree/ disagree questions. One is "forced choice." In this, a test may ask an applicant, "Which is truer about you: I'm a good worker/ I get along with others?" Instead of rating themselves as high or low across the board, asking respondents to discriminate in this way leads to more nuanced feedback.

A second approach, developed for workplace assessments, asks for someone's judgment of a situation. This is similar to a technique Robert Sternberg used for his tests of practical intelligence. For example:

You're working in a group and are responsible for a project that's due in a week. One of the members of the group is criticizing and holding back progress. What should you do?

A. Take this person aside and tell them to skip the rest of the meetings.
B. Criticize them in front of the group.
C. Talk to the teacher/supervisor.

A third technique to make results of surveys more comparable across cultures, which was used beginning in the 2012 PISA tests, is called "anchoring vignettes." In a section about classroom management, students were given three descriptions of teachers with a low, medium, and high degree of control over their classrooms, and it asked in each case to agree or disagree with the statement, "Ms. Johnson is in control of her class." Then they answered the same question for their own teacher. The response to the fictional situation provides context to "anchor" the student's judgement to the real situation.

Schools are also considering more naturalistic indicators of MESH factors. Kyllonen mentions a study at an Italian law school that tracked, over seven years, the time that went by between a student being notified she was accepted and when she actually registered for classes. That little moment of procrastination turned out to be an accurate predictor of whether a student is likely to stick it out in the program. "If we could get more measures like this, this would be a really interesting and productive development," he said. Similarly, behavior and attendance records can be powerful indicators both of the general atmosphere at schools and of the outlook of individual students.

Or you can get more information by simply asking teachers about their students. As an optional supplement to the GRE, Kyllonen has developed something called the Personal Potential Index, a fifteen-minute questionnaire that people who know the applicant can complete to provide an outside perspective on qualities like knowledge, creativity, resilience, communication skills, planning, organization, teamwork, ethic, and integrity. Similarly, for her 2008 dissertation at Stanford, Carmit Segal showed that student misbehavior in eighth grade, based on teacher "yes-no-don't know" ratings on five items (whether the student rarely completes homework, is consistently inattentive, or is frequently absent, tardy, or disruptive) independently predicted workforce earnings twenty years later, controlling for educational attainment and achievement test scores.

MONKEY LOVE

However we measure it, social and emotional skills like grit are shaping up to be the *g* factor of our time: seductively powerful keys to how and why people succeed. Just as Lewis Terman once declared, "There is nothing about an individual as important as his IQ," it is tempting to overemphasize, oversimplify, and overessentialize these qualities about which we still know very little.

In May 2015 Angela Duckworth herself co-authored a paper in which she cautioned that measures of "grit" including self-report questionnaires weren't ready to be used for high stakes. "I feel like the enthusiasm is getting ahead of the science," she told me in an interview.

Similarly, Carol Dweck told me, "we have to be careful. I take a lesson from the self-esteem movement"—the idea, promulgated starting in the 1970s, that building up children's self-esteem was the key to spurring achievement. "That started with tremendous optimism, and it was completely misguided and, in the end, harmful. We have to be rigorous about implementing noncognitive measures and do it carefully. We have to assess it appropriately and do all these things in the service of learning and creating outcomes."

Most troubling to me is the ways in which measuring and holding schools accountable for the social and emotional health of their students, if done in the wrong ways, might, once again, worsen the effects of inequality. Faced with poor "school climate" scores, will a CORE district school get creative about addressing student behavior, hire an extra social worker, or get more aggressive about screening out so-called troublemakers?

The psychometricians of the nineteenth and early twentieth century were convinced that they were unveiling ground truths about human nature. But their preexisting biases infected their experimental design and ended up reflecting social conditions instead. Modern-day scientists are no less susceptible to this problem. For example, a 2012 experiment re-created Mischel's marshmallow test, telling children they could have two marshmallows instead of one if they waited for fifteen minutes. But this time the experimenters added a condition: in one case, the adults repeatedly broke promises to the child subjects, while in the other condition they were shown to be reliable. The children in the "reliable adult" condition waited far longer. The study's lead author, Celeste Kidd at the University of Rochester, was inspired by her work at a homeless shelter. She wrote in the paper that the results imply that children rationally consider whether delaying gratification will actually pay off. In an unstable environment, such as that created by extreme poverty, "the only guaranteed treats are the ones you have actually swallowed." In other words, what looks like impulse control, like IQ before it, may be little more than a proxy measure for social class.

It would certainly be ironic if, in the name of recognizing a wider set of qualities essential for success, we ended up dunning children for internalizing factors in their environment that are largely out of their control. MESH measures should be used to channel resources and support to students, never to track or stigmatize them.

GROSS NATIONAL HAPPINESS

With that large caveat in mind, as new colors in the sixty-four-crayon box of assessment—as one of multiple measures—MESH measurements have a lot of potential. The movement for alternative testing in education parallels other efforts to create alternative metrics that move away from strictly economic definitions of success. Entire nations, like the Central Asian kingdom of Bhutan, and individual cities like Somerville, Massachusetts, and Santa Monica, California, have created Gross National Happiness indexes—scores that combine statistics on poverty, public health, and crime with citizens' survey responses about their health and well-being.

For the time being, Kyllonen said, NCLB is standing in the way of opening up assessment to take advantage of new insights about the importance of social and emotional learning. But he thinks it's "just a matter of time" before these measures are widely adopted into accountability formulas. The evidence for their importance is just too strong and converging from all directions.

For Gabrieli MESH addresses an "existential crisis" in education. "The educational system almost overwhelmingly does today what it did yesterday without a lot of reflection," he said. "We've been trying to raise third grade reading scores for 20 years—with limited success, but [at least] we know what is promising because we have those scores. The same is not true for MESH competencies, which are valued but not measured. It's one thing to become highly aware of the need to accomplish something, but if you don't start measuring something, you don't start valuing it."

When I look at schools starting to measure school climate and asking whether students have someone who cares about them, I see a scientifically informed reorienting of priorities. Paying attention to MESH means we could stop obsessing about the so-called achievement gap and start asking some more important questions: Are all of our kids safe, happy, even loved?

Team Robot and Team Monkey offer a lot to think about. But the very fact that the traditional powers that be currently embrace these approaches all but ensures that they represent incremental improvements, in limited dimensions, over our current ways of testing.

If we're committed to reinventing education, Team Butterfly and Team Unicorn represent a step beyond.

6

MEASURING WHAT MATTERS

"We do not see things as they are, we see them as we are."

—Anaïs Nin

"The assessments that we will need in the future do not yet exist."

—Gordon Commission report, 2013

TEAM BUTTERFLY

Joe Bower, a teacher and blogger in Red Deer, Alberta, Canada, and editor of the book *De-Testing and De-Grading Schools*, is an absolutist. He wants to throw all tests out the window. "The bad news is, we're deluding ourselves if we think we can quantify real learning," he said. "The good news is, it can always be described and observed. The coolest things kids do in school can be told through stories and qualitative evidence. Any time we want to talk about what's really going well in schools, it's got to be in a medium other than numbers. It's gotta be through anecdotal rather than quantitative means."

Instead of tests and grades, Bower uses a technique called performance assessment. He describes it this way: "With performance assessments the kids are doing something in a context and for a purpose. They are creating projects, writing stories. All this is collected in a portfolio like that of an artist or an engineer—a rich collection of stuff."

Whereas a bubble test "drops from the sky," at a performance assessment school curriculum development, teaching, and professional development are all connected as possible processes of evaluation and, furthermore, to real-life situations and challenges.

Imagine getting rid of all the unwieldy accountability structures and requirements of NCLB, all the reams of boring, deadening multiple-choice questions, in favor of assessments that fully integrate with the process of learning. Checks and balances, true rigor, personalization, and professionalism for both students and teachers. No more erasing parties. No more happy and sad bubbles. Communities would participate in evaluating student work, an idea that goes back to the earliest days of the republic.

This is more or less what Team Butterfly offers. And it's gathering allies in some surprising places.

PRIDE AND PERFORMANCE

On a cloudy afternoon in January I am sitting in a coffee shop near Hunter College waiting for a seventeen-year-old girl named Micaela Beigel, a student at a New York City public school called Urban Academy Laboratory High School. We have never met before, but I am here to pass judgment on one of her most important qualifications for high school graduation.

Beigel is tall and round-faced with a tiny, glittering nose stud. She introduces herself forthrightly with none of the diffidence of your stereotypical teen. She is toting a copy of Jane Austen's *Pride and Prejudice*, heavily marked up and leafed with Post-It notes. I've been asked to reread the book too.

For the next forty-five minutes we discuss the novel—as a character study of Lizzie Bennett, as a portrait of female friendship, as a model of marriage, as a reflection on women's changing roles, as the basis for centuries of adaptations and related works. Beigel's ideas are more sophisticated than those of many college graduates I've met. She challenges a simplistic feminist critique that I put forward, referring to another class she's taken on images of women in Disney: "Just saying that *Pride and Prejudice* correlates with the marriage structure doesn't mean that's the only thing it's about. It's like the *Little Mermaid*: yes, she trades her voice to get a man, but she's also struggling with identity, growing up, self-confidence, determination. You need to look at all the things that come out of the story."

Urban Academy is a member of the New York Performance Standards Consortium, a group of twenty-eight regular public six-through-twelfth-grade and high schools across New York State that have been thriving for over a decade without giving any state tests at all. Their model is now spreading across the country, in part because of the standardized testing backlash.

Instead of cramming for tests, students like Beigel learn in order to *do* things. They complete tasks designed to correspond as closely as possible to the work that artists, scientists, researchers, and other professionals do in the real world. To graduate, Urban students must present a literary essay, a social studies research paper, a science experiment, and an application of higher-level mathematics. Within reason, students can choose topics that interest them. Besides discussing *Pride and Prejudice* with me, Beigel did her "criticism proficiency" on a Roman Vishniac retrospective at the International Center of Photography, for which she interviewed attendees and led a discussion and Q&A with her classmates on the power of media. She wrote an argumentative paper on culpability in the My Lai massacre and a critique comparing the book and film versions of *A Clockwork Orange*, and she is putting together a book of photographs she took at her upstate summer camp. For her science requirement she took a class at Hunter College and conducted a psychological study of people's attitudes toward book and movie genres, applying basic statistical concepts such as correlation.

Beigel struggled in her previous, high-pressure school. After transferring she flourished at Urban, which allowed her to lean into her passions. "This is an alternative system where I get to explore new things and create. I rediscovered why I like learning—I used to feel bad about reading for fun." And, not for nothing, "I got into a good college." She'll start in the fall at Goucher.

Performance schools are wide open to the world. Students get feedback from all directions. They present their work to fellow students, teachers from other schools who haven't taught the students, academic experts, and other professionals. That's how I got here. After interviewing Ann Cook, the former codirector of Urban Academy and the leader of the Consortium, I asked whether there was any way to observe the performance assessment process up close, and she said I was perfectly qualified to be an English evaluator.

Since 1865 New York State's Board of Regents has offered a set of subject-area examinations. In 2000 the state rewrote the exams and standards and required all students to pass at least five Regents Exams, making the Regents diploma, once a kind of honors diploma, mandatory for all students. "Once Regents Exams became high stakes, test prep became the curriculum," said Cook. She saw public schools that catered to diverse needs and interests, like vocational and technical education or the arts, disappearing, victims of the single standard of success. She was part of a group of high school leaders across the state interested in other ways of assessing student work. "When the Regents started on the standards kick, we got really serious and organized the Consortium formally," receiving waivers from the state to use performance-based assessments in lieu of exams. Their website is emblazoned with the tagline, "The alternative to high-stakes testing."

"I'm a terrible test taker. A week of three-hour exams? It's the worst situation ever," said Beigel of the Regents. "It just sucks and I hated it. The Regents should definitely be gotten rid of because it's a waste of money. I already take the SATs, and that's the college entrance examination, so it actually means something."

Performance learning allows students an unusual level of personalization and autonomy. This model at first seems shockingly subjective if you've been spending your days looking at percentiles and proficiency scores. I know that leading up to our chat Beigel read the novel several times over three semesters, watched many adaptations, and worked intensively with an academic mentor trained and experienced in giving her feedback. But as an outside evaluator, I was given zero instruction walking into the conversation. She asks me to sign off on a state-issued rubric, but her teacher, Sheila Kosoff, informs me that's just a formality. "The rubric is for the state's requirement and not what we actually use to assess the student. Your own feedback of the experience in e-mail is more useful. It allows us to reflect and tweak as needed. The rubric is a little dry and vague." So I simply dash off my impressions of Beigel's performance, more or less as set forth here, and that's that.

On reflection I realize, as Walter Lippman reminded his readers in 1926, that multiple-choice tests offer no more than the illusion of precision. By contrast, performance tasks put human judgment back into the equation. The process reflects the real world, where rubrics don't hold much sway either. At crucial points in life—job interviews, work presentations, cocktail parties—everyone is going to have to convince a stranger that they know their stuff. And Beigel clearly did.

BUT DOES IT WORK?

Performance assessment is not new. For decades performance tasks have been part of the certification of professionals, including nurses, nursing aides, social workers, doctors, therapists, pharmacists, and teachers. In regular K–12 schools performance assessment, along with related approaches, including project-based learning and portfolios, had a moment of popularity in the 1980s and 1990s. For example, the state of Kentucky implemented a high-stakes assessment system in 1992 that included student portfolios of work, performance tasks, and tests featuring open-ended questions. A 1996 RAND research report found that teachers and principals thought the system was good for instruction and raised expectations for students but was burdensome and stressful to put in place. In 1998 the state dropped it.

Alongside praise for performance assessment, researchers have raised a range of concerns. One is about psychometric reliability and validity. It's impossible to specify a single "correct" answer for each performance task. Nor can you fully capture feedback with reference to the kind of four-point scale often used to grade performances: Outstanding, Good, Competent, Needs Revision. Also, students are encouraged to redo and resubmit work (i.e., "needs revision") until it's as good as it can be. And many tasks are done in groups. In short, everything that makes performance assessment more like work in the real world also makes it harder to compare results across large populations of students.

Another concern is balance. It made me a little uneasy to hear how Beigel was able to graduate as a fully formed liberal arts maven without dipping more heavily into the higher maths and hard sciences, but some performance standards schools do a better job of encouraging balance than others do. Besides, if she's anything like me, as an undergrad she'll briefly reconfront distribution requirements before putting microscope slides and cosines behind her for good.

It's harder to cover a broad and complex domain such as "English Language Arts" within the specific format of a performance task such as "Read and discuss Jane Austen's *Pride and Prejudice*." A multiple-choice test can sample more subtopics within a discipline, even if it does so shallowly. Sometimes students have trouble transferring concepts and understanding from a very specific performance format to a broader context, a concept known as generalizability. As psychometrician Bob Mislevy wrote in a 2013 academic paper, performance assessments, especially when high stakes, will ideally cover as wide a range of tasks as possible in order to get at the balance and generalizability issues: "For licensing physicians, for example, the National Board of Medical Examiners (NBME) currently uses 12 tasks in its computer-based patient management test and 12 simulated patient tasks in its clinical skills examination." Of course, these problems—balance and generalizability—arise in traditional drop-from-the-sky standardized multiple-choice tests too. It's very possible for students to score well on the fourth-grade math exam without being able to make change for a dollar in real life, and vice versa.

Subjectivity is, surprisingly, less of an issue than it may seem. Research has established that scoring on performance tasks, given an established rubric, is broadly reliable from one trained evaluator to another, although that may not be as true of untrained evaluators working without a rubric, like me.

TEAM BUTTERFLY IN SCHOOLS

If high-stakes standardized testing deprofessionalizes teaching, performance assessment is the antidote. In these settings teachers shoulder the responsibility for creating all assessments and are constantly working with colleagues and other experts inside and outside the school to improve instruction and learning. "One indicator I think is important is that the city has a 35 percent attrition rate for teachers with five or fewer years of experience, compared to the Consortium's rate of 13 percent," Cook said. "In contrast to a test-driven environment, Consortium schools allow for an emphasis on a more professional way to teach. I think you'd probably find a higher level of commitment to problem solving and innovation in Consortium schools along with a much higher tolerance for valuing conversations with one's colleagues."

What about money? Doesn't performance assessment cost more to implement? In fact, it probably costs less, all told, says Cook. Money that would be paid to outside vendors for tests, prep materials, and tutoring sessions is instead spent on professional support and development for teaching staff. Many outside evaluators, like me, are volunteers. There is no instructional time lost outside the curriculum to test administration, prepping, coaching, or remediation. All of the school's resources are thus coordinated behind supporting teachers. The nonprofit Performance Assessment Review Board, Inc., a body of educators, test experts, researchers, and members of the legal and business world, monitors the entire New York system, systematically sampling student work, holding the annual moderation studies, and buying bagels and coffee for an eight hundred–person annual conference. Serving thirty-nine schools, they have a budget of less than half a million dollars.

Despite their decade-long record of success, the Consortium hasn't been touted as an innovation by the Gates Foundation or the city's Department of Education. Perhaps that's because, as Ann Cook adamantly maintains, their approach is fundamentally at odds with any kinds of high-stakes testing. "You can't do *both* systems well. You can't graft a performance assessment system onto a test-based system," she explained.

Still, the Team Butterfly approach is drawing interest from educators across the country. A group of chief state school officers known as the Innovation Lab Network, representing California, Colorado, Iowa, Kentucky, Maine, New Hampshire, Ohio, Oregon, Virginia, Vermont, West Virginia, and Wisconsin, have adopted performance-based learning as one of their six "critical attributes" for a successful school, and several of those states are moving toward including a performance assessment option in public schools. Vermont is taking similar steps, and there is a New England Secondary School Consortium that all use performance assessment. But most interesting to me is what's happening in one of the Innovation Lab states, Kentucky.

MY OLD KENTUCKY HOME

Ann Cook tells me that in October 2012 a delegation of educators from Kentucky made a trip to a "moderation study" by the Performance Assessment Consortium in New York. At these events performance educators from several states compare notes on student work, teacher assignments, and scoring guidelines. A teacher from another school will actually read your students' essays, and vice versa, to see if the scores match up as a means of validating the work done at each school. This provides a form of quality control through peer review.

At the last minute Dr. Amy Swann, a principal at Bate Middle School in Danville, Kentucky, tagged along with the delegation. She was electrified by a high school math project that asked students to design their own amusement park ride. "What I saw was, this is so much better, so much deeper. We'd been doing project-based learning already, and it just seems like the natural next step. I said, let's take this to Danville."

Swann, a teaching superstar with a philosophy degree who used to manage a record store, determined to adopt the performance assessment model at the middle school level. The entire Danville Independent School District, led by Superintendent Carmen Coleman, with the backing of the state education commissioner, applied to skip all spring 2014 standardized tests, with the exception of the ACT and ACT practice tests for college admission, in favor of performance assessments. Jettisoning the tests required the approval of the state legislature, a bill that passed the House but was shot down in the Senate. But though the school was forced to put kids through state tests, they completely remade their curriculum in favor of performance assessment.

I visited Bate Middle School, housed in a leaky red-brick building from the 1970s, in the spring of 2014 to watch the seventh graders present their math and science performance-based assessments. When the bell rang at the end of the day the students, dressed in their Sunday best, filed into the cafeteria for a snack of cheese crackers and Capri Sun before heading off to classrooms around the school to present their projects in front of panelists.

At first blush it looked like any middle school science fair, with experiments involving baking soda rockets presented on posterboards. But when Charlie Hall, a blond, apple-cheeked twelve-year-old in a shirt and tie, cued up the first presentation in the school library in front of a panel that included Coleman and two visiting officials from a neighboring district, it was clear that deeper learning was going on. Student after student held the stage for twenty minutes each, confidently discussing their projects and fielding questions on the steps of the scientific method, background research, the difference between independent and dependent variables, possible sources of bias or error in their experiments, math concepts like median and mean, and real-world applications.

Most striking to me was the way the students listened closely and gave each other thoughtful and supportive feedback. At that age I don't remember ever being asked my opinion of a classmate's work. The kids I spoke to at Bate seemed to know that what they're doing is special, and they can feel that it's relevant. "Let's get this straight; who is going to be bubbling in answers at their job? No one," said Hall, whose experiment involved testing stress-reduction techniques for his Doberman, Rosie. "We're getting skills that we're actually going to need later on in life. It's really cool."

Bate's a good national test case for this approach, precisely because it's in no way exceptional. It's 60 percent free and reduced lunch and 36.3 percent minority. About a fifth of the students are special ed. Five years ago, when Coleman took over as superintendent of the Danville Independent School District, the school was on the state "watch list" because of its low achievement. When the state commissioner made a surprise visit to the school to decide whether to shut it down, the previous principal and teachers blamed the scores on the kids for being "bad" and "rough," said Swann.

What makes the Danville experiment particularly noteworthy is that Kentucky was out ahead of the nation in adopting the Common Core. Swann believes the standards are worthwhile, but the Pearson-published tests they used in the spring of 2013 were "your same old multiple choice." "I feel like on a standardized test you're really showing what kids don't know," said Swann. "In the performance you can show what they do know. You can honestly scaffold it for special needs. It's twenty-first-century skills, not just paper and pencil but speaking and listening, teamwork. It's about applying what you learned, not just recalling content. It seems to go so much deeper and mean so much more."

Standardized testing leads to standardized teaching, says Swann; performance tasks are differentiated and individualized. "One of my gripes with standardized testing is that we've become so focused on what's going to be on the test at the end of the year for specific grade levels. From August to April I have to teach this content, and it doesn't matter if the kid is way up *here*, I have to pull them back down so they'll do better on this content and review it. And for the low-end kids, if I rush them through it, maybe it'll at least look familiar to them." In the seventh-grade math and science PBATs that I observed, one special ed student on the autism spectrum, normally uninterested in school work, earned an Outstanding, the highest score, for his presentation on surface tension.

In the fall of 2013 Swann held a meeting to explain the new approach and ask for parents' buy-in. "Parents showed up, and I went through what learning looks like when you're preparing for a standardized test [vs.] a performance-based assessment and showed pictures of our kids and the different activities they're doing. And the teachers came up and talked about what the kids were doing. The parents absolutely loved it. But one raised her hand and asked, 'Are they going to make you go back to the old system? Because I don't want to go back. I love that my kids are challenged, more engaged— they want to be in school.' Middle schools aren't always the happiest places, but kids and staff are happy here.'"

Both Swann and Coleman left Danville at the end of the 2014 school year—Swann to institute project-based learning at low-performing, high-poverty schools in several states with a consultancy called MatchBook Learning, and Coleman for a position at the University of Kentucky, where part of her work will involve founding a consortium in that state that is similar to New York's. They have been in touch with school leaders in Texas and other states to implement the model as well. "Danville's got to be our model," said Coleman.

TEAM UNICORN

The approaches to assessment we've covered so far stake out complementary territories:

Team Robot tests conventional subjects (math, reading, writing) in unconventional ways (invisible, integrated, electronic).

Team Monkey tests unconventional qualities (mindset, grit) in conventional ways (multiple-choice surveys).

Team Butterfly integrates learning with assessment and covers twenty-first-century skills, without quantifying the outcomes in a way that's familiar or easily comparable from student to student or school to school.

The final approach to testing is an attempt to have it all. It addresses twenty-first-century skills and social and emotional learning. It's highly engaging for students, like the best performance assessment. Yet it's data-rich and generalizable, like the best standardized assessment. I call it Team Unicorn because its existence is still unproven.

It starts with a form of media that's often been demonized for its impact on children: video games.

INSIDE THE GLASSLAB

I am the mayor of a little city. My goal is to cut air pollution while maintaining the energy supply and keeping the economy humming. I build a brand-new solar plant, then immediately bulldoze the coal plant. Oops, the sun just went down, and now there are brownouts across the city!

SimCityEDU: Pollution Challenge! debuted in November 2013. It's the product of a $10.3 million private-public collaboration between the nonprofit Institute of Play, the Entertainment Software Association, the Gates and MacArthur Foundations, the large video game company Electronic Arts, Pearson, and ETS. The creators, a multidisciplinary team known as GlassLab, are based in Redwood City, in the heart of Silicon Valley. They have big dreams. They want to use game-based assessments to start measuring what really matters in the twenty-first century: how we learn and how we think.

"We have all these high-stakes assessments focusing the majority of their testing on rote learning and not authentic application of skill and problem solving," said Seth Corrigan, the director of education and evaluation for GlassLab. "We're never going to transform education and prepare kids for success if we don't transform assessment to look at higher-order skills. Everything pointed to games as the way to do that."

In the past ten years or so, learning scientists have become fascinated with video games for many reasons. First of all, games are fun, even addictive, to play. Second, they are capable of simulating complex situations to a degree of detail that becomes translatable to the real world, which is why they are used to train fighter pilots and Cisco network engineers.

And like Team Robot's learning software, games can stealthily record an amazing level of detail about the learning process. "A student who sits down in front of a paper-pencil test gets each question right or wrong. Zeros and ones," said Corrigan. "That's all the information you've got to work with after the student leaves the room." By contrast, *SimCityEDU: Pollution Challenge!* is tracking my mouse movements each fraction of a second. They're keeping track of how many times I take a certain action, when in relation to other events, and how much time I spend accessing information relevant to the game. Was it a hard or easy question or decision? How quickly did I pull the trigger? Am I speeding up or slowing down? How often do I look at the air-quality map to check the effects of my decisions? Do I shut down the coal plant as an experiment before charging ahead to bulldoze it? (Whoops!) If Team Robot moved us from a snapshot to a film strip, the moment-by-moment data collection turns up the fidelity to the level of HD video.

But the vital connection between games and learning is not data. It's the player-learner's state of mind. Michael John, senior creative director at Electronic Arts who oversees GlassLab's creative product development, says a lot of what makes a good game is about finding the optimal level of challenge. "I've made lots of games for middle school kids, and the worst thing they can tell you is 'It was too easy.' You have to strike a really careful balance to make the games feel fun and the accomplishments feel satisfying." It turns out that this balance is also widely considered the best one for learning. Pioneering developmental psychologist Lev Vygotsky called it the "proximal zone of development"—poised between boredom, when things are too easy, and anxiety, when they get too hard. Or as Lee Peng Yee, a professor of math instruction at Singapore's National Institute of Education, famously put it, "If you think you can catch the bus, you will run for it."

SimCityEDU seems to keep kids running at their own top speeds for their own personal bus. Denise Cruz, a beta tester who teaches at Robinswood Middle School in Orlando, decided to use the game with two groups of English Language Arts students, a remedial class and a gifted group. The game motivated her struggling readers to pay close attention to its short written instructions. The gifted kids enjoyed it just as much. "We modified things based on where we were trying to take the kids," said Cruz.

They're also generalizing their learning to the real world. "Kids are relating their experience in the simulation to the area where they live," she said. "For instance, close to where they live there is a factory. They see an arrow showing the wind direction [in the game] and they're going, 'Oh my gosh, when the wind blows that factory is sending pollution to our neighborhood! How could they even zone that area like that?' One full day we took talking about that issue." Michael John, the game designer, says this is part of the elemental appeal of games: "They have the ability to put you *in* a context, instead of just around a context. Once something is realized as a world it becomes a lot more resonant than somebody else's story that I'm reading," he said. "All games do that if they're done well." The immersive power of games is part of their fundamental appeal.

FLUID TESTS

Instead of just finding out what students already know, game-based assessments, by recording the pattern of students' decisions within a rich context, might be able to find out something far more important: how well they learn and how they think.

It would be more helpful for educational purposes and more hopeful for individuals to understand a student's capacity for growth and her particular learning strengths and weaknesses rather than merely take that snapshot of whether she is above proficient or below proficient in a specific subject at a given point in time. One way to get at this is so-called dynamic testing. This, again, is from Vygotsky. He posited a test-teach-retest model. The idea is to get a sense of how the student assimilates new information in a particular domain. This could be thought of as testing for teachability. *Pollution Challenge!* creates a probabilistic model of how the students' level of skill changes while playing the game. In other words, it could be seen as an automated dynamic test. "Traditionally folks have looked at assessments as filtering mechanisms or ranking systems that put you at the top or bottom of the heap," Corrigan said. "The damn thing is, that's not actionable."

As each ten-minute challenge is completed within *SimCityEDU*, students get on-screen feedback about what went right, what went wrong, and what to try next (e.g., "Can you use fewer bus stops to get all the kids to school?") Teachers see a dashboard with updated charts that display each student's level of competency in systems thinking as they move from a "black box" concept of one input affecting one output toward the ability to weigh the relative effects of multiple variables. The lesson plans that come with the game will include conversation prompts that help students move along to the next step in that trajectory. This feedback is designed to motivate students and inform better teaching.

TO THE FUN FAIR

Game-based assessments are being designed specifically to test twenty-first-century literacies. With its realistic simulations of energy and pollution, *SimCityEDU: Pollution Challenge!* conforms to the Next Generation Science Standards, created in parallel to the Common Core. It includes reading tasks that align with the Common Core. But *Pollution Challenge!* is not primarily designed to teach or test either science or reading—it's a game-based test of systems thinking.

Systems thinking isn't a binary value—"Yes, I understand systems thinking" vs. "No, I don't." Students progress along a trajectory, which Corrigan described this way: "It starts out with black-box thinking: I know something is causing pollution, but I don't know what it is. Then it's billiard-ball causality—a single independent variable A causes dependent variable B to occur. Then it's multivariate causality: the ability to identify multiple independent and dependent variables." Unlike Team Robot's assessments of mastery in, say, the rules of algebra, Team Unicorn's game-based assessments model students' mastery of more abstract, higher-order cognitive and noncognitive skill sets like collaboration, leadership, persistence, focus, and even mindset and values.

Dan Schwartz is a professor of education at Stanford, where he creates video game–based assessments he calls "choicelets," which focus on how students make choices. "In our assessments we make little fun games, and to do well at the games you need to learn something, so they're not just measures of what the student already knows but attempts to measure whether they are prepared to continue learning when they're no longer told exactly what to do," he said.

For example, Schwartz's team built a game called *Posterlet* in which students are asked to design posters for a fun fair. The students then can choose to hear feedback on their posters from a focus group of three animal characters. From each member of the focus group, the players can choose to hear either positive or negative feedback. The animal characters evaluate the posters based on fairly well-established design principles like symmetry, compatible colors, appropriate font size, and so on: Are there colors on top of each other that are hard to see? Is the text too difficult to read? Too small? Then the students can choose to revise their posters based on the feedback, display them for the fair, and see how many tickets they sell. After that they can go back for a second or third round of revisions.

The idea of this game, says Schwartz, is not primarily to teach or test the students' understanding of graphic design principles but rather to test their motivation to improve and their understanding of how to take criticism and respond to feedback. "The more negative feedback you choose, the more your poster improves," said Schwartz. "Choosing negative feedback is a better way to learn." Another Schwartz-designed "Choicelet" tests students' willingness to make several attempts to solve a problem, sorting through and evaluating their own efforts.

"When I talk to superintendents, they understand the importance of the achievement tests, but they have their own things they want to promote, like collaboration and design thinking," said Schwartz. "So we sort of give them a chance to find out how they're doing because there aren't any assessments out there that can do that." An initial experiment with *Posterlet* compared two schools that based their curricula on "design thinking" principles, including the idea that failure is a desirable part of a process of creative iteration. At the school that the experimenters thought was doing a better job overall, based on surveys and interviews with the teachers and students, the students also sought negative feedback at a higher rate.

CHOCOLATE-COVERED BROCCOLI

Game-based assessments are in their infancy. They have several cycles of development ahead of them to be tested and tweaked. They need to be given to large numbers of students in the real world to de-termine their predictive power, their validity, and their comparability and generalizability across different contexts. "There's a hunt for ground truth," as Corrigan puts it. An independent research firm is observing students at two schools in the Bay Area as they play *SimCi-tyEDU: Pollution Challenge!* and having them think aloud about their gameplay decisions to get at the effects on problem solving and learn-ing. "They're looking for a good connection between the kinds of de-cisions the student says that they're making and the actual steps in their gameplay," said Corrigan. "We'll look at both sorts of informa-tion and make sure the game requires the sort of systems thinking we say it does."

Designing good game-based assessments, from what I can tell, is damn hard. It requires learning scientists, psychometricians, and game designers to collaborate in unprecedented ways. Game design-ers are used to an agile design process in which they run tests and make big changes along the way, whereas test writers are used to pro-ducing a completed test and then field-testing it on huge numbers of students for reliability and validity before releasing it all at once. Plus, the industry's best game designers are in demand to work on block-busters with hundred-million-dollar budgets like *Call of Duty* and *Grand Theft Auto*. Those who choose to lend their skills to the na-scent field of educational software are rare true believers.

So to build a learning and testing game, these teams must ana-lyze a content domain (e.g., pollution) and a cognitive domain (e.g., systems thinking), then create rules that make sense as a game and also according to the real-world laws of physics, biology, or energy exchange. The challenge for the designers is to produce games that gather useful data while avoiding the "chocolate-covered broccoli" syndrome common to many educational media products—a thin coating of cool over a large serving of good-for-you.

SimCityEDU, as a beta version, has some chocolate-broccoli problems. At one point the game asks you to fill out a diagram show-ing the cause and effect between, say, sulfur dioxide, coal plants, and air pollution. This was added on at the request of the assessment team to provide a more explicit basis of evidence for systems think-ing. But it feels more like stopping play to fill out a worksheet. Still, the overall experience was fun enough to keep me motivated through the boring parts.

The second GlassLab game, *Mars Generation One: Argubot Academy*, was produced in collaboration with NASA and released in April 2014. Set on a Mars colony, with pieces recognizable from Pokemon and Magic card games, the game both teaches and tests the elements of argumentation, including claims, evidence, and reasoning. GlassLab is making its assessment infrastructure available for use by other game developers. Future games will attempt to tackle other higher-order skills like collaboration, which requires modeling the behavior of various members of a team.

GlassLab's games are currently available to classrooms, schools, districts, and parents through multiple commercial and public channels. Getting the GlassLab and Choicelet projects, or others like them, to scale in classrooms across the country is crucial to Team Unicorn's long-term goal: upsetting the status quo of multiple-choice, static standardized testing and replacing it with an evidence-based model of continuous formative feedback for continuous improvement in higher-order skills.

MY TWO BRAINS

Game-based assessment creates a simulated situation and analyzes large amounts of data about students' behavior within it. Other Team Unicorn approaches involve building computer systems that gather and crunch information about students in more naturalistic settings. If game-based assessment is like Laser Tag, with students running around within an artificially constructed and wired environment, then these approaches are more like putting computer chips in the ears of a herd of migrating antelope—letting students explore a natural learning landscape at will while quietly collecting data on them in the background.

Two of the rapidly expanding frontiers of research in computer science are machine learning and artificial intelligence. Both, as their names suggest, build computer simulations that can learn and behave like human brains—some are actually called "neural networks."

Some researchers in these fields are returning the favor, trying to improve our understanding of how human brains learn and behave through the analysis of huge amounts of information.

In an early example of the potential of such technology, Deb Roy, a cognitive scientist then at MIT, in 2005–2006 constructed a system of cameras and computers all over his house that captured and analyzed a total of two hundred thousand hours of video and audio of his son's first year. The system was able to document the "birth of a word"—that is, when and how each word in his son's vocabulary emerged, including the subtlety of learning interactions between him and his caregivers. For example, just before the baby was about to learn a new word, his mother, father, grandmother, and nanny seemed to pick up on his cues—they started using it and repeating it more often, in shorter sentences.

At its most intriguing, Team Unicorn technology highlights the social, emotional, and human aspects of learning. For example, *SimCityEDU* was produced in collaboration with Columbia's Ryan Baker, whose research is at the forefront of "educational data mining." This field, still small, has been expanding rapidly in the past decade in response to the growing interest in big data and its analysis.

Baker has spent the last ten years working on educational software that guesses how learners feel while they're learning. His technology is embedded within systems currently being used by tens of thousands of students in classrooms from kindergarten through medical school. His systems intuit when students are gaming the system, drifting off-task, or making careless errors. They have found that medical residents show the highest rates of gaming the system, trying to trick the software into letting them move on without learning anything, at rates up to 38 percent for a program that was supposed to teach them how to detect cancer.

Using this evidence on the timing of actions and their meaning within the game or program, the engagement detectors model a range of emotional states, like delight, boredom, confusion, flow, frustration, and what Baker memorably calls WTF behavior. For instance, think back to when the students at Garfield High, protesting the MAP tests in Seattle, hit the answer "A" over and over until the test was invalidated. If that test had had an engagement detector built in, it would have known immediately that something was up. It might even have been able to figure out, from the speed of pressing the buttons, that the students were excited or angry.

Experimenters rate the performance of these computer systems against the impressions of trained human observers, who walk up and down aisles in a classroom to see whether students seem checked in or checked out. Vis-à-vis the humans, Baker says, the computers are currently only fair but are improving steadily. One of Baker's engagement detectors predicted, 69 percent of the time, which students would actually go to college five to seven years later, based not on their academic performance but on the students' apparent attitudes toward and engagement in the process of learning.

Baker envisions tools like these working like an espresso maker, not a vending machine: they are meant to enhance teacher performance, not replace teachers. They're not designed to make independent determinations of student learning or engagement but to provide important information to the teacher and student.

"High tech doesn't get rid of the teacher. It allows them to focus on what people are best at," said Baker. "Dealing with students' engagement, helping to support them. I would like to see that every kid get an educational experience tailored to their needs on multiple levels: cognitive, emotional, social. And I think that we can do that. Also I would simultaneously envision teachers having much more useful information about their kids." This may be what most distinguishes Team Unicorn from Team Robot: the former understands the limitations of what they are building.

Norma and Vivienne Ming, a married couple who have a research startup called Socos, are building machine learning systems that try to assess students' learning using only unstructured, passively collected data. For example, in two published research papers they analyzed discussion posts written in an online forum by college students taking biology and economics. By parsing student writing alone, the Socos system was able to predict students' final grades within one week; by the end of the course they knew within two and four percentage points what each student's final grade would be without looking at assignments, tests, or the textbook. The system went beyond the "bag of words" approach, instead using a new algorithm and a complex concept-matching classification. It identified independent concepts in relation to each other, whether near or far, and from more general to more specific. In spring 2014 the Mings began a trial with small audio recorders worn by bilingual kindergartners in an Austin school to see whether they could model students' language acquisition over time by analyzing the words they produce and hear both in and out of class.

Capturing so much data about students could entirely change the field of learning research, says Baker. Think of designing studies "that capture, say, 75 percent of the richness of qualitative methods with ten times the scale of five years ago." When researchers look at the effectiveness of a particular method of teaching reading or math, a typical sample size is around fifty students. It's this research literature that formed the basis of some of the Common Core State Standards, for example. But educational data mining allows you instead to design a study that goes into detail with fifty thousand students.

For example, Baker says, one educational data mining paper looked at the difference between brief and extended confusion. Extended confusion, it turns out, is terrible for motivation, but brief moments of confusion are a key part of the process for learners who exhibit the greatest amount of growth.

BRAIN GAMES

Some of the most forward-looking work of AI specialists, neuroscientists, and others on Team Unicorn hearkens back to the earliest days of anthropometry—trying to measure the functioning of the nervous system and the workings of the brain directly. They're even using some of the same tools. And the enterprise may turn out to be just as foolhardy as it was back then, but the experiments are intriguing nonetheless.

Researchers such as Jan Plass at New York University are putting EEG headsets, cameras, and electrodes on people while they work with learning software, combining measurements of brainwaves, eye gaze, and galvanic skin response (sweating, heartbeat, body temperature) with the input from the keyboard to get a close-up view of learning in progress. Although this is too invasive a setup to be used on a daily basis, it could be used, like a treadmill "stress test" of cardiovascular fitness, to get a hyper-rich, moment-by-moment reading of a student's emotional and mental states and the conditions under which they best acquire new knowledge.

Some computer-brain interfaces are already being tested that aim to not just diagnose but also improve students' performance in school. Atentiv is a startup launched in February 2014, based on research at Duke University. It's a video game with a brain-computer interface designed to diagnose and treat attention disorders. To play it, a kid straps on a Bluetooth headset that reads the electrical signals coming from his frontal lobe and then completes the Stroop Task, a common performance test of concentration. (A typical Stroop Task item asks you to read, out loud, the word "blue" appearing in red letters.) The modified EEG system calibrates the player's unique signature patterns of focus and distraction. Research has shown that people diagnosed with ADD have characteristic EEG patterns.

Once the system is calibrated to the player, he starts playing a video game that involves a runner crossing an obstacle course. When the player focuses, as measured by brainwaves, the runner speeds up; when he gets distracted, the runner slows down. Kids learn how to control attention and manage distractions. Atentiv's early trials showed that 75 to 85 percent of kids improve their symptoms over time—without drugs—as measured by tests, parents' perceptions, and direct readings of the brainwaves.

I spoke to the mother of one study participant, Sandra in Newton, Massachusetts, who asked to preserve her family's anonymity. Her nine-year-old son, Hayden, took part in a clinical trial three times a week for eight weeks. "I really saw a tremendous difference both at home and at school. I was thrilled," she told me. Hayden's handwriting got neater. He slept better. His homework improved. His teacher was no longer calling with discipline problems. He got along better with his sister and with friends. He was easier to get off to school in the morning.

Atentiv assesses attention, yes, but the most important feedback it gives is directly to the player. It's a widget for teaching mindset. "For Hayden, it helped him realize he was capable," said Sandra. "Just the way the game and training materials talked to him about it: saying there's nothing wrong with you, you're not dumb. Look, your brain is like a Ferrari and we're going to teach you to look at the green and red light."

Part of this may be a placebo effect. This experimental effect needs to be duplicated across large numbers of young people, and we also need to know whether it persists over time. But if it gave Hayden the confidence to cultivate his own attention and self-control, a game like Atentiv could function more or less like the feather in Dumbo's trunk: a little bit of "magic" that helps someone soar.

THE FOUR TEAMS AND THE FUTURE OF TESTING

This tour through the alternative precincts and emerging frontiers of testing has, I hope, demonstrated that it's no longer necessary to peg our entire school system to the results of weak, limited, static measures of math and reading alone. Testing doesn't need to be invasive or anxiety producing. It shouldn't be used to label children in lasting, damaging ways while perversely ignoring some of the factors most important to success. In the best-case scenarios the activity of testing fades into the background of the real work of teaching and learning. You don't drive by staring at the dashboard; you mostly keep your eyes on the road.

To get rid of bad tests once and for all we need a positive and coherent vision of what will replace them. I think it should include something from all four teams. But I'd want to start with Team Butterfly.

Team Butterfly is a humanistic approach. It's a way of "doing school," not just "doing testing"; it deeply integrates learning and assessment. It invokes tradition yet speaks to the needs of students today. The performance-assessment students I've met are remarkable for their joy and engagement with learning for its own sake. They are aware of working on the skills that really matter. Successful performance-assessment teachers and school leaders are modeling self-reflection and peer review at the school level as well as the student-to-student level. I'd like to see my daughter attend a high-quality performance-assessment school.

But if high stakes are attached or the model is foisted on unwilling participants, performance assessment, like any other test, can be highly susceptible to fudging. In regular New York City public schools students who opt out can submit portfolios of projects instead of tests. "Schools love portfolio students because you can always make sure they get 4s," the highest scores, one principal told me anonymously.

If students stopped taking state tests, how would we know how well they're really doing? What about equity and accountability? How do we keep schools honest?

What about this: use real-world metrics that actually matter.

According to the most recent data available, from 2008 to 2012 Performance Assessment Consortium schools in New York City have nearly identical demographics to the city's public schools as a whole in terms of poverty, minority groups, English language learners, and those with disabilities. But their five-year graduation rate is 10 points higher—76.0 percent vs. 66.1 percent. Their dropout rate is 5.3 percent vs. 11.8 percent. And their graduates are far more likely to stay in college: 93 percent make it to their sophomore year, compared to 80 percent across New York State.

THE BUTTERFLY EFFECT

Did you find those numbers convincing? I did. Part of the Consortium's edge may be that these are small schools with self-selected students and highly dedicated teachers. But you can say, at a minimum, that given these numbers, individualized project-based learning sans bubble tests is not hurting these students' academic progress and may be better preparing them to succeed.

Maybe the problem with data-driven accountability is our choice of data. Rather than relying solely on any standardized test, we now have the ability to keep track of what happens to students. And rather than relying on standardized proficiency targets, districts, schools, and students can use better information to create individualized growth targets. Call this the butterfly-effect approach. It uses data to paint a fuller, more individualized picture of school outcomes, drawing connections between, say, a middle schooler acting up in class and her performance in college six years later.

One advocate of this approach, perhaps surprisingly, is Julian Vasquez Heilig, the researcher who exposed the Texas Miracle, now at California State University in Sacramento. He thinks that better data can avoid the unintended consequences created by a narrow reliance on standardized test scores. "One of the interesting requirements of Race to the Top was more information systems," he said. In 2009 all fifty states committed to creating data systems with twelve key elements. These included tracking each student by a unique statewide identifier and seeing what happens when they leave school: Do they graduate? Enroll in college? Do they need remediation in college? And sometimes, do they persist and get their degree? Because of this new level of detail, made possible by ever-growing computer power, test-score snapshots could soon be replaced with long-range indicators of success. "We don't need the testing companies to tell us who's 'college ready,'" said Heilig. "We can tell you which students are remedial, what they majored in, whether they persisted in college."

Though it's early still, better data is already shaping educational decision making. In 2010, in response to Race to the Top and internal advocacy by then-Mayor Michael Bloomberg and the philanthropic community, New York City's Department of Education began publishing the results of tracking individual students through the pipeline from ninth grade all the way to the city's public community college system, the City University of New York (CUNY).

The good news was that, compared to a decade earlier, more public school students were graduating from high school, more were earning GEDs, and more were going to college. The number of graduates attending CUNY community and four-year colleges each year jumped by ten thousand over the years 2002 to 2012.

The bad news was that 77.6 percent of high school graduates who enrolled in CUNY community colleges in the fall of 2013 needed high school–level instruction, also known as remediation, in reading, writing, or math. That number was up from 71 percent a few years before, partly because more kids were going to college. The tracking data told us something that the test scores were hiding: despite passing four Regents Exams, as required, with a score of 65 or better, four of five students were arriving at college unable to read, write, do math, or all three at a college level.

The giant cruise liner that is New York City's school system, from middle school through college, began to turn under the impact of these new currents of data. The Department of Education created a series of programs that push college-level instruction and expectations into high schools. President Obama has visited and saluted Pathways in Technology Early College High School (P-Tech), in Brooklyn, the first of a group of high schools created in partnership with IBM and other companies that keep students for six years so they can earn technical associate's degrees for free. There are twelve further "early college high schools" that give students the chance to earn college credits, even associate's degrees, in high school.

CUNY, for its part, introduced special programs called Accelerated Study in Associate Programs (ASAP), CUNY Start, and Guttman Community College. All three are designed to move students through the basics by putting them through long hours in a few core classes with the same small group of classmates and specially trained teachers. ASAP has been around the longest, since 2007. Of that first class, over half, 55 percent earned their associates' degree within three years, compared to 24.7 percent of similar students in the broader CUNY system. According to an independent study, the graduation rates were so much higher that ASAP, though it cost far more per student, cost about 10 percent less per graduate. Similarly, 60 to 70 percent of Start students gain proficiency in a given subject after just one semester, compared to just one in five who take regular remedial courses.

Under Mayor Bill DeBlasio, elected in 2013, and his superintendent Carmen Fariña, New York City is stepping back from the heavy emphasis on data, including ending letter grades for schools based largely on test scores. But DeBlasio used similar kinds of long-term research-based indicators to build the case for his signature policy proposal, universal pre-K.

ENVISIONING A DIFFERENCE

The butterfly-effect is not magic. Goodhart's law still applies. When the stakes are high and resources are scarce, any individual factor, from performance tasks to dropout rates to college admission rates, is still susceptible to being gamed just like test scores. That's why Hammond's principle of multiple measures is so important. Most Team Butterfly schools, for example, still have most kids taking the ACT or SAT, which acts as a kind of backup measure to provide a basis for comparability and soothe worried parents.

Innovative schools, districts, and even states around the country are moving toward a multiple-measures approach that incorporates ideas from both Team Monkey and Team Butterfly. Charter schools are heavily identified with a "no excuses" attitude and obsession with test scores. But it is the data itself that has been leading some charters away from looking at test scores alone. The growing consensus among charter leaders and other reformers is that long-term college outcomes matter more than annual state test scores.

KIPP, perhaps the most lauded group of charter schools in the nation, has been going through a public reexamination of some of its core tenets since the publication of a 2011 report following its first group of students. Among these students, who entered eighth grade in 1995, one-third had graduated from college. Although that compares favorably to just 8 percent of non-KIPP students from similar backgrounds, it still fell far short from what KIPP expected. KIPP has since announced that they're refocusing on the long-term destiny of their students, including equipping them with better social and emotional skills, so they will be able to learn and succeed away from the highly structured environment.

Bob Lenz is the Chief of Innovation at Envision Schools, a small but influential group of three charter public high schools in the San Francisco Bay Area. They are adopting the butterfly-effect approach. "My point of view is pretty similar to yours," he told me. "If we can get the assessments right, it should start to change what happens in schools." Change tests, and you change teaching and learning and, ultimately, "get the kinds of schools our kids need."

"We developed our performance standards with the help of Linda Darling-Hammond at Stanford to get at not only core academic knowledge but deeper competencies—critical thinking, collaboration, project management—and we also believe that kids need to be reflective and metacognitive about their learning," Lenz said.

Envision schools judge themselves on two major metrics: the quality of student work as aligned with Common Core and college-ready standards and the percentage of graduates who persist through the first year of college. Students create portfolios of work that are shared and exhibited publicly in the tenth and twelfth grades. Graduating seniors do a dissertation-style defense of their portfolios. As in the New York Performance Assessment Consortium schools and in the tradition of the old "examinations," Lenz sees public exhibition as another means of holding Envision accountable.

As for those numbers: 70 percent of Envision students are low income, and 75 percent are African American or Latino; 98 percent of their graduates go to college, with 73 percent to a four-year college; 80 percent of the kids are first in their family to go to college, and nine of ten persist in college for at least a year after graduation. "The high number of kids going to school is great, but knowing that they're sticking is huge," said Lenz. Envision has a consultancy that works with schools around the country to spread these ideas far and wide.

OAKLAND VS. MONTGOMERY COUNTY

Again, Envision and KIPP schools are small, with highly committed staff and all kinds of extra support. Can the butterfly-effect approach be customized for the needs of different communities, especially at schools that are struggling on the basics? Heilig suggests that it can and should. "There are lots of other ways and outcomes that we have available to us now to understand how schools are performing," said Heilig. "For example, how many kids go to county lockup? That's something we care about as a society, but we [currently] can't hold our communities, schools, or districts accountable for that."

Heilig has proposed "community-based accountability," in which educational leaders come together with parents and community members to set short- and long-term goals, to be measured with multiple indicators. The process respects local starting points and priorities. In a community like Oakland, California, where young black men are as likely to get killed as they are to graduate high school college-ready, stopping the violence should be job number one. Whereas in affluent Scarsdale or Montgomery County, Maryland, Michael McGill and Joshua Starr have the luxury of focusing on creative problem-solving abilities and technology literacy.

The state of California actually included a first step toward community-based accountability in the budget passed in 2013: a "local control funding formula" that rewards school districts for taking local steps toward bigger goals. Progress toward these goals is determined in part by surveys administered by the Healthy Kids Survey.

Briana Lamb, seventeen, is a senior at Fremont High School in South Central Los Angeles who has been organizing on behalf of the Local Control Funding Formula. She told me about her struggle to get an education in resource-strapped urban schools. "At the beginning of my junior year," she said, "I was assigned four 'home' periods," meaning blank spots in her schedule. Almost half the seniors, she said, head home at noon. "We had a long-term sub in Algebra I. She said, 'I'm not a math teacher. I can't help you. I'm sorry. Maybe you can help each other.' A lot of kids are like, 'What's the point of going to class because the teacher can't teach me.'"

She and her fellow students are getting mugged at the school gate, dealing with gang violence and problems at home. At school there is one mental health counselor for hundreds of students. "My sophomore year, my mother passed away and my father was sick. I couldn't focus on school. But nobody took the time to see—'Why aren't you passing?' Everybody just assumed I didn't care about school. They mentioned to me that the GED is always an option, and I was only a sophomore." Lamb managed to beat the odds and is headed to Cal State Northridge.

"If your school is only focused on getting a passing grade on a test, that influences teaching to the test and nudging low performers out of school," said Heilig. "If schools are focused on the fact that they don't want 5 percent of their kids going to jail anymore, that changes how you do school." Community-based accountability should not be used as an excuse for lowering expectations of any student. It's a means of trying to blunt the force of Goodhart's law by choosing more suitable targets for schools and communities to try to live up to.

SPY GAMES

In a few years, thanks to the spread of statewide longitudinal data systems, student records could include individual progress on particular measurable goals year after year. The same accountability systems that today track students from high school into college could correlate the behavior records, attendance, health, interactions with the law, and even the love of school of third and fourth graders with their outcomes many years later. Education Secretary Arne Duncan, for one, supports this approach. "Hopefully, some day, we can track children from preschool to high school and from high school to college and college to career. We must track high-growth children in classrooms to their great teachers and great teachers to their schools of education," he said in a 2009 speech.

Whether this and the whole big-data approach sounds like an incredible advance or a creepy invasion depends on your point of view, and sometimes on the time of day. We live in an age in which people are up in arms about government surveillance while voluntarily sharing intimate information with a long list of commercial platforms and apps. The long-term tracking of kids, in particular, even when they are identified with numbers rather than names and as groups rather than as individuals, has some parents and privacy experts spooked.

Most public school districts today are already storing their records, including demographics, grades, and attendance, with third-party "cloud" providers under agreements that leave that information open to be sold to vendors or accidentally exposed to hackers. If we put large numbers of students under minute-by-minute surveillance of the actual learning process, as comes with the spread of learning analytics, we'd need some pretty good assurances that this detailed data would be safe.

Student data, like health data, is extremely sensitive. What if the information is used for marketing? Or for hiring decisions? Or for tracking or otherwise stigmatizing young people? Does it matter whether these systems are government owned or in the hands of private vendors? What kinds of safeguards do we need to ensure that student information isn't stolen or used for profit? The law is just starting to grapple with these questions and build the right kinds of protections.

A California state bill and a federal bill introduced in 2014 each cover some of the following principles:

- Making sure that contracts covering the storage of student data don't allow it to be sold or used for marketing purposes, or for any purpose that is not educational.
- Parents should be allowed to access and amend student data.
- Data should be deleted when it is no longer required for an educational purpose.
- In the case of actual harm such as a data breach, make sure there are penalties and reporting responsibilities in place.

These important policy issues need to be addressed because the combination of performance assessment plus "stealth assessment" plus data-driven community-accountability ratings arguably represents a huge step forward over what we have right now. It offers the opportunity to cut out the middleman—test scores—in favor of real learning plus real numbers.

WHAT IS TO BE DONE?

Eliminating high-stakes testing should create a big opening for new ways to improve schools. But it will never happen without a vision of how we get there. The push for change has to come from families who are not only fed up but also can see the alternatives clearly. Mentioned throughout the book, the Stanford researcher Linda Darling-Hammond's work describes a complex ecosystem of tests, standards, and accountability that comes the closest to what I would like to see happen in schools. With gratitude to her, here is what I'd like to see replace The Tests.

First, students' experience in school is defined by Team Butterfly: interdisciplinary, interest-driven, individualized projects. Students work together and separately to build, make, read, write, conduct experiments, solve problems, and present their work. "How am I doing?"

is a question answered continuously, by self-reflection, teacher feedback, peer review, and public exhibition as well as by referring to external standards such as the Common Core. Team Unicorn–style games
and simulations could soon take their place alongside "analog" performance tasks, generating even more evidence about students' acquisition of twenty-first-century skills and values and helping to provide a
basis for comparison across different schools.

Second, national, standardized assessments are given sparingly—say, at the seventh- and twelfth-grade levels—as an additional
way to validate the results of performance assessments at individual
schools, to identify gaps, and maybe for college admission. These
don't have to be stop-and-test or bubble-heavy; they could be essay
exams or portfolios graded by disinterested experts. Or they could be
the sum of Team Robot–style, invisible, integrated interactions with
learning software over time. That way they could model student
growth, not just achievement. These same software systems provide
another source of ongoing feedback to students, teachers, and parents—just like the readings from the dashboard and the GPS that
drivers use to stay on track.

Third, at the school and district level, these multiple measures
of student learning (Butterfly and Robot) are combined with other
key indicators. For students these include Team Monkey social and
emotional measures. For schools they include trends like discipline,
attendance, graduation rates, and college persistence.

Teachers, like students, are evaluated using multiple measures
of their own professional practices as well as all of these student outcomes and by using self-reflection, student feedback, peer review, and
public exhibition.

THREE NEW KINDS OF ACCOUNTABILITY

Overhauling assessment is important, but overhauling accountability is even more important. It's not just the measures but what the
measures are used for that really matters. The most humanistic, beau-
tifully nuanced, portfolio-based assessment system in the world
could still be misused as a bludgeon to punish teachers and close

schools. Likewise, standardized tests, even at their most limited, re-ductive, and dry, are being used today by intrepid school leaders like my friend Linda to holistically motivate better achievement.

The emphasis of an accountability system should not be on the "accounting" part but the "ability" part. Rather than using test scores to punish students, teachers, and schools, we should use all the infor-mation available to help them do better. "We can't fire our way to great-ness," in the words of the Economic Policy Institute's Elaine Weiss.

Darling-Hammond talks about "reciprocal accountability." This means our schools aren't just beholden to our communities; our com-munities are also beholden to our schools. "Resource accountability" means holding districts and states accountable for the inputs that our school system receives, not just holding schools to account for the outcomes. Right now schools, students, and teachers are graded as "failing" and punished—not districts, not states, not politicians, not the federal government. In a climate in which state aid per student is falling in most states, in which only fourteen states even attempt to give poor schools more aid than rich schools, perhaps it's time to make sure the fingers point in both directions.

"Community accountability," Heilig's approach, means widening the lens to take in other measures that affect young people, like health and violence, and relating those back to the work that schools are do-ing, highlighting the potential for collaboration. The Broader, Bolder education agenda is another example of this. The "community schools" approach means making schools the hub of crucial social services, like mental health and health care, and even services for par-ents like job placement, language classes for immigrants, help getting Internet access, and housing assistance. All of these services comple-ment the educational mission and, in many cases, make it possible.

One day I would like to see the education reform discussion merge into a bigger conversation about what kind of world we are creating for our children. Child welfare, foster care, juvenile justice, and maternal health are all part of this conversation. So are minimum wage, the pay gap, and maternity leave. So are the rise of childhood ADD, autism, asthma, allergies, and type 1 diabetes. As test scores have repeatedly shown us for generations, good performance is extremely difficult to achieve unless a child is brought up in a good environment.

Of course there are massive political and economic forces arrayed against this integrated vision—there are folks in Congress right now who want to end the school lunch program. But education reform has been an unusually bipartisan cause for the last thirty years. I believe better evidence can help drive reformers on both sides of the aisle toward a more holistic definition of "leaving no child behind." The emergence of universal pre-K onto the national agenda, in both right- and left-wing jurisdictions, is an early encouraging sign of this direction. Even if you view education narrowly as a means to create economic growth and law-abiding citizens, the long-term research shows that equalizing resources among poor and rich children is the very best way to do that.

Whether all of this happens, though, will ultimately be up to you and me. Middle-class, educated parents and other concerned citizens are the most powerful force in transforming the education system.

In the meantime, those of us with kids have to face a rocky transitional period. The final chapter is about the very personal quest to get through this period with our sanity intact.

PLAYING AND WINNING
THE TESTING GAME

O n the wettest, slushiest morning of a wet, slushy February, I
bundle up my daughter Lulu and schlep her a few blocks to
the Williamsburg, Brooklyn, outpost of FasTracKids. Founded in
1998, this chain now has over two hundred locations in forty-nine
countries, offering academic enrichment and test prep to children as
young as my daughter, two years old. They claim to be one of the
fastest-growing franchises of any kind in the world. We are here for a
free sample of the Discovery class, for the youngest children, which
happens Mondays, Wednesdays, and Fridays from nine in the morning to twelve noon.

The bright, colorful room has midget tables and chairs, bins of
toys and art supplies—just like Lulu's nursery school. But looming
over everything is a large interactive electronic whiteboard. After free
play (with only educational toys) and circle time, when they go over
the days of the week, Lulu, wearing the pink and green tutu and yel-
low rain boots she picked out, gathers with the other kids around the
big screen to watch a video and play an interactive counting game.
Then they have counting worksheets to fill out, followed by handwriting practice.

The Discovery class looks like a nursery school, but it's technically not licensed as one. "We don't provide care," said the director. Parents or nannies sit in the lobby, watching the kids on a closed-circuit camera, ready to step in should their child need a diaper change or a hug. Academics are the only activity here—no dance, no yoga, nothing you'll find in "those play-based programs," as the director said dismissively.

I can't help it. I'm proud to see Lulu, who's twenty-six months at the time, correctly count and identify the number three on the big screen. She's having a great time and doesn't want to leave the class, but by the time we get home she's a whiny, exhausted mess, demanding an early nap.

Over four hundred kids come to this location for enrichment, including the entire enrollment of a nearby charter elementary school. FasTracKids holds prep classes for the entrance tests into New York City's Gifted and Talented public school programs and competitive private schools. They run for fourteen weeks, two and a half hours on Saturdays—this for four-year-olds. The director tells me they had a 95 percent success rate on admissions last year. Their afterschool enrichment program, which also starts at age four, runs seven days a week and uses a curriculum called Eye Level that, the director points out, one-third of all Koreans have used. He pulls a workbook titled *Basic Thinking* from the shelf. It is page after page of rote subtraction problems. *Critical Thinking* is a workbook of geometry puzzles.

The director freely admits that their all-academics, all-the-time approach hasn't fully caught on with the hipster parents of Brooklyn. When he goes to open houses where play-based preschools are attracting new parents, "They look at me like I have three heads," he said. "But a year later they'll be on the phone." He ducked his head, impersonating an embarrassed parent calling up, saying, "Um, can we have some help?"

I wrote this book partly to resolve a personal dilemma about how to educate my child. It depresses me to think of immersing Lulu in a high-stakes testing environment that will snuff out her intrinsic interest in learning at an impressionable age or try to stuff her irrepressible individuality into a box.

Tests make school into a competition with winners and losers. The schools that do well at this game are sacrificing something important in the process. Children are internalizing the idea that what really matters is not the excitement of discovery but rather the scores they post at the end of the year. I have this little being in my life who does spontaneous dances in honor of delicious cheese and loves to take out the appendix of her giant chicken puppet. Won't testing squash all of that out of her?

Of course, there are big and small ways for our family to opt out. There are independent schools where standardized tests are never part of the curriculum. There is homeschooling.

But my husband and I both work full time and we love our careers, so long-term homeschooling is out. Private school is complicated. My husband attended a private school from kindergarten through twelfth grade and mostly loved it, whereas I was a public school kid and thrived. Twelve years of private school tuition would stretch our budget while pinching our other life choices, like where to live and how much to work. I also see a downside to bringing up my daughter immersed in a warm bath of near-homogeneous affluence and the values that often come with it. Finally, although I wouldn't sacrifice my daughter to my ideals, as someone engaged in the future of education, I feel a pull to participate in the school system that 90 percent of kids attend.

I take some comfort in the research that says private schools, ironically, don't do much for student achievement, at least on the average and as imperfectly measured by national and international tests. A 2006 national comparison of scores on the NAEP, the Nation's Report Card, for example, found no significant differences between public and private school fourth and eighth graders, after controlling for socioeconomic factors and race. The exceptions were fourth-grade math, where public school kids did better, and eighth-grade reading, where private school kids did better. Similarly, an international analysis of PISA scores completed in 2012 found that 90 percent of the apparent test-score edge at private schools came from the socioeconomic advantages of their students and disappeared when you compared them to similarly affluent public schools.

If my daughter turns out to have special needs or specialized interests, we'll certainly consider the customized attention a private school can offer or even homeschooling if that becomes a better option for the family. I have a secret fantasy of taking her on a "roadschooling" trip across the country or out of the country for a year. Still, whatever route we choose, there will likely be some tests to face along the way—entrance exams, exit exams, OLSATs, APs, ACTs, SATs. I'm confident that changes will come through the system by the time she graduates high school, but we'll need to make some decisions before 2029. And sometimes sitting through a test or two will, frankly, be easier than opting out of every single one.

But after learning so much about the damage these tests do, I can't subject Lulu to test prep for the sake of test prep. She's not going to Saturday cram schools or filling out workbooks at home. She certainly won't be exchanging the arts, movement, and social development of her small, warm, community-oriented religious nursery school for some prefab chain with big video screens.

The hell of it is that traditional test prepping doesn't even work very well. A 2009 review of the research by the National Association for College Admissions Counseling, a group of high school guidance counselors and college admissions officers, found that coaching produced about a 2 percent improvement in scores on the SAT and about a 3 percent improvement on the ACT. The big test-prep companies make misleading marketing claims and use outdated practice tests to give students an artificially inflated sense of how their scores are improving.

As for gifted program testing of four-year-olds, which my neighbors, apparently, are devoting their weekends to at FasTracKids, it may serve as a status symbol. But it also does very little to predict how students will actually perform as they go through school. As Po Bronson and Ashley Merryman reported in their best-selling book *NurtureShock*, in almost three out of four cases students who place into gifted programs on entrance into kindergarten aren't performing as well by high school. Four years old is just too early on in brain development to make lasting determinations based on any test. Some kids are simply faster out of the gate, less fidgety, more cooperative and outgoing, but it doesn't make them "smarter" in any fundamental sense.

Because of the dawning doubts about the validity of testing young children, the rampant coaching, and the associated anxiety and obsession, New York City's most prestigious private schools announced in the fall of 2013 that they were dropping or making optional the Wechsler Preschool and Primary Scale of Intelligence, known as the WPPSI, for use in kindergarten admissions. "Due to the increased prevalence of test prepping, the results of the WPPSI are tainted and their credibility is in question," the schools' association announced, noting that the test was never designed to make lifelong determinations about intelligence based on the test results of four-year-olds. But the reprieve was brief; in the spring of 2014 a few of the schools announced that they would adopt the Admission Achievement for Beginning Learners, a cheaper, iPad-administered test that, as the name suggests, actually expected four-year-olds to have mastered certain academic skills and knowledge. The new test was expected to be much harder.

Your family may be in a similar situation to mine. You're not in a position to opt out of every test. Maybe your kid needs to post a high score on a particular test to have the best opportunities for her future. Maybe the best way to conquer a case of test anxiety is to conquer the test itself.

So can we split the difference here? Can we preserve a healthy attitude toward learning for its own sake while also asking our kids to hit the highest bar possible?

After speaking with dozens of experts I assembled a set of proven strategies that will not only help our kids do better on tests but will also help them do better in life in general.

I use the acronym, TEST, to remember these win-win strategies.

- **Manage the Test**: Realize what the tests are for and how they work and come up with a strategy to take them well.
- **Manage Emotions and Energy**: Use good habits to manage your child's emotions and energy.
- **Manage Self-motivation**: Successful people set their own goalposts instead of abiding by external marks. Motivation and effort matter most. Parents need to step back and allow children to take the lead in discovering their own interests.

- **Manage your Tone:** Instead of focusing on preparing your child, focus on your own attitude and the messages you're sending as a parent.

MANAGE THE TEST

Manage the Test: Playing and Winning the Testing Game

When kids are spending hours, days, or weeks on test prep, with nerves running high, they need to know that these tests have no magic powers. A test is a tool to serve your child—don't let it define your child. There's a lot to be gained by demystifying tests, getting students to think explicitly about who writes them, why, and how and about what the scores really mean. The benefits of this kind of critical investigation will show up in test scores, yes, but also in other ways.

With a middle or high school student you can start by reading the first three chapters of this book. Talk about how the tests are just written by people, people who work for big companies, people who make mistakes.

Then, tackle some actual test questions together. Practice questions can be found online. In Rhode Island in March 2013 the Providence Student Union, a group of high school students who have been creative in their protests against the test-happy status quo, organized an event at a local library at which several dozen state legislators, city officials, professors, and others sat down to try answering questions from the actual high school state test and then discuss their experience with students who were preparing to take the test. Parents who have taken the tests report a much better understanding of what their kids are going through.

Manage the Test: The Wizard's Rules

Jami Craig, an elementary school teacher I talked to, turned the test into a contest for her students to win. She printed out a picture from the Internet of some generic "mean old white guys" and told her students, "These are the test makers! We're going to beat them!" to an enthusiastic chorus of "boos."

That's pretty similar to Bob Alexander's mental strategy. He's the "wizard" of test prep who took Laela Gray in Florida from failing to acing the third-grade FCAT in just two sessions. His books are titled *Demystifying the SAT, Demystifying the ACT,* and *Demystifying the FCAT.* "Most students, when they hear the words 'standardized test,' it's panic time," he said. "I show them that's a beautiful thing. If they weren't standardized, they wouldn't be predictable."

It's the predictability of the tests, he says, that make them easy and even fun to beat. "The very first lesson is to help them understand that these tests are games. You calm the kids down and start developing their confidence." The first time they sit down together, Alexander often asks kids who they are playing against when they play a video game. "After awhile they realize they're playing against the programmer who created the challenge inherent in the game—and that's exactly what's happening with these tests."

You could take this advice a step farther and actually play a video game with your kid, whatever they enjoy, be it *Fruit Ninja, MineCraft,* or *SimCity.* Then talk to them about the process of playing, which is also the process of learning to play. You might be mad for a minute when you get killed, but screwing up is just a chance to start over and try again. You get better by practicing. Asking for help can actually be fun—"walkthrough" videos in which kids explain to other kids how they beat a certain level on a game are a popular genre on YouTube. Video games as test prep—who knew?

Thinking about the way the tests are put together has broader benefits, Alexander says. "One of my principals said, 'You told me you were going to sell me an SAT prep class. It's not an SAT prep class, it's a critical thinking course!' The teachers said that when the kids came to school, they systematically approached learning more effectively than the kids who were not in the SAT class. And I said, but John, if I told you it was a critical thinking course, you wouldn't have bought it. You bought an improvement in test scores. I believe to do that you've got to teach kids to be analytical and critical thinkers. And that's why my score increases are better than anything that Kaplan or Princeton brags about. I teach kids how to think."

Alexander often begins by showing his students the actual item specifications that Florida's state testing authority makes available online as guidelines for the people who write the test items. "I describe it to my students as the rule book that the test writer must follow," he said. Looking at the rule book gives students clues both as to what kinds of traps to be wary of and how to prioritize their time. You can find the ones for your state tests by Googling "item specification" and the name of your state test.

On the Oklahoma state tenth-grade reading tests, to give a random example, 75 to 85 percent of the questions test recall, basic comprehension, context clues, and summarization skills. Only 15 to 25 percent of the questions call for interpreting an author's intentions or synthesizing information from two or more texts. That means that most of the test questions should be fairly easy.

Here are ten more insights into test preparation from Alexander's accumulated wisdom.

1. Decide on an individualized strategy based on what you are trying to accomplish on a specific test. Are you merely looking to pass, as with most state tests, or do you need a near-perfect score, as with entrance exams? If the former, you don't even need to look at the hardest questions. If the latter, then you need to spend lots of time on the hardest questions.

2. Real SATs, ACTs, and so on are the best way to prepare and are available online for a price. Most commercial test-prep chains like Kaplan administer practice tests that are harder than the real tests. This artificially inflates students' sense of how much their classes are helping but doesn't help with confidence or familiarity with the actual test.

3. Most standardized tests are pitched low in terms of content and derive the desired level of difficulty from the tricky ways the question is written. For example, says Alexander, 90 percent of the topics on the math SAT are also covered on the eighth-grade FCAT state exam. That's why becoming familiar with question formats can be more important than covering every possible concept you might encounter.

4. On reading comprehension questions don't waste time reading the questions before reading the passage. Most

questions on state tests will tell you exactly where to look for
the answer.

5. Don't read passages too closely. Read for MOPP: Main idea,
   Organization, author's Purpose, and Point of View. "Look at
   the passages as a work of art, rather than the details," said
   Alexander. "You have to be an engaged, analytical, critical
   reader."

6. Don't bother drilling vocabulary. "You can study your butt off
   and you're not likely to remember more than one hundred
   new words," said Alexander. "About 4 percent of the words a
   kid has learned are likely to show up on test day. What is the
   probability that those four words show up on a question that
   the kid was going to miss?" Instead, rely on context clues
   and building general reading fluency.

7. On many reading tests the three "distractors" or incorrect
   answers will be plausible statements not supported by the
   facts of the passage. Whereas in school you are rewarded
   for relating what you learn to real-life experience, in the
   artificial test environment that's a no-no. You must ignore
   what you know and concentrate only on what is written in
   the test.

8. On the math SATs and many state tests questions progress
   from easier to harder within a section. By knowing where he
   is in the section, a kid can get a clue about how hard or easy
   a test question is likely to be, and, depending on his strategy,
   he knows how much time he should spend with it.

9. When questions are asked about the meaning of a word, it's
   often the less common definitions of a common word.

10. On math questions there's often a distractor that involves
    simply adding or subtracting the numbers in a problem.
    "Let's say a product is bought by a merchant from a
    wholesaler and he marks up the price 80 percent from what
    he pays for it and then puts it on the shelf," said Alexander,
    giving an example off the top of his head. "Then he has a
    sale and marks it down 30 percent. And the question is,
    What's the price on sale as a percentage of what the
    merchant originally paid? Kids will say, 80 percent up and

30 percent down so it's 50 percent more." The real answer is 26 percent more, but that deceptive answer will be staring you in the face.

Manage the Test: Out of the Classroom and into the World

As parents, we can help our kids improve on tests by taking academics out of the artificial classroom context and relating them back to everyday life. Andrea Kuszewski is a behavioral therapist, behavioral consultant, and cognitive neuroscientist who works one-on-one with young people diagnosed with autism spectrum and other serious learning disabilities. She's had students whose tested IQ scores rose over 20 points, just like the girls in the Skeels and Dye experiments of the 1930s. She often writes for outlets such as *Scientific American* about the malleability of intelligence. "Intelligence and creativity was my area of study in my PhD program," she said. "I left my PhD program because my mentor was of the old-school philosophy that intelligence is fixed and genetic." Her experience taught her differently. "By the time I got to grad school I had worked as a therapist and seen kids' abilities change over time using methods that did not teach to the test." Not only was the measured IQ of her students going up, "I saw them improve in other areas of their life. They know they're getting better. They're happier."

Kuszewski, even more than Alexander, believes in test preparation that has nothing to do with conventional "test prep." "Standardized tests will probably always be around in some form," she said. "I found if you thoroughly know the material and take the time to study in a way that you get deep meaning, you will score better on all tests of achievement. It is a time investment in the beginning of learning that reaps dividends in the longer term."

Deep meaning, she says, comes by hitting a topic in different contexts, in different media, and from all directions, an approach she calls "multimodal presentation." "I'm constantly flooding them with different ways to think. Every single skill I translate to a natural environment. While we're walking to the park, we're talking about colors, counting, making predictions. At the museum it's shapes, geometry.

We're going to McDonald's—will you have enough money left over for an ice cream cone if I give you a $5 bill?"

The reasoning behind this approach is simple: multimodal presentation leads to deeper learning that sticks. "I know a student has mastered a certain concept when they're able to apply it totally unrelated to a specific task," Kuszewski said. Psychometricians would call this principle "generalizability."

Presenting material in this way takes time, creativity, and relentlessness. But the results are impressive. "If you want to teach kids how to think more creatively, innovatively, in ways that are going to actually get them ahead—instead of presenting them with answers, ask them questions," Kuszewski said. And communicating your belief that intelligence can improve over time can only help your children along the way.

Manage the Test: Rules for Getting Smarter

Kuszewski's five principles for anyone who wants to grow his or her intelligence, whether they be children or adults, are as follows. I've added some concrete suggestions to try with your school-age child.

1. Seek Novelty—Bring home new toys, games, or apps that introduce a math, science, or reading concept in a new way.
2. Challenge Yourself—Reviewing material for a test can get boring. Make sure you're staying on your kids' edge of difficulty. Throw in an element of speed or competition to keep things tough and interesting. Prizes are always appreciated (like that ice cream cone).
3. Think Creatively—Creativity in this sense is less about artistic expression and more about "divergent thinking," the ability to generate many solutions to a problem or to apply understanding or ideas from one domain to another. You can present your kid with the exercises from Sternberg's Rainbow Project, like coming up with new captions for a cartoon. Or play a game in which you take turns telling a story given a certain opening sentence. Instead of rushing to the right

answer, ask them to come up with three new ways to solve a math problem. How would they do it with clay or string instead of paper and pencil? How could they do it in their heads?

4. Do Things the Hard Way—Spend a fun day together writing with the wrong hand, eating dinner blindfolded, or finding a shortcut home without using GPS.

5. Network—Exposure to different learning and teaching styles is motivating and can stretch your kids' understanding. If they don't understand your or a teacher's explanation of a particular point, how about a virtual tutor on a YouTube video? Or encourage your kid to find new study partners. Even helping a younger sibling with homework can illuminate a child's understanding of a topic.

MANAGE EMOTIONS AND ENERGY

Preparing your children emotionally and physically to do their best on tests and in school goes far beyond putting them to bed early and giving them a good breakfast. The 25 to 40 percent of students who experience test-related anxiety severe enough to depress scores especially need tools to deal with those feelings before their emotions sabotage them.

Manage Emotions and Energy: Mindfulness and Meditation

One positive consequence of the extreme stress caused by pervasive testing is a renewed focus on the importance of mindfulness techniques to control anxiety. Meditation and relaxation are starting to be taught in schools around the country and the world. Leaf Middle School in Brooklyn is one that takes advantage of the David Lynch Foundation's Quiet Time program. The foundation is one of the most prominent supporters of meditation training in public schools. They have trained teachers and school leaders all over the country in the specific mantra-based technique called Transcendental Meditation. Quiet Time schools have two fifteen-minute daily meditation sessions practiced by teachers as well as students. Many scientific journals have published the results of the foundation's studies, showing an average 10 percent improvement in test scores, a narrowing of the achievement gap, and a reduction of symptoms of ADHD and other learning disorders at these schools. Quiet Time schools have seen a sharp drop in violent conflicts and school suspension rates as well as improved teacher morale.

Visitacion Valley Middle School, located in a low-income part of San Francisco, became the first school to adopt Quiet Time in 2007, and it reportedly triggered a tiny revolution at the school. This school is in such a violent neighborhood that it employs a full-time grief counselor to help students deal with frequent shootings. In the first year of practicing daily fifteen-minute sessions of meditation, the number of suspensions fell by 45 percent. Within four years the suspension rate was among the lowest in the city. Daily attendance rates climbed to 98 percent, well above the citywide average. Grade point averages improved markedly, and students started getting into elite high schools. Across the state of California, in schools using the Quiet Time program, twice as many students have become proficient in English on state tests, compared with students in similar schools where the program doesn't exist; the gap is even bigger in math. In the annual California Healthy Kids Survey, the students at Visitacion Valley recorded the highest happiness levels in San Francisco.

Small studies with students from elementary school through high school and across the socioeconomic spectrum support the idea that even a few weeks of mindfulness training can boost academic performance, improve behavior, reduce the impact of stress on the body as measured by cortisol levels, lessen symptoms of ADD and depression, and improve school climate.

Amy Saltzman, a physician and mindfulness coach in the Bay Area, works with youth both in schools and in one-on-one private sessions. She came to the work both as a researcher and as a mother. "When my son was three and my daughter was six months old," she said, "she was very mobile—crawling, pulling down her brother's block tower. He asked if he could meditate with me" to help manage his own stress and have quiet time with his mother away from his sister. "When I started teaching him, I started experimenting, learning what worked and what didn't. At the same time, I was reading in both the professional and lay literature about the epidemics of ADHD and anxiety and depression and teen suicide and cutting and drug use in tweens and teens. I thought, why are we waiting until people are forty for them to learn these skills? Why can't kids learn these skills when they are eight? So they can use them when they fail a test, break up with a boyfriend or girlfriend, don't get into the college of their choice?"

Asking kids to check in with their bodies for the signs of stress is a simple place to start. "Sensations in the body are often the first way you know something's up," Saltzman said. "You're grinding your teeth or stomach's really tight or you have a headache."

She works with kids in learning to rest in what she calls the "still quiet place." That's the natural pause between the in-breath and the out-breath. "This stillness and quiet is always with you," Saltzman said. Her voice, even on the phone, has an undeniably soothing effect. "It's a reliable place to go to for comfort. It's there when you're anxious or arguing with your best friend. From this place you can learn to watch your thoughts or feelings without letting them run your life."

After exploring the "still quiet place," she works with kids on listening to and managing their internal dialogue. "I end up talking to kids about what I call Unkind Mind. I give them some fun little puzzles to do and then I ask them to say out loud or write down what they tell themselves as they're trying to do the puzzles. Things like, 'I'm stupid,' 'I can't get this,' 'This is impossible.' Then we identify that type of thinking as Unkind Mind. I tell the kids, 'You can watch Unkind Mind. You don't need to believe it or take it personally. You can watch it come and go, and go back to taking the test and doing your best.' Over time they realize that the negative internal chatter doesn't need to drive their behavior." Instead, when the negative tape starts running during a test, students can do what they've practiced: "Close my eyes for one minute to uncouple from those thoughts and feelings, then take a deep breath and refocus and come back to the question."

But mindfulness doesn't mean that negative emotions and stress magically disappear, Saltzman says. "What's more likely is that you will feel it, but it won't have you freeze up and not be able to take the test at all."

Saltzman teaches mindfulness skills to children typically in a series of eight weekly sessions, but she can also bundle them into a single lesson plan specifically to help with test preparation. Until recently, in California students took the STAR test, so Saltzman turned STAR into its own acronym:

> *S* is for if you're Stuck or Struggling, you can STOP.
>
> *T* is for Take a deep breath, one or several, that allows your nervous system to settle.
>
> *A* is Accept you have to take a test even though you don't want to be there, or you don't know the answer to this one, or you're feeling a little stressed out. Have that moment of acceptance, let yourself be the way you are.
>
> And one fourth-grade boy remembered the *A* as ALL IS WELL: even if you're nervous and don't know the answer, all of that is fine.
>
> And then *R* is for RESUME or RESTART—sharpen your pencil and come back.

"That's a really basic tool for the kids to use in the heat of the moment."

Of course, there is more than one way to encourage students to develop mindfulness. Saltzman admits her son now has a natural sense of equanimity and doesn't meditate. But her daughter, the active baby, has a steady practice and even teaches meditation to others, sometimes with the help of one of Saltzman's CDs. Other kids might prefer to approach mindfulness through movement, such as yoga or martial arts.

Manage Emotions and Energy: The Healthy Body–Healthy Mind Checklist

Practices to support emotions and energy have benefits far beyond test scores, like healthy, happy kids. If you're concerned about your kid's test performance, before you sign up for test prep run through the following checklist.

1. Are they getting enough sleep on a regular basis? Ten to eleven hours a night is optimal in the elementary school years, and eight to nine hours for teenagers. Short or disrupted sleep is associated with lower grades in school and a much higher chance of failing a grade. Sleepiness interferes with attention, motivation, and memory.

2. What does screen time look like in your house? Two hours a day, from all sources, is the maximum amount sanctioned by the American Academy of Pediatrics, but school-age kids are actually spending an unbelievable average of seven hours and thirty-eight minutes a day using entertainment media— often multitasking across multiple screens. Almost half of even our youngest school kids, five- to eight-year-olds, have a TV in their bedrooms. There's an association between heavy media use, lower grades, and sleep problems.

3. What about diet? Is it dominated by processed foods? Do you eat together as a family? Frequent family meals, at least five times a week, are associated with higher grades for teenagers in some surveys. Quick, scattered meals full of convenience foods may be a symptom of overscheduling, which makes it hard for kids to do their best in school or on tests.

4. Is there a way to work in at least thirty minutes of physical activity on school days? Many test-crazed and budget-cramped schools have cut back on recess and PE, which is unfortunate, as research connects regular exercise with increased blood flow to parts of the brain associated with memory, faster learning of vocabulary words, better cognitive flexibility, higher grades, and better test scores.

Manage Emotions and Energy: Learning to Feel Better

Research points to the role of social and emotional skills in success. There's a corresponding awareness dawning that being a high-functioning, happy, confident, kind human being isn't written in DNA. Children can learn emotional intelligence through direct instruction in the five core competencies: self-awareness, self-management, social awareness, relationship skills, and responsible or ethical decision making. The Collaborative for Academic, Social, and Emotional Learning (CASEL) has reported in their review of dozens of studies on the subject that participants in classroom- and school-based programs demonstrated significantly improved social and emotional skills, attitudes, behavior—not to mention an average 11-percentile-point gain in academic achievement. "I think if you care about academic performance, you have to care about more than academic performance," said CASEL CEO Roger P. Weissberg, a chair in psychology at the University of Illinois at Chicago, summing up the research.

CASEL asks parents to sign a pledge committing to a set of behaviors to encourage social and emotional learning at home, which include the following five.

1. Focus on strengths. When your child brings home a test, talk about what went right before you go into what went wrong.
2. Commit to fair and consistent consequences for misbehavior.
3. Ask your children how they feel. Introduce emotion-based vocabulary at a young age. Studies show that parents tend to do this more often and more extensively with girls than with boys.
4. Give kids choices where possible, and respect their wishes.
5. Ask questions that help kids solve their own problems instead of leaping in with a solution.

Manage Emotions and Energy: Mindset

Yet another way of taking a step back from the testing process is to gain more perspective on the process of thinking and learning itself. As described in Chapter 5, mindset research, begun by Carol Dweck, demonstrates that simply reminding students that brains can learn and change and that abilities like intelligence are not fixed and innate has real measurable effects on performance on standardized tests as well as on grades in challenging courses, from seventh-grade math to university-level organic chemistry.

A simple experiment tried by Khan Academy, a website with free math exercises, demonstrates this point. The site set up a test in which some visitors would see this slogan next to a math problem: "The more you learn today, the smarter you'll be tomorrow." Those ten words, along with a link to further explanation, led to a 5 percent increase in problems attempted, badges earned, and return visits to the site.

In two separate published studies in the mid-2000s seventh graders were given workshops at which they were taught about the nature of the brain, particularly a concept known as neuroplasticity, the moldability of the brain. They were told that every time they stretched themselves and learned something new, their brain formed new connections, just like a muscle that grows stronger with use. They were also invited to apply this lesson to their schoolwork by approaching new, difficult assignments as challenges to be overcome. A control group was given a workshop covering basic study skills. The growth-mindset group showed an improvement in their math grades and achievement test scores, whereas the control group showed no improvement in scores and a decline in grades. Teachers, meanwhile, saw more of an improvement in the growth-mindset students' motivation.

Dweck says inducing a growth mindset doesn't mean telling kids to try hard. "Just exhorting children to exert effort is not effective," said Dweck. "But if you're talking about how you can get smarter and grow your brain if you work at something, you're giving them actionable information and a reason to try hard. Kids are thrilled by the idea that they can actually make a difference in their brains." There is a Carol Dweck–endorsed Brainology curriculum available for $79 per student online, aimed at middle schoolers.

Traditional tests reinforce the damaging idea that abilities are fixed at a point in time. Growth-mindset messages can counteract this idea. They defang the test by reminding students that they are only an invitation to work harder on problem areas and do better next time.

MANAGE SELF-MOTIVATION

For our kids to do well on tests, they have to want to do well. This sounds simple, but in an age of helicopter parenting, it's often an overlooked point.

One of the key insights Andrea Kuszewski draws on in her work is that motivation is central to learning. She refers me to a series of studies on mice, dopamine, motivation, and learning. Dopamine is the neurotransmitter most strongly associated with motivation—not primarily with pleasure itself (those are the group of chemicals known as endorphins) but with pleasure *seeking*. Mice with their dopamine receptors temporarily "knocked out" can learn—that is, be conditioned, say, to complete a maze, with a reward—but their motivation is impaired. The harder the task, the longer it takes for them to do it. They're bored and checked out, even if they're starving. By contrast, mice with dopamine artificially elevated by 70 percent learn more and faster. They leave the start box of a maze more quickly than regular-dopamine mice, require fewer trials to learn, pause less often in the runway, resist distractions better, and proceed more directly to the goal.

You can stimulate short-term motivation with rewards—remember the experiment from Chapter 5, with the M&Ms and the 10-point IQ boost? But for the long term that's horribly counterproductive. External rewards have a tendency to destroy intrinsic motivation. "I work with kids with Aspergers syndrome, mostly," said Kuszewksi. "They're very low motivation outside their topics of interest." She once had an eleven-year-old student obsessed with trains. He knew all the schedules and could even identify the model of a train by the sound of the clicking on the tracks. "The parents were saying, he won't do his math. I think we're going to restrict all access to anything to do with trains until he sits down and learns it. I was like, 'No, we'll do the 100 percent opposite. You have the golden ticket to get him motivated: it's trains! We're going to use that.' I devised a whole set of word problems that centered around trains: Say the green line has six trains, how much money would you need to replace the seats? He was really super into figuring these things out. Using something they're already interested in, you can always find a way to teach." Tapping into your kids' passions as a way to strengthen their mastery of academics is ideally something a dedicated teacher can do. As a parent, you know your child best, so you're in an even better position to open the way.

Manage Self-Motivation: The Maker Movement

More and more students are making connections between doing what they love and learning at makerspaces. "It's sort of a mash-up of a shop class, a computer lab, an art class, and maybe a bio lab," said Dale Dougherty, founder of *Make* magazine, which is like a *Popular Science* for the twenty-first century, and chief instigator of the maker movement. Makerspaces are places, either attached to schools or freestanding, where kids of all ages pursue projects ranging from computer programming to crafts, gardening to knitting, science to art. Sometimes they use gadgets like laser cutters, Arduino open-source hardware kits, and 3-D printers; sometimes they use old soda bottles and duct tape.

Makers often connect in online communities where they share step-by-step accounts of their projects, tips, and encouragement. One young star of the movement is Sylvia, who, at age eight, started making a YouTube show with her dad that features her doing all kinds of projects, from basic screen print to electricity-conducting play dough. There are annual Maker Faires all over the country that are like mad-scientist conventions, featuring everything from giant flame-throwing dinosaurs made of scrap metal to potato clocks.

The maker movement has drawn a lot of interest because of the urgency to reconnect American kids with math and science. Maker Corps, a nonprofit spinoff of *Make*, served ninety thousand families with maker-related programming in the summer of 2013, and *Make* got a grant from the Defense Advanced Research Projects Agency (DARPA) to open one thousand makerspaces at schools around the country. These, by design, don't have a fixed curriculum, explains Dougherty. "I'm trying to push the idea of inviting and giving kids the opportunity to make based on their own interest and connected to the development of a passion of discovery, of something they really want to do." In other words, interest-driven learning. As a mark of how seriously the movement is being taken at elite levels, MIT announced in the fall of 2013 that it would start accepting a maker project or portfolio as part of applications.

For the past eight years Kimberly Sheridan, a professor at George Mason University, has been studying alternative contexts for learning. She wrote an influential 2007 book called *Studio Thinking* that elucidated the habits of mind associated with education in the arts. These include observing, stretching and playfully exploring, and reflecting on what you've made.

Right now Sheridan is studying makerspaces. "One of the spaces I've been looking at is a place called Mt. Elliott Makerspace in East Detroit," she said. "A lot of makerspaces are full of mainly middle- or upper-middle-class kids of highly educated parents. This community is aiming not to be that. It's in the basement of a church, is free, and is open to anyone who is interested." Once the students get there, unlike anywhere else in their lives, there is no one to tell them what to work on. Sheridan is studying how they discover their inner sense of what to do.

"It's powerful feedback for a student to design his or her own educational environment," she said. "They're making their own decisions. It's a huge amount of agency. We're trying to figure out how to characterize and assess this. How does someone develop more autonomy in decision making, more efficacy in handling new problems? If you're given this unstructured support and space for making things, how do you become somebody who has the agency and drive to create things?" Makerspaces are set up as labs for the development of unstructured problem solving, one of the four key areas for jobs of the future. If you want to raise kids who create and collaborate with robots instead of kids whose jobs will one day be replaced by robots, these are a great place to start. For the past few summers *Make* has run a free online "summer camp" through Google Plus that's a way for students to connect, try new projects, and share what they've learned.

Manage Self-Motivation: Backyard Time

We would all like to see our kids mature into people with agency and a drive to create. Interest-driven learning seems like the perfect antidote to our overtested school environment. Here's what we often miss, though: by its nature, interest-driven learning is not something we can force on our kids. It's an alchemical process, something you create the conditions for—unstructured time, materials and opportunities, freedom of choice—and then step back. Sometimes you have to send your kids into the backyard to play and see what they come up with.

My parents, both college professors, had a knack for sharing their own passions and inspiring this kind of learning in my sister and me. I remember going to the library or the bookstore and coming back with armloads of books about our latest geeky obsessions: mushroom hunting, butterfly collecting, bird watching, chess, logic puzzles, crochet, cross-stitch, ceramics, calligraphy, Shakespeare, Charlie Chaplin. My home menagerie peaked at two parakeets, a lizard, a hamster, a goldfish, a cat, and a dog. Later it was vegetarian cooking, composting and gardening, the Beatles, and the acoustic guitar.

Family vacations were a learning bonanza. When I was eleven we traced the legends of the Anasazi on a road trip to New Mexico; when I was thirteen we delved deeply into the art of the Renaissance on a trip to Italy. Before our trips we listened to language tapes in the car and used maps and atlases to plot our course. We visited museums, castles, and every ancient ruin in sight, writing journal entries and making sketches. When we came home my mother crafted scrapbooks to memorialize the trip. I still remember the things I learned during those travels.

Here are five possible contexts for self-motivated learning.

1. summer camp
2. a family vacation
3. an afterschool activity
4. a museum or library
5. an online community

Manage Self-Motivation: Write It Down

A deceptively simple technique to tap into motivation and self-direction is through a regular journaling practice. Research strongly associates notebooking with creativity. One of Sheridan's creative "habits of mind" is envisioning, the process of picturing what you will work on next, through thumbnail sketches, drafts, and improving through a conscious process of revision. Keith Sawyer, a psychologist at the University of North Carolina at Chapel Hill who has written several books on creativity, said, "This comes up over and over again from various kinds of creativity research: the importance of externalizing your ideas and getting what's in your mind out there into the world. Exceptional minds do this instinctively. They pick up a piece of clay even before they have the idea." Externalizing ideas is a form of metacognition—thinking about thinking—associated with high levels of creative performance.

Decades of research going back to the 1980s show that writing down goals can make you more productive, and writing specifically about areas of emotional upset can be therapeutic. Writing can help surface and sort out unresolved emotions. It's associated in teenagers and adults with lower stress in the body, fewer doctor visits, and better performance at school and on the job. Dr. Jordan Peterson at the University of Toronto has developed a curriculum known as Self-Authoring that combines a personality self-assessment with a mini-autobiography and identifying your most important goals for the future. When the curriculum was first tested on eighty-five students who were struggling academically at McGill University in Montreal, their average GPA rose 29 percent in a single academic year. Peterson's team is currently developing a version of the curriculum aimed at high school students.

Is there a way to make a regular notebook time part of your family rituals? At bedtime, at weekly dinners, or even in the car? Maybe you could fill out a version of the Self-Authoring questionnaire alongside your child, found at selfauthoring.com for $29.95. I did it, and it was a transformative experience.

MANAGE YOUR TONE

Manage Your Tone: Focus on Your Own Attitude and the Messages You're Sending as a Parent

The last letter of this acronym is the one I myself most need to hear. Instead of focusing on preparing children for the next test, maybe we need to try looking at our own attitudes, health and balance, and the messages we're sending as parents.

One of my wisest mama friends is Julie, an acupuncturist specializing in fertility who is originally from Texas. I came to see her when I was trying to get pregnant, and she ended up pregnant just a few months after me. She's married to Scott, a psychoanalyst. One day at a playdate I mention that he must bring an interesting perspective to the development of their daughter Anna. "Basically, we both think the most important thing you can do as a parent is work on your own shit," she said. This rings incredibly true to me, particularly in our educated, middle- and upper-middle-class subculture, in which we're assuming that basic needs are met, and we are largely dealing instead with poverty of the spirit. And nowhere more so than in testing and related dilemmas.

Who is to blame for America's high-stakes testing obsession, unique in history and in the world? Testing companies are collecting the cash, politicians are passing the laws, but as parents, we are the ones who have allowed this to happen.

Test-based accountability is a motor built of mistrust and anxiety that creates more mistrust and anxiety in its wake. If we trusted our teachers and school leaders to do the right thing, we wouldn't agree to subject students to these tests. And as long as we don't trust them, nothing will get any better.

There are real economic and social causes for the ratcheting up of anxiety and mistrust. Economic inequality in America is at levels not seen since the 1920s. People are exposed to more volatility in their lifetimes because of the erosion of pension plans and employer-sponsored health care; the rise of consumer debt and part-time, freelance, contract, temporary, and other flimsy work arrangements; and the rapid cycling of the economy from boom to bust. Entire industries are rising and falling in the matter of months it takes for a smartphone to become obsolete.

More and more kids are moving back home after college: 21.6 million young adults (age eighteen to thirty-one) are now living with their parents, according to one report. Not coincidentally, in recent years nearly half of new college graduates are either unemployed or underemployed in a job not requiring a college degree.

Selective colleges are far more selective than they were a generation ago and are about twenty times more expensive, and our kids are competing with the top students from around the world, both to get in and after they get out. If the way to success is a ladder, then America's is getting narrower at the top, and families are hanging on for dear life, whipping around up there in the stiff winds of social change.

The professionals who work with our kids say that the kids are reading our messages loud and clear, the mixed messages that say, "You can do anything!" and "I'm afraid you're not good enough!"

Gever Tulley is a brilliant educator with an impish grin and the ability to instantly gain the trust of almost anyone, from toddlers on up. He first became known for the book *Fifty Dangerous Things You Should Let Your Children Do* and its accompanying TED talk. One of his many hobbies is paragliding near his home, in the breathtaking coastal cliffs south of San Francisco. We met when we both spoke at a conference in Atlanta in 2010 and immediately recognized each other as kindred spirits. Since 2011 he's run Brightworks out of a repurposed warehouse in a hip neighborhood in San Francisco. It's the alternative school of my dreams, where kids work with "real tools, real materials, and real problems." Students of all ages are busy alongside teachers known as "collaborators," responding to "provocations," following creative "arcs," building multidisciplinary projects to explore topics like wind and the sea.

When I speak with him, Brightworks students happen to be exploring measurement, from space to time. One recent "provocation" asked students to design a chair. "It was really designed to be a context to appreciate precision and accuracy in measurement," Tulley told me over Skype, speaking with his usual precision and accuracy. "Their first batch of chairs was super wobbly, so I would have to say it worked perfectly. They became collectively disgusted with their own chairs. Three or four iterations later, they're actually chairs you might see in a store."

Building a chair is a typical Tulley assignment and a perfect performance assessment. An eight-year-old needs little help to make the task relevant to her own life—everyone needs to sit, after all. Nor does she need much help to appraise her own work—either the chair is wobbly, or it's straight. The "collaborator" steps in merely to help figure out what went wrong and what to do better the next time.

Creative, interdisciplinary curriculum and lots of personal attention from an overachieving staff of award-winning, internationally known, distinguished educators—if I were privileged enough to send Lulu to a school like this, surely testing would be the farthest thing from my mind. But Tulley says his parents often have a hard time letting go of the numbers. "We face this question all the time of testing, primarily from an anxiety standpoint from the parents who want to know how their kids compare to other kids. It's not always completely healthy," he said. "Abstractly, they buy into the notion that they don't want their kids to be abusively tested. . . . But it only takes one question from a dubious grandparent that leads to us getting a flurry of e-mails at 3 a.m."

Many of his parents actually go so far as to pay independent agencies to give their kids a battery of standardized intelligence and aptitude tests. "More than 90 percent of the time it highlights the things we're already working with that child on. With a student-teacher ratio of eight-to-one, the teachers really do know the children and are shaping the provocation to meet that child at their challenge," he said. Yet although the parents are entrusting their children to his team, day in and day out, they're not fully trusting the team's judgment. The testing culture has gotten into their heads.

Manage Your Tone: "We Always Do Extra Credit"

Does it seem that your child is putting pressure on himself or absorbing it from the environment? Peers are important, as is the atmosphere at school. But it's ultimately we the parents who need to look within.

For the children Amy Saltzman sees privately in her mindfulness practice as well as at schools, it's the parents who are creating much of the stress they experience. One of the questions on her intake form is "What are your family mottoes?"

"One girl wrote: THE SMITHS ALWAYS DO EXTRA CREDIT. The parents said, 'She's putting all this pressure on herself.' But I was able to say, 'Do you understand the mixed message you're giving?

You're stressing her out, you're stressing yourself out. You should just stop it.' The parental habit of thinking, worrying, obsessing about achievement and 'good' colleges really plays into the kids' anxiety. The kids want to do well, but what we do as parents and in the school culture just makes it worse." Saltzman says parents' internal conflict, including her own (and mine), is betrayed in all kinds of ways, like when a kid comes home from school and parents ask, "How did you do on the test?" rather than "What interested you today?"

Suniya Luthar is a psychologist who taught at Columbia University Teachers' College and is now at Arizona State. She started her career working with inner-city families who faced obvious environmental stressors like gang violence and drug abuse. But fifteen years ago, while gathering a control group for a study, she made a startling discovery: upwardly mobile, upper-middle-class communities today are producing youth who are statistically more at risk than the norm. Problems such as drug and alcohol use, delinquency, depression, anxiety, self-harming, and eating disorders emerge around seventh grade at a higher rate in rich communities than in middle-class ones and even "high-risk" poor communities. She's since reproduced these findings at schools on the East Coast, West Coast, and Midwest. Luthar traces these problems to a severe anxiety about status, as expressed in signifiers like, yes, test scores.

"It's at puberty that kids first get preoccupied with, where will I go to college?" she said. "When kids come to this point, their very sense of self-worth depends on how much they can accomplish and achieve in terms of these benchmarks that have been drawn up by us, educators, and parents. Things get very dangerous for them if their sense of self becomes threatened."

Obsession over test scores, whether state tests, APs, PSATs, or SATs, is the template for a more general preoccupation with excelling based on certain metrics. In the extreme version of this syndrome, no class or activity is undertaken for its own sake; everything is about the grade, the award, or the line on the résumé. And too many of our kids are breaking under this pressure. "Our values are disproportionately oriented toward achievement," said Luthar. "We need to be watchful of how much we, ourselves, believe in the merits of accomplishment as opposed to decency." When she's not quite two and a half, I ask my daughter on a whim, "Is it better to be nice or smart?" "Smart," she answers without missing a beat.

Luthar says mothers and daughters, especially, are feeling the toll of this dynamic. "I've got a bunch of suggestions for mothers. We have repeatedly found our daughters are suffering more than our sons, with problems across multiple domains. The males are often externalizing aggression"—cheating, stealing, driving drunk, selling drugs. "For the daughters, it's depression, anxiety, self-harming, and also the rule breaking, delinquency, substance use, eating problems. The standard for girls is 'effortless perfectionism'—do it all without seeming like you really tried."

This hits me like a sock in the gut. Isn't this just a miniaturized version of the "having it all," "lean in" myth that I struggle with as a wife, mother, and writer? Getting up to run six miles at 6 a.m., putting organic, home-cooked meals on the table every night, lying in bed making to-do lists at three in the morning? Is it foolish to think I can raise a self-directed, joyful, conscientious, outgoing, highly motivated, and spirited daughter without her internalizing the overachieving image that I model for her every day? If we can't be compassionate with ourselves, how can we be with our kids?

"The high expectations that we have of ourselves as mothers leave us feeling psychologically depleted," said Luthar. "We can't be that steadfast comfort and support." As the overachieving mother of two overachieving young adults, she knows whereof she speaks. Her son is working long hours as a consultant in Dubai; meanwhile, she struggles to tell her daughter, a college sophomore, to "chill out" and not work too hard.

In order to be a safe refuge for our kids, Luthar says, we need more than anything to take refuge ourselves. "I say to mothers: take care of yourself. I don't mean go to yoga or get a manicure or a facial. I mean, don't let yourself come to a point where you feel isolated, alone, and like no one cares for you. Make sure you feel seen and loved, tended and defended. That is the one dimension that falls by the wayside."

Like Saltzman, she says a little social and emotional learning is in order for parents too. "Be watchful of your own value system and what you convey to your kids. A raised eyebrow can convey a lot. Stop and think: what do you truly cherish? Where do you draw the line? Enough of this race to the top, I'm not doing it." Being insufficiently "tended and defended" may sound like a caviar problem. But truly, social and emotional support is vital for families of all walks of life. And it's incumbent upon society's most privileged to interrogate our values relentlessly because they are inevitably imposed on others.

Manage Your Tone: The Questions to Ask

If you recognize any piece of this syndrome yourself, it's time to ask some tough questions that get down to root causes.

What if my kid doesn't score as high as she might have on a test? What is it I'm really afraid of? That she's not really all that special? That the world won't realize he's as wonderful as I know he is? That she won't be successful? That his life will be ruined if he doesn't get into this kindergarten or that college? That he'll be missing out on his best chance at happiness? Or am I really afraid of how that score will reflect on me and the job I'm doing?

Like Joshua Starr, the Montgomery County superintendent, we all want our kids to be both straight-A students and great people. But if we had to pick just one, which would we choose? Do our kids know that?

"I'm hoping that people will pay attention to these issues," Luthar said. "This is about you and me, our kids, so we had better pay attention."

Finding and forming connections with likeminded parents is essential. So is enlisting our kids' teachers as allies. I'm firmly convinced that a future of fewer tests, better tests, and happier, healthier, more successful kids is well within our grasp. But we all have to work together to create it.

Joe Bower, the editor of *De-Testing and De-Grading Schools*, has seen teachers, parents, and students go through a detox process when they give up relying on grades or tests for external validation of their progress. "At some point they fall off the bandwagon and get the shakes."

He told the story of a student named Sara, a high achiever in his English language arts class who came to him at the end of eighth grade, clearly upset. "I'm worried that you haven't prepared me for high school," she said. He asked her to pull out her portfolio. "I said, prove what you've learned, show me some evidence." So they did, getting down a box full of thick manila folders, 8½-by-11. It was full of examples of deep, multidisciplinary learning, like a paper on Lois Lowry's allegorical novel *The Giver* and an essay on the particle model of matter, both with comments on the first and second draft that were evidence of improvement. She had researched, written, and illustrated a large poster on breast cancer in honor of her beloved aunt, who had been diagnosed with the disease.

"I asked her again, 'Have you been learning?' 'Oh, big time,' she said. 'Well, can you tell me a better way to prepare for high school than to be learning a lot in grade eight?' She looked at me, she paused and closed her portfolio, and went out for recess."

ACKNOWLEDGMENTS

This book would not exist without the support of my agent, Jim Levine, who first suggested the focus of it and who believed in me. Thank you.

Benjamin Adams and the rest of the team at PublicAffairs have been unfailingly helpful and encouraging of my particular voice and vision.

Thanks to the amazing teams at Fast Company, the Hechinger Report, and NPR where I did some of the initial reporting that led me into this topic.

Emily Davis, Saurav Sarkar, and Rebeca Ibarra were my awesome amanuenses.

I can't believe I have work that lets me call up the very smartest people all day long. Everyone I interviewed was thoughtful, generous, and helpful. Bob Alexander, Bob Schaeffer, Rick Roach, and Julian Vasquez Heilig especially so.

Thanks to my good friend Linda Rosenbury, who gets me so inspired about education.

And, as always and for everything, to Adam.

NOTES

INTRODUCTION

A $2 billion industry controlled by a handful of companies:

Matthew M. Chingos, "Strength in Numbers: State Spending on K-12 Assessment Systems," Brookings Institution, November 2012, www.brookings .edu/~/media/research/files/reports/2012/11/29%20cost%20of%20assessment%20chingos/11_assessment_chingos_final.pdf.

The "big four" testing companies are Harcourt Educational Measurement, CTB McGraw-Hill, Riverside Publishing (a Houghton Mifflin company), and NCS Pearson.

"The Testing Industry's Big Four: Profiles of the Four Companies That Dominate the Business of Making and Scoring Standardized Achievement Tests," Frontline, www.pbs.org/wgbh/pages/frontline/shows/schools/testing /companies.html.

On Goodhart's and Campbell's Law:

Donald Campbell, "Assessing the Impact of Planned Social Change," Public Affairs Center, Dartmouth College, Hanover, NH, December 1976, https://www.globalhivmeinfo.org/CapacityBuilding/Occasional%20 Papers/08%20Assessing%20the%20Impact%20of%20Planned%20 Social%20Change.pdf. Emphasis in quoted material is added by the author.

See also Marilyn Strathern, "'Improving Ratings': Audit in the British University System, " *European Review* 5, no. 03 (July 1997): 305–321.

Elizabeth Warren:

Elizabeth Warren and Amelia Warren Tyagi, *The Two Income Trap: Why Middle-Class Mothers and Fathers Are Going Broke* (New York: Basic Books, 2003).

Jill Lepore, "Reading Elizabeth Warren," *New Yorker*, April 21, 2014.

Thirty-three tests per year:
    Eleanor Chute, "With More Than 270 Tests at Pittsburgh Schools This
Year, When Is Enough Enough?" *Pittsburgh Post-Gazette*, November 2, 2013,
www.post-gazette.com/local/city/2013/11/03/With-more-than-270-tests-at
-Pittsburgh-schools-this-year-when-is-enough-enough/stories/20131103
0067.

In one Florida high school:
    Diane Ravitch, "A Florida High School Student Speaks Truth to Power,"
Diane Ravitch's blog. February 20, 2013, http://dianeravitch.net/2013/02
/20/a-florida-high-school-student-speaks-truth-to-power/.

CHAPTER 1

1. We're testing the wrong things:
    "MIT Neuroscientists . . . " Anne Trafton, "Even When Test Scores Go
Up, Some Cognitive Abilities Don't," *MIT News Office*, Massachusetts Insti-
tute of Technology, December 11, 2013, http://newsoffice.mit.edu/2013
/even-when-test-scores-go-up-some-cognitive-abilities-dont-1211; Daniel
Koretz, *Measuring Up: What Educational Testing Really Tells Us* (Cambridge,
MA: Harvard University Press, 2009).

2. Tests waste time and money:
    Howard Nelson, *Testing More, Teaching Less: What America's Obsession with
Student Testing Costs in Money and Lost Instructional Time*, American Federa-
tion of Teachers, www.aft.org/pdfs/teachers/testingmore2013.pdf; Jennifer
McMurrer, *Choices, Changes, and Challenges: Curriculum and Instruction in the
NCLB Era* (Washington, DC: Center for Education Policy, 2007), www
.cep-dc.org/displayDocument.cfm?DocumentID=312.

**3. They are making students hate school and turning parents into
preppers:**
    George Mandler and Seymour B. Sarason, "A Study of Anxiety and
Learning," *Journal of Abnormal and Social Psychology* 47, no. 2 (April 1952):
166–173; J. C. Cassady, "Test Anxiety: Contemporary Theories and Implications for Learning," in *Anxiety in Schools: The Causes, Consequences, and Solutions for Academic Anxieties*, ed. J. C. Cassady, pp. 7–26 (New York: Peter
Lang, 2010); Ray Hembree, "Correlates, Causes, Effects, and Treatment of
Test Anxiety," *Review of Educational Research* 58, no. 1 (Spring 1988): 47–77;
Michael W. Eysenck and Manuel G. Calvo, "Anxiety and Performance: The
Processing Efficiency Theory," *Cognition and Emotion* 6, no. 6 (November
1992): 409–434; Arthur S. Otis, *Otis Group Intelligence Scale: Manual of Di-
rections for Primary and Advanced Examinations* (Yonkers-on-Hudson, NY:
World Book Co, 1920); Lisa Miller, "Ethical Parenting: Is There Such a
Thing? Just Ask Your Children," *New York*, October 6, 2013, www

.lisaxmiller.com/ethical-parenting-is-there-such-a-thing/5303/; "Affluent Students Have an Advantage and the Gap Is Widening," *New York Times*, December 22, 2012, www.nytimes.com/interactive/2012/12/22/education /Affluent-Students-Have-an-Advantage-and-the-Gap-Is-Widening.html?_r=0; James Marshall Crotty, "Global Private Tutoring Market Will Surpass $102.8 Billion by 2018," *Forbes*, October 30, 2012, www.forbes.com/sites/james marshallcrotty/2012/10/30/global-private-tutoring-market-will-surpass-102 -billion-by-2018/.

4. They are making teachers hate teaching:

The MetLife Survey of the American Teacher: Challenges for School Leadership, February 2013, www.metlife.com/assets/cao/foundation/MetLife -Teacher-Survey-2012.pdf; State of the States 2013: Connect the Dots: Using Evaluations of Teacher Effectiveness to Inform Policy and Practice," National Council on Teacher Quality, October 2013, www.nctq.org/dmsView /State_of_the_States_2013_Using_Teacher_Evaluations_NCTQ_Report; Linda Darling-Hammond, Audrey Amrein-Beardsley, Edward H. Haertel, and Jesse Rothstein, "Getting Teacher Evaluation Right: A Background Paper for Policy Makers," American Educational Research Association and National Academy of Education, September 14, 2011, http://prezi.com/nlly65 uqldln/getting-teacher-evaluation-right-a-background-paper-for-policy -makers; Linda Darling-Hammond, *Getting Teacher Evaluation Right: What Really Matters for Effectiveness and Improvement* (New York: Teachers College Press, 2013); "*According to Its Pension System, D.C. Teacher Turnover Hasn't Increased*," December 13, 2013, Teacher Pensions Blog, www.teacherpensions .org/blog/according-its-pension-system-dc-teacher-turnover-hasnt-increased. **Carolyn Abbott:** Aaron Pallas, "The Worst Eighth-Grade Math Teacher in New York City," *A Sociological Eye on Education*, The Hechinger Report, May 15, 2012, http://eyeoned.org/content/the-worst-eighth-grade-math-teacher -in-new-york-city_326. **A veteran fourth-grade teacher in Florida:** Iquit youcantfireme, "In Pursuit of Happiness," *YouTube*, May 21, 2013, www.you tube.com/watch?v=uH9vxq1iJVM.

5. They penalize diversity:

"Closed Schools, Chapter 2: Elementary and Secondary Education," Digest of Education Statistics: 2012, U.S. Department of Education, National Center for Education Statistics, 2013, NCES 2014–2015, http://nces .ed.gov/programs/digest/d12/ch_2.asp; Patrick Michels, "Faking the Grade: The Nasty Truth Behind Lorenzo Garcia's Miracle School Turnaround in El Paso," *Texas Observer*, October 31, 2012, www.texasobserver.org/faking-the -grade-the-nasty-truth-behind-lorenzo-garcias-miracle-school-turnaround -in-el-paso; Manny Fernandez, "El Paso Schools Confront Scandal of Students Who 'Disappeared' at Test Time," *New York Times*, October 13, 2012,

www.nytimes.com/2012/10/14/education/el-paso-rattled-by-scandal-of
-disappeared-students.html; Jennifer Booher-Jennings, "Below the Bubble: 'Educational Triage' and the Texas Accountability System," *American Educational Research Journal* 42, no. 2 (January 2005): 231–268; "National
disaster . . . " Alan Schwarz, "The Selling of Attention Deficit Disorder," *New
York Times*, December 15, 2013, www.nytimes.com/2013/12/15/health/the
-selling-of-attention-deficit-disorder.html; Valerie Strauss, "Mom: My Autistic Son 'Is Lost in a Sea of Standards' at School," *Washington Post*, October
31, 2013, www.washingtonpost.com/blogs/answer-sheet/wp/2013/10/31
/mom-my-autistic-son-is-lost-in-a-sea-of-standards-and-expectations/.

6. **They cause teaching to the test:**

Jennifer McMurrer, *Choices, Changes, and Challenges: Curriculum and Instruction in the NCLB Era*, (Washington, DC: Center for Education Policy,
2007), www.cep-dc.org/displayDocument.cfm?DocumentID=312; Howard
Nelson, *Testing More, Teaching Less*, American Federation of Teachers, July
2013, www.aft.org/pdfs/teachers/testingmore2013.pdf; Diane Ravitch, "First
Grade Teacher: How I Conquered the Testing Monster," Diane Ravitch's
blog, June 17, 2013, http://dianeravitch.net/2013/06/17/first-grade-teacher
-how-i-conquered-the-testing-monster/.

7. **The high stakes tempt cheating:**

Robert Kolker, "Cheating Upwards," *New York Magazine*, September 16,
2012, http://nymag.com/news/features/cheating-2012-9; Jack Gillum and
Marisol Bello, "When Standardized Test Scores Soared in D.C., Were the Gains
Real?" *USA Today*, March 27, 2011, http://usatoday30.usatoday.com/news
/education/2011-03-28-1Aschooltesting28_CV_N.htm; Chelsea J. Carter,
Dave Alsup, Joe Sutton, and Darrell Calhoun, "Grand Jury Indicts 35 in
Georgia School Cheating Scandal," *CNN*, March 29, 2013, www.cnn.com
/2013/03/29/us/georgia-cheating-scandal; Linda Calbom, *K-12 Education:
States' Test Security Policies and Procedures Varied*, US Government Ac-
countability Office, May 16, 2013, www.gao.gov/products/GAO-13-495R;
Rachel Aviv, "Wrong Answer," *New Yorker*, July 21, 2014, www.newyorker
.com/magazine/2014/07/21/wrong-answer?currentPage=all.

8. **They are gamed by states until they become meaningless:**

John Cronin, Michael Dahlin, Yun Xiang, and Donna McCahon, *The
Accountability Illusion* (Washington, DC: Thomas B. Fordham Institute,
2009), http://edexcellence.net/publications/the-accountability-illusion
.html.

9. **They are full of errors:**

"Errors Plague School Testing: AJC Investigation," *Atlanta Journal-Constitution*, September 15, 2013, www.ajc.com/news/news/local/errors
-plague-school-testing-ajc-investigation/nZwp4; Kathleen Rhodes and

George Madaus, *Errors in Standardized Tests: A Systemic Problem* (Chestnut Hill, MA: National Board on Educational Testing and Public Policy, 2003), www.bc.edu/research/nbetpp/statements/M1N4.pdf; David Sadker and Karen Zittleman, "Test Anxiety: Are Students Failing Tests—Or Are Tests Failing Students?" *Phi Delta Kappan* (June 2004), Myra Sadker Foundation, www.sadker.org/PDF/test_anxiety.pdf; Stephanie Banchero and Darnell Little, "School Test Data Tardier Than Ever," *Chicago Tribune*, November 23, 2006, http://articles.chicagotribune.com/2006-11-23/news/0611230051 _1_student-test-results-school-report-cards-parents-and-schools; Diana B. Henriques and Jacques Steinberg, "Right Answer, Wrong Score: Test Flaws Take Toll," *New York Times*. May 20, 2001, www.nytimes.com/2001/05/20 /business/right-answer-wrong-score-test-flaws-take-toll.html. For more on the pineapple question, see Leonie Haimson, "The Pineapple and the Hare: Pearson's Absurd, Nonsensical ELA Exam, Recycled Endlessly Throughout Country," *NYC Public School Parents*, April 19, 2012, http://nycpublic schoolparents.blogspot.com/2012/04/pineapple-and-hare-pearsons-absurd .html.

10. The next generation of tests will make things even worse:

"Beyond the Bubble Tests: The Next Generation of Assessments—Secretary Arne Duncan's Remarks to State Leaders at Achieve's American Diploma Project Leadership Team Meeting," U.S. Department of Education, September 2, 2010, www.ed.gov/news/speeches/beyond-bubble-tests-next-generation -assessments-secretary-arne-duncans-remarks-state-l; A Public Policy Statement, Gordon Commission on the Future of Assessment in Education, Princeton, NJ, 2013, www.gordoncommission.org/rsc/pdfs/gordon_commission _public_policy_report.pdf; Andrew Ujifusa, "Tests Aligned to Common Core in New York State Trigger Score Drops," *State Ed Watch, Education Week*, August 7, 2013, http://blogs.edweek.org/edweek/state_edwatch/2013 /08/_one_interesting_aspect_of.html; Andrew Ujifusa, "Scores Drop on Ky.'s Common Core–Aligned Tests," *State Ed Watch, Education Week*, November 2, 2012, www.edweek.org/ew/articles/2012/11/02/11standards.h32.html; President's Council of Advisors on Science and Technology (U.S.), Executive Office of the President, *Report to the President Prepare and Inspire: K–12 Education in Science, Technology, Engineering and Math (STEM) for America's Future*, September 2010, www.whitehouse.gov/administration/eop /ostp/pcast/docsreports.

CHAPTER 2

In 1795, at an astronomical observatory in Greenwich:

C. Radhakrishna Rao and S. Sinharay, *Psychometrics* (Amsterdam: Elsevier North-Holland, 2007).

"Gaussian distribution" . . . :
>   Saul Stahl, "The Evolution of the Normal Distribution," *Mathematics Magazine* 79, no. 2 (2006): 96, www.maa.org/sites/default/files/pdf/upload _library/22/Allendoerfer/stahl96.pdf.

Lambert Adolphe Jacques Quetelet:
>   Adolph Quetelet, *A Treatise on Man, and the Development of his Faculties* (Edinburgh, UK: William and Robert Chambers, 1842), https://archive.org /details/treatiseonmandev00quet; John B. Juan Huarte de San Juan Carroll, *Human Cognitive Abilities: A Survey of Factor-Analytic Studies* (Cambridge: Cambridge University Press, 1993).

Galton:
>   Francis Galton, *Anthropometric Library* (London: William Clowes and Sons, Limited, 1884), http://galton.org/criticism/10-14-02/venn-1889-j -anthro-cambridge-anthropometry.pdf; Karl Pearson, *The Life, Letters and Labours of Francis Galton* (Cambridge: Cambridge University Press, 2011), http://galton.org/pearson/.

Jastrow at the World's Fair:
>   *Report of the Committee on Awards of the World's Columbian Commission: Special Reports upon Special Subjects or Groups, Volume 1* (U.S. Government Printing Office, 1901). For more on the World's Fair, I recommend Erik Larson, *Devil in the White City* (New York: Vintage 2010).

Cattell:
>   Lyle V. Jones and David Thissen, "A History and Overview of Psychometrics," *Handbook of Statistics* 26 (2007): 1–27, www.stat.cmu.edu/~brian /905-2009/all-papers/jones-thissen-2007.pdf; Jonathan Plucker, "James McKeen Cattell . . . ," *Human Intelligence: Historical Influences, Current Controversies, Teaching Resources*, www.intelltheory.com/rcattell.shtml.

Wissler:
>   Jonathan Plucker, "Clark Wissler," *Human Intelligence: Historical Influences, Current Controversies, Teaching Resources*, www.intelltheory.com /wissler.shtml.

Binet:
>   Jonathan Plucker, "Alfred Binet . . . ," *Human Intelligence: Historical Influences, Current Controversies, Teaching Resources*, www.intelltheory.com /binet.shtml; Christine Brain, *Advanced Psychology: Applications, Issues and Perspectives* (Cheltenham: Nelson Thornes, 2001).

Gould:
>   Stephen J. Gould, *Mismeasure of Man (Revised and Expanded)* (W.W. Norton and Company, 2006).

Terman:

Lewis M. Terman, "Were We Born That Way," *The World's Work* 44 (Doubleday, Page & Co., 1922), 655–660.

"There is nothing about an individual as important as his IQ . . . ":

Lewis M. Terman, "The Binet-Simon Scale for Measuring Intelligence," *The Psychological Clinic* 5, no. 7 (December 15, 1911): 199–206.

Army Alpha:

Daniel J. Kevles, "Testing the Army's Intelligence: Psychologists and the Military in World War I," *Journal of American History* 55, no. 3 (1968): 565–581; Paul F. Ballantyne, *Psychology, Society, and Ability Testing (1859–2002): Transformative Alternatives to Mental Darwinism and Interactionism*, 2002, www.igs.net/~pballan/C4P1.htm.

Otis:

Arthur S. Otis, *Otis Group Intelligence Scale* (Yonkers-on-Hudson, NY: World Book Company, 1920).

Walter Lippmann:

Walter Lippmann, "The Mental Age of Americans," *New Republic*, October 25, 1922; "The Mystery of the A Men," *New Republic*, November 1, 1922; "The Reliability of Intelligence Tests," *New Republic*, November 8, 1922; "The Abuse of the Tests," *New Republic*, November 15, 1922; "Tests of Hereditary Intelligence," *New Republic*, November 22, 1922; "A Future for the Tests," *New Republic*, November 29, 1922.

Twenty-Sixth Yearbook of the National Society for the Study of Education . . . :

Guy Montrose Whipple, ed., *Yearbook of the National Society for the Study of Education* 26 (Bloomington, IL: Public School Pub., 1926).

Henry Goddard:

The quote comes from *The Kallikak Family*, Goddard's book-length investigation of a "feeble-minded" little girl born in an almshouse and admitted to a reformatory. He travels to the town where her family is from and discovers her to be the product of no less than six generations of "defectives and delinquents," 143 of whom are, respectively, "derelict," "reckless," "witless," "weak," "vicious," "sexually immoral," and, above all, "feeble-minded." Henry Goddard, *The Kallikak Family* (New York. MacMillan, 1912), http://scholarworks.gsu.edu/cgi/viewcontent.cgi?article-1006&context-col_facpub.

Harold Skeels:

Harold M. Skeels, "Adult Status of Children with Contrasting Early Life Experiences: A Follow-Up Study," *Monographs of the Society for Research in Child Development* 31, no. 3 (1966): 1–65.

OSS:

Louie M. Banks, *The Office of Strategic Services Psychological Selection Program*, 1995, www.ossreborn.com/files/OSSPsychologicalSelectionProgram.pdf.

Thurstone and multiple intelligences:

Don Baucum, *Psychology* (Hauppauge, NY: Barron's Educational Series, 1999).

Lindquist:

David Holmgren, "Lindquist, Everet Franklin," *The Biographical Dictionary of Iowa* (Iowa City: University of Iowa Press, 2009), http://uipress.lib.uiowa.edu/bdi/DetailsPage.aspx?id=233.

Literacy tests:

Rebecca Onion, "Take the Impossible 'Literacy' Test Louisiana Gave Black Voters in the 1960s," *Slate*, June 28, 2013, www.slate.com/blogs/the_vault/2013/06/28/voting_rights_and_the_supreme_court_the_impossible_literacy_test_louisiana.html.

Rebecca Onion wrote a follow-up post giving more background on her quest for an archival version of these tests, including some interesting speculation on their origins:

"Update: On the Hunt for the Original Louisiana Literary Test," *Slate*, July 3, 2013, www.slate.com/blogs/the_vault/2013/07/03/louisiana_literacy_test_update_the_hunt_for_the_original_document.html.

Of the 50 million students in American public schools, 22 million receive free and reduced-price lunches:

US Department of Agriculture, National School Lunch Program Factsheet, 2013, www.fns.usda.gov/sites/default/files/NSLPFactSheet.pdf.

North Carolina . . . :

Michael Freemark and Anne Slifkin, "Economic Status Biggest Factor for Successful Students," *News and Observer*, November 14, 2013, www.newsobserver.com/2013/11/14/3371552/economic-status-biggest-factor.html.

Sternberg:

Robert Sternberg, "The Rainbow Project: Enhancing the SAT Through Assessments of Analytical, Practical, and Creative Skills," *Intelligence* 34 (2006): 321–350.

CHAPTER 3

For more on *A Nation at Risk*, and the Sandia Report, see:

Gerald Bracey, "Righting Wrongs," *Huffington Post*, December 3, 2007, www.huffingtonpost.com/gerald-bracey/righting-wrongs_b_75189.html.

Check out FairTest's list of publications at:

FairTest, www.fairtest.org/resources/publications.

On the global use of standardized tests:

Strong Performers and Successful Reformers in Education: Lessons from PISA for the United States (Paris: OECD, 2011), www.oecd.org/pisa /46623978.pdf; Valerie Strauss, "How the First Standardized Tests Helped Start a War—Really," *Washington Post*, December 3, 2012, www.washington post.com/blogs/answer-sheet/wp/2012/12/03/how-the-first-standardized -tests-helped-start-a-war-really; Sherisse Pham, "High Test Scores, but China Education Flawed," *ABC News*, December 9, 2010, http://abcnews.go.com /Politics/chinas-education-prepares-students-tests/story?id=12348599; Roman Dolata, *The Reform of the Matura Exam-Evaluation and Recommendations*, Institute of Public Affairs, 2004, www.isp.org.pl/files/4193050760737 287001117523865.pdf; Jian Xueqin, "The Sad Truth of China's Education," *The Diplomat*, June 3, 2011. http://thediplomat.com/2011/06/the-sad-truth -of-chinas-education; Jason Strother, "Drive for Education Drives South Korean Families into the Red," *Christian Science Monitor*, November 10, 2012, www.csmonitor.com/World/Asia-Pacific/2012/1110/Drive-for-education -drives-South-Korean-families-into-the-red; Hanna Sistek, "South Korean Students Wracked with Stress," *Al Jazeera*, December 8, 2013, www.aljazeera .com/indepth/features/2013/12/south-korean-students-wracked-with-stress -201312884628494144.html; Jiyeon Lee, "South Korean Students' 'Year of Hell' Culminates with Exams Day," *CNN*, November 13, 2011, www.cnn.com /2011/11/10/world/asia/south-korea-exams/.

$263 million . . . :

Marguerite Clarke, George Madaus, Catherine Horn, and Miguel Ramos, "The Marketplace for Educational Testing," *Statements* 2, no. 3 (April 2001), www.bc.edu/research/nbetpp/publications/v2n3.html.

96 percent . . . :

"The Testing Industry's Big Four," *Frontline*, March 2002, www.pbs.org/ wgbh/pages/frontline/shows/schools/testing/companies.html.

No Excuses:

Samuel Casey Carter, *No Excuses: Lessons from 21 High-Performing, High-Poverty Schools* (Washington, DC: Heritage Foundation, 2000), http:// samuelcaseycarter.squarespace.com/storage/NoExcuses-SCC.pdf.

NBA Players under six feet tall:

This unofficial census can be found at the fansite NBA All Star, www.allstar nba.es/players/players-by-height.htm. There are eight NBA All-Star Players under six feet tall, compared to twenty-nine who are over seven feet tall.

Sandy Kress:

Nate Blakeslee, "Crash Test," *Texas Monthly*, May 2013, www.texasmonthly .com/story/crash-test.

Indeed, by 2011, before a majority of states had waivers from the consequences of the law . . . :
Alexandra Usher, *AYP Results for 2010–11—November 2012 Update* (Washington, DC: Center on Education Policy, November 1, 2012), www .cep-dc.org/displayDocument.cfm?DocumentID=414.

In May 2001 the *New York Times* ran a series of front-page exposés:
Diana B. Henriques and Jacques Steinberg, "Right Answer, Wrong Score: Test Flaws Take Toll," *New York Times*, May 20, 2001, www.nytimes.com /2001/05/20/business/right-answer-wrong-score-test-flaws-take-toll.html; Diana B. Henriques and Jacques Steinberg, "When a Test Fails the Schools, Careers and Reputations Suffer," *New York Times*, May 21, 2001, www .nytimes.com/2001/05/21/business/21EXAM.html.

Julian Vasquez Heilig:
Julian Vasquez Heilig and Linda Darling-Hammond, "Accountability Texas-Style: The Progress and Learning of Urban Minority Students in a High-Stakes Testing Context," *Educational Evaluation and Policy Analysis* 30, no. 2 (2008), 75–110.

Walt Haney:
Walt Haney, "The Myth of the Texas Miracle in Education," *Education Policy Analysis Archives* 8, no. 41 (2000), n41, http://epaa.asu.edu/ojs/article /view/432/828; George W. Bush, "Acceptance Speech to the Republican National Convention," Madison Square Garden, New York, NY, September 2, 2004, www.presidency.ucsb.edu/ws/?pid=25954.

Mayor Michael Bloomberg and test scores:
Diane Ravitch, "Obama's Race to the Top Will Not Improve Education," *Huffington Post*, August 1, 2010, www.huffingtonpost.com/diane-ravitch /obamas-race-to-the-top-wi_b_666598.html; Economic Policy Institute, "Broader, BOLDER Approach to Education," 2014, www.boldapproach.org.

Race to the Top:
"The Race to the Top," White House, www.whitehouse.gov/issues /education/k-12/race-to-the-top; "President Obama, U.S. Secretary of Education Duncan Announce National Competition to Advance School Reform," US Department of Education Press Release, July 24, 2009, www2 .ed.gov/news/pressreleases/2009/07/07242009.html.

PARCC and Smarter Balanced:
Arne Duncan, "About PARCC," *Partnership for Assessment of Readiness for College and Careers*, November 2, 2010, www.parcconline.org/about -parcc; "Member States," *Smarter Balanced Assessment Consortium*, www .smarterbalanced.org/about/member-states.

"World-class standards . . ." :

Arne Duncan, "Secretary Arne Duncan's Remarks at the 2009 Governors Education Symposium," US Department of Education, June 14, 2009, www2.ed.gov/news/speeches/2009/06/06142009.html.

This became the most prescriptive piece . . . :

Sam Dillon, "Administration Takes Aim at State Laws on Teachers," *New York Times,* July 23, 2009, www.nytimes.com/2009/07/24/education/24 educ.html?_r=0.

There were historic deficits at the state level . . . :

"State Budget Update: July 2009," National Conference of State Legislatures, (Denver: CO, July 2009), www.ncsl.org/documents/fiscal/statebudget updatejulyfinal.pdf; Gates Foundation, "History," Bill and Melinda Gates Foundation, www.gatesfoundation.org; Gates Foundation, "Foundation Fact Sheet," www.gatesfoundation.org/Who-We-Are/General-Information /History.

Arne Duncan recruited both chief of staff . . . :

Sam Dillon, "After Complaints, Gates Foundation Opens Education Aid Offer to All States," *New York Times,* October 27, 2009, www.nytimes.com /2009/10/28/education/28educ.html.

$335 million . . . :

Nick Anderson, "Gates Foundation Gives $335 Million for Teacher Effectiveness," *Washington Post,* November 20, 2009, www.washingtonpost.com /wp-dyn/content/article/2009/11/19/AR2009111902211.html. For more on Gates and the Common Core, see Lindsey Layton, "How Bill Gates Pulled Off the Swift Common Core Evolution," *Washington Post,* June 7, 2014, www .washingtonpost.com/politics/how-bill-gates-pulled-off-the-swift-common -core-revolution/2014/06/07/a830e32e-ec34-11e3-9f5c-9075d5508f0a _story.html.

NAACP:

Lawyers Committee for Civil Rights under Law, National Association for the Advancement of Colored People (NAACP), NAACP Legal Defense and Educational Fund, Inc., National Council for Educating Black Children, National Urban League, Rainbow PUSH Coalition, and Schott Foundation for Public Education, "Framework for Providing All Students an Opportunity to Learn Through Reauthorization of the Elementary and Secondary Education Act," July 2010, http://naacp.3cdn.net/bbe013962d37e1c6a9_com6 btgji.pdf.

Hedge funds and charter schools:

Some argue that hedge funds' interest in charter schools can be traced to a generous tax credit: "Under the New Markets program, a bank or private equity firm that lends money to a nonprofit to build a charter school can receive a 39% federal tax credit over seven years. The credit can even be piggybacked on other tax breaks for historic preservation or job creation. By combining the various credits with the interest from the loan itself, a lender can almost double his investment over the seven-year period." Read more: Juan Gonzalez, "Albany Charter Cash Cow: Big Banks Making a Bundle on New Construction as Schools Bear the Cost," *Daily News*, May 6, 2010, www.nydailynews.com/new-york/education/albany-charter-cash-big-banks -making-bundle-new-construction-schools-bear-cost-article-1.448008# ixzz351EZfISa; Diane Ravitch, *The Death and Life of the Great American School System* (New York: Basic Books, 2010).

South by Southwest:

A video of Bill Gates' keynote address is accessible at the South by Southwest EDU website, http://sxswedu.com/news/watch-bill-gates-sxswedu-keynote -video-now.

Rupert Murdoch:

Ian Quillen, "News Corp.'s Purchase of Wireless Generation Follows Hiring of Klein," *Education Week*, December 8, 2010, www.edweek.org/ew /articles/2010/12/08/14newscorp.h30.html.

When I interviewed Gates in March 2013 . . . :

Anya Kamenetz, "Bill Gates on Education: We Can Make Massive Strides," *Fast Company*, April 15, 2013, www.fastcompany.com/3007841 /tech-forecast/bill-gates-education-we-can-make-massive-strides.

Rick Roach:

Valerie Strauss, "Revealed: School Board Member Who Took Standardized Test," *Washington Post*, December 6, 2011, www.washingtonpost.com/blogs /answer-sheet/post/revealed-school-board-member-who-took-standardized -test/2011/12/06/gIQAbIcxZO_blog.html; Marion Brady, "When an Adult Took Standardized Tests Forced on Kids," *Washington Post*, December 5, 2011, www.washingtonpost.com/blogs/answer-sheet/post/when-an-adult -took-standardized-tests-forced-on-kids/2011/12/05/gIQApTDuUO_blog .html.

The extensive literature of test criticism, see:

Alfie Kohn, *The Case Against Standardized Testing* (Portsmouth, NH: Heinemann, 2000); W. James Popham, *Transformative Assessment* (Alexandrian, VA: Association for Supervision and Curriculum Development, 2008); Sharon Nichols, *Collateral Damage: How High-Stakes Testing Corrupts America's Schools* (Cambridge, MA: Harvard Education Press, 2013); Jim Horn, *The Mismeasure of Education* (Charlotte, NC: Information Age Publishing, 2013).

Things Fall Apart . . . :

NAEP, The Nation's Report Card, National Center for Education Statistics, http://nationsreportcard.gov/data_tools.aspx; PISA OECD, "Programme for International Student Assessment: Results from PISA 2012 Country Note," www.oecd.org/unitedstates/PISA-2012-results-US.pdf; *Answering the Question That Matters Most: Has Student Achievement Increased Since No Child Left Behind?* (Washington, DC: Center on Education Policy, 2007), http://eric.ed.gov/?id=ED520272; Thomas Dee and Brian Jacob, "The Impact of No Child Left Behind on Student Achievement," *Journal of Policy Analysis and Management* 30, no. 3 (2011): 418–446, www.nber.org/papers /w15531.

The only states without NCLB waivers as of June 2014 were California (though a group of the largest districts within the state has its own special waiver), Montana, Nebraska, North Dakota, Vermont, and Delaware. Iowa and Wyoming had waivers under review: "Index Page for the ESEA Flexibility Page," US Department of Education, December 13, 2013, www.ed.gov /esea/flexibility; "Ohio ESEA Flexibility Request," Washington, DC: US Department of Education, 2013, www2.ed.gov/policy/eseaflex/oh.pdf; Bruce D. Baker et al., "Is School Funding Fair? A National Report Card," National Center for School Funding Fairness, January 2014, www.schoolfunding fairness.org; Texas Education Agency, "House Bill 3 Transition Plan," Texas Education Agency, June 18, 2014, www.tea.state.tx.us/student.assessment /hb3plan; Texans Advocating for Meaningful Student Assessment, www .tamsatx.org.

For more on Robert Scott, and the backlash in Texas, see:

Jeffrey Weiss, "How the Texas Testing Bubble Popped," *Dallas Morning News*, March 2014, http://res.dallasnews.com/interactives/2014_March /standardized_tests/part2.

Seattle:

Jackie Micucci, "How Garfield High Defeated the MAP Test," *Seattle Magazine*, August 2013, www.seattlemag.com/article/how-garfield-high -defeated-map-test.

In a single week in February . . . :

FairTest, "Testing Resistance and Reform News: February 5–11, 2014," February 11, 2014, www.fairtest.org/testing-resistance-reform-news-february -5-11-2014.

Washington State:

Joy Resmovits, "Washington Becomes First State to Return to No Child Left Behind," *Huffington Post*, April 24, 2014, www.huffingtonpost.com /2014/04/24/washington-no-child-left-_n_5207245.html.

California:

Sharon Noguchi, "California Switches Testing Plans, but May Still Risk Losing $3.5 Billion in Federal Funds," *San Jose Mercury News*, November 22, 2013, www.mercurynews.com/education/ci_24580452/california -switches-testing-plans-but-may-still-risk; Dennis Van Roekel, "NEA President: We Need a Course Correction on Common Core," *NEA Today*, February 19, 2014, http://neatoday.org/2014/02/19/nea-president-we-need-a -course-correction-on-common-core; Vicki Phillips, "A Letter to Our Partners: Let's Give Students and Teachers Time," June 10, 2014, http://college ready.gatesfoundation.org/LinkClick.aspx?fileticket=wPhuLSxJgV4% 3D&portalid=0.

SAT overhaul:

Todd Balf, "The Story Behind the SAT Overhaul," *New York Times Magazine*, March 6, 2014, www.nytimes.com/2014/03/09/magazine/the-story -behind-the-sat-overhaul.html.

China's growing resistance:

Ian Johnson, "Class Consciousness," *New Yorker*, February 3, 2014, www.newyorker.com/reporting/2014/02/03/140203fa_fact_johnson; Lauren Ingeno, "U.S.-style Liberal Arts Colleges Plant Foothold in China," *McClatchy DC*, August 12, 2013, www.mcclatchydc.com/2013/08/12/199129 /us-style-liberal-arts-colleges.html; NTDonChina, "Montessori Education Takes Off in China," YouTube, April 12, 2013, www.youtube.com/watch ?v=kZdx-L8Z7r4; Leonard Singapore Lim, "Heng Concerned over Exam Focus and Social Mobility," *Straits Times*, March 16, 2013, www.edvantage .com.sg/content/heng-concerned-over-exam-focus-and-social-mobility.

Canada:

Rachel Giese and Caroline Alphonso, "The Debate over Standardized Testing in Schools Is as Divisive as Ever," *Globe and Mail*, May 31, 2013, www.theglobeandmail.com/news/national/education/the-debate-over -standardized-testing-in-schools-is-as-divisive-as-ever/article12299369 /?page=all; Debbie Kasman, "Global Education Perspectives: Canada Grapples with Testing Too," *ParentMap*, January 15, 2014, www.parentmap.com /article/global-education-perspectives-canada-grapples-with-testing-too.

Mexico:

"Mexico Chucks Test Bonuses, National Exam," *Frontera NorteSur*, February 5, 2014, University of New Mexico, http://fnsnews.nmsu.edu/mexico -chucks-test-bonuses-national-exam; Eva Hershaw, "Profiting from Education Reform in Mexico," *Texas Observer*, October 7, 2013, www.texasobserver .org/profiting-education-reform-mexico; Andalusia Knoll, "Despite Repression, Mexican Teachers Continue to Resist Education Reform," *Truthout*, Sep-

tember 25, 2013, www.truth-out.org/news/item/19038-despite-repression
-mexican-teachers-continue-to-resist-education-reform.

Israel:

Shahar Chai, "Education Minister Drops Standardized Tests," *Ynetnews*,
August 12, 2013, www.ynetnews.com/articles/0,7340,L-4416883,00.html.

CHAPTER 4

In the United States . . . :

William J. Reese, *Testing Wars in the Public Schools* (Cambridge, MA: Harvard University Press, 2013).

Deutermann:

Jeanette Deutermann, Long Island Opt-Out Info Facebook Group, www
.facebook.com/groups/Longislandoptout/?ref=br_tf.

Other opt-out organizations and resources:

The National Center for Fair and Open Testing, fairtest.org; United Opt
Out, http://unitedoptout.com; Scrap the MAP! (Seattle), http://scrapthe
map.wordpress.com; More Than a Score (Chicago), http://morethanascore
chicago.org; Colorado Parents Opt Out of State Tests, www.facebook.com
/pages/Colorado-Parents-Opt-Out-of-State-Tests/517015661652082.

CHAPTER 5

For the employers' view, consider remarks made by Lazslo Bock . . . :

Adam Bryant, "In Head-Hunting, Big Data May Not Be Such a Big Deal,"
New York Times, June 19, 2013, www.nytimes.com/2013/06/20/business
/in-head-hunting-big-data-may-not-be-such-a-big-deal.html; Thomas Friedman, "How to Get a Job at Google," *New York Times*, February 22, 2014,
www.nytimes.com/2014/02/23/opinion/sunday/friedman-how-to-get-a-job
-at-google.html.

A 2012 research paper by Patrick Kyllonen:

Patrick C. Kyllonen, "Measurement of 21st Century Skills Within the
Common Core State Standards," K-12 Center at ETS, Invitational Research
Symposium on Technology Enhanced Assessments, Educational Testing
Service, May 2012, www.k12center.org/rsc/pdf/session5-kyllonen-paper
-tea2012.pdf.

A study published by Oxford University economists:

Carl B. Frey and Michael A. Osborne, "The Future of Employment: How
Susceptible Are Jobs to Computerisation?" September 17, 2013, www
.oxfordmartin.ox.ac.uk/downloads/academic/The_Future_of_Employment
.pdf25. Also see Anya Kamenetz, "The Four Things People Can Still Do Better Than Computers," *Fast Company*, July 19, 2013, www.fastcompany
.com/3014448/the-four-things-people-can-still-do-better-than-computers.

Try your hardest. Keep going. Be kind. Bounce back:
> Paul Tough, *How Children Succeed: Grit, Curiosity, and the Hidden Power of Character* (New York: Mariner, 2013).

Walter Mischel, a Columbia psychologist, is known for his famous marshmallow test . . . :
> Jonah Lehrer, "Don't!: The Secret of Self-Control," *New Yorker*, May 18, 2009, www.newyorker.com/magazine/2009/05/18/dont-2.

Christopher Jencks, a Harvard professor . . . :
> Christopher Jencks, *Who Gets Ahead?: The Determinants of Economic Success in America* (New York: Basic Books, 1979).

James Heckman, a Nobel Prize–winning University of Chicago economist . . . :
> James J. Heckman, Jora Stixrud, and Sergio Uzrua, *The Effects of Cognitive and Noncognitive Abilities on Labor Market Outcomes and Social Behavior* (Cambridge, MA: National Bureau of Economic Research, 2006), www.nber.org/papers/w12006.

Carol Dweck, a Stanford psychologist . . . :
> Carol S. Dweck, *Mindset: The New Psychology of Success* (New York: Random House, 2006); Angela L. Duckworth, Christopher Peterson, Michael D. Matthews, and Dennis R. Kelly, "Grit: Perseverance and Passion for Long-Term Goals," *Journal of Personality and Social Psychology* 92, no. 6 (2007): 1087–1101.

M&M effect:
> Calvin V. Edlund, "The Effect on the Behavior of Children, as Reflected in the IQ Scores, When Reinforced After Each Correct Response," *Journal of Applied Behavior Analysis* 5, no. 3 (1972): 317–319; Charles Q. Choi, "IQ Tests Measure Effort, Too," *Livescience*, April 25, 2011, www.livescience.com/13862-intelligence-iq-tests-motivation.html.

David Williamson Shaffer:
> His website is http://edgaps.org/gaps/about/epistemic-games-university-of-wisconsin-madison/david-williamson-shaffer.

"pseudo-quantitative precision heuristic":
> Robert J. Sternberg, "College Admissions: Beyond Conventional Testing," *Change: The Magazine of Higher Learning*, September–October 2012, www.changemag.org/Archives/Back%20Issues/2012/September-October%202012/admissions_full.html.

Jose Ferreira:
> Anya Kamenetz, "What If You Could Learn Everything?" *Newsweek*, July 10, 2013, http://mag.newsweek.com/2013/07/10/what-if-you-could-learn-everything.html.

For example, when Knewton first produced a remedial math course for college freshmen at the University of Arizona:

Steve Kolowich, "Arizona St. and Knewton's Grand Experiment with Adaptive Learning," *Inside Higher Ed*, January 25, 2013, www.insidehighered.com /news/2013/01/25/arizona-st-and-knewtons-grand-experiment-adaptive -learning.

Kimberly O'Malley is the senior vice president of school research:

"About Kimberly O'Malley," Person, Research and Innovation Network, http://researchnetwork.pearson.com/author/kimberlyomalley; Valerie Shute and J. Michael Spector, "SCORM 2.0 White Paper: Stealth Assessment in Virtual Worlds," Unpublished manuscript, 2008, www.zotero.org/groups /e-assessment/items/itemKey/RTX8HZ4C.

Automated Scoring:

Caralee J. Adams, "Essay-Grading Software Seen as Time-Saving Tool," *Edweek*, March 10, 2014, www.edweek.org/ew/articles/2014/03/13/25 essay-grader.h33.html 19 Jun 2014; Mo Zhang, "Contrasting Automated and Human Scoring of Essays," Educational Testing Service, R&D Connections, no. 21, March 2013, www.ets.org/research/policy_research_reports /publications/periodical/2013/jpdd.

Les Perelman:

Anya Kamenetz, "Three Rules for Robograding, and Other Ed-Tech Innovations," The Hechinger Report, August 15, 2013, http://hechingerreport .org/content/three-rules-for-robograding-and-other-ed-tech-innovations _12901.

Gallup student survey:

Gallup Student Poll, www.gallupstudentpoll.com.

YouthTruth:

YouthTruth Student Survey, www.youthtruthsurvey.org.

California Healthy Kids survey:

California Healthy Kids Survey, http://chks.wested.org.

School Climate Survey, http://cscs.wested.org.

OECD PISA questionnaire:

PISA Products, OECD, www.oecd.org/pisa/pisaproducts.

Buzzfeed infographic:

Jake Levy, "Where in the World You Can Find the Best Schools—And the Happiest Kids," BuzzFeed, January 15, 2014, www.buzzfeed.com/jakel11 /where-in-the-world-you-can-find-the-best-schools-and-the-hap.

In Korea, in February 2013 . . . :

Lee Joo-hee, "Park Pledges a Happier Korea," *Korea Herald*, February 25, 2013, www.koreaherald.com/view.php?ud=20130225000785.

Christopher Gabrieli:
　　His website is Transforming Education, www.transformingeducation.org. Gabrieli's group, Transforming Education, is advising the California Office to Reform Education. John E. Deasy, "District News," Los Angeles Unified School District, March 1, 2014.
According to Todd Balf, who wrote for the *New York Times* about the spring 2014 relaunch of the SATs . . . :
　　Rachel Nolan, "Behind the Cover Story: Todd Balf on the Coming Changes to the SAT," *The 6th Floor Blog, New York Times*, March 10, 2014, http://6thfloor.blogs.nytimes.com/2014/03/10/behind-the-cover-story-todd-balf-on-the-coming-changes-to-the-sat.
West Point:
　　L. Eskreis-Winkler, E. Shulman, S. Beal, and A. L. Duckworth, "The Grit Effect: Predicting Retention in the Military, the Workplace, School and Marriage," *Frontiers in Personality Science and Individual Differences,* in press.
Anchoring vignettes:
　　"ANNEX A6: Anchoring Vignettes in the PISA 2012 Student Questionnaire," *OECD*, www.oecd.org/pisa/keyfindings/PISA-2012-results-Annex%20A6-VolIII-VolIV.pdf.
Personal Potential Index . . . :
　　"ETS Personal Potential Index: For Faculty and Other Evaluators: About ETS PPI," ETS, https://www.ets.org/ppi/evaluators/about.
Kyllonen mentions a study at an Italian Law School . . . :
　　Marco Novarese and Viviana Di Giovinazzo, *Promptness and Academic Performance* (Munich, Germany: University Library of Munich, 2013).
Similarly, for her 2008 dissertation at Stanford . . . :
　　Carmit Segal, "Misbehavior, Education, and Labor Market Outcomes," *Journal of the European Economic Association* 11, no. 4 (2013): 743–779.
2012 experiment re-created Mischel's marshmallow test . . . :
　　"The Marshmallow Study Revisited," *University of Rochester,* October 11, 2012, http://rochester.edu/news/show.php?id=4622.
Gross National Happiness:
　　Mallika Rao, "The 'Wellbeing Index': Santa Monica Joins U.S. Cities Tracking Happiness," *Huffington Post*, April 23, 2013, www.huffingtonpost.com/2013/04/23/wellbeing-index-santa-monica_n_3118641.html.

CHAPTER 6
Joe Bower:
　　Joe Bower and P. L. Thomas, eds., *De-testing and De-grading Schools: Authentic Alternatives to Accountability and Standardization* (New York: Peter Lang

Press, 2013); New York Performance Standards Consortium, performance assessment.org.

Since 1865 New York State's Board of Regents . . . :

"History of Regents Examinations: 1865 to 1987," *Office of State Assessment*, New York State Education Department, August 22, 2012, www.p12 .nysed.gov/assessment/hsgen/archive/rehistory.htm.

Regents diploma, once a kind of honors program, mandatory for all students:

New York State Education Department, Office of Elementary, Middle, Secondary and Continuing Education, *General Education and Diploma Requirements* (Albany: New York State Education Department, 2000), www.p12 .nysed.gov/ciai/gradreq/intro.html.

For example, the state of Kentucky . . . :

Daniel Koretz et al., "Perceived Effects of the Kentucky Instructional Results Information System (KIRIS)," 1996. www.rand.org/pubs/monograph _reports/MR792.html.

As psychometrician Bob Mislevy wrote in a 2013 academic paper . . . :

Bob Mislevy et al., "Psychometric Considerations in Game-based Assessment," GlassLab Research, Institute of Play, 2014, www.ets.org/research/policy _research_reports/publications/white_paper/2014/jrrx.

Innovation Lab Network . . . :

The website is www.ccsso.org/What_We_Do/Innovation_Lab_Network .html.

Vermont is taking similar steps . . . :

Chris Sturgis, "Vermont Breakaway on Proficiency-Based Policy," January 20, 2014, www.competencyworks.org/2014/01/vermont-breakaway-on -proficiency-based-policy.

New England Secondary School Consortium:

Currently consists of fifty-five high schools that support "proficiency -based learning." To learn more, see New England Secondary School Consortium, http://newenglandssc.org.

"moderation study":

Martha Foote, "The New York Performance Standards Consortium College Performance Study," Performance Standards Consortium, June 2005, http://performanceassessment.org/consequences/collegeperformancestudy .pdf.

Bate Middle School:

Check out the video case study from the Partnership for 21st Century Skills, www.p21.org/exemplar-program-case-studies/1294-case-study-bate-middle -school; and see Charlie's video about his dog, Rosie, on YouTube: "The Case of

the Hungry Hound," YouTube, March 26, 2014, www.youtube.com/watch
?v=Mzi6V54YvY8; Matchbook Learning, www.matchbooklearning.com.

Glasslab:
Learn more at Institute of Play, www.instituteofplay.org/work/projects
/glasslab.

Lev S. Vygotsky:
Lev S. Vygotsky, *Mind in Society: The Development of Higher Psychological Processes* (Cambridge, MA: Harvard University Press, 1980); see also Robert J. Sternberg, *Dynamic Testing: The Nature and Measurement of Learning Potential* (Cambridge: Cambridge University Press, 2001).

Lee Peng Yee:
He served as an adviser to Scholastic's Math180 program. Thanks to Tyler Reed at Scholastic for introducing me to his ideas. See Math180, Scholastic, http://teacher.scholastic.com/products/math180/authors-advisors.htm.

Dan Schwartz:
His lab at Stanford University is called the AAA Lab, http://aaalab.stanford .edu.

Deb Roy:
Watch his TED talk at Deb Roy, "The Birth of a Word," Ted, www.ted .com/talks/deb_roy_the_birth_of_a_word; Brandon C. Roy, Michael C. Frank, and Deb Roy, "Relating Activity Contexts to Early Word Learning in Dense Longitudinal Data," *Proceedings of the 34th Annual Meeting of the Cognitive Science Society*, 2012, Sapporo, Japan.

Ryan Baker:
Cristobal Romero et al., eds., *Handbook of Educational Data Mining* (Boca Raton, FL: CRC Press, 2011); Ryan Baker et al., "Better to Be Frustrated Than Bored: The Incidence, Persistence, and Impact of Learners' Cognitive-Affective States During Interactions with Three Different Computer-Based Learning Environments," *International Journal of Human-Computer Studies* 68, no. 4 (2010): 223–241.

Norma and Vivienne Ming:
Norma C. Ming and Vivienne Ming, "Automated Predictive Assessment from Unstructured Student Writing," *DATA ANALYTICS 2012, The First International Conference on Data Analytics*, 2012; Socos's website is www .socos.me/about.html.

Jan Plass:
Jan L. Plass (faculty page), New York University, http://steinhardt.nyu .edu/faculty_bios/view/Jan_Plass.

Atentiv:
Anya Kamenetz, "Could a Video Game Replace ADD Medication?" *Digital/Edu*, November 27, 2013, http://digital.hechingerreport.org/content

/could-a-video-game-replace-add-medication_1055; also see Atentiv, http:// atentiv.com.

According to the most recent data available . . . :

Performance Standards Consortium, "Educating for the 21st Century: Data Report on the New York Performance Standards Consortium," 2013, www.nyclu.org/files/releases/testing_consortium_report.pdf; Julian Vasquez Heilig, "A Refresher: What Is Community-Based Accountability?" *Cloaking Inequality*, April 15, 2014, http://cloakinginequity.com/2014/04/15/a -refresher-what-is-community-based-accountability.

In 2010, in response to Race to the Top . . . :

"New York City Graduation Rates Class of 2012 (2008 Cohort)," *Graduation Outcomes Highlights*, NYC Department of Education, http://schools .nyc.gov/NR/rdonlyres/31DFBEE6-2620-4792-BE7A-01B00F2E5B56 /0/2012GraduationRatesPUBLICFINALWebsite.pdf; Elizabeth Walters, "Too Unschooled for School," *Village Voice*, October 23, 2013, www.villagevoice .com/2013-10-23/news/too-unschooled-for-school; *Remediation: Higher Education's Bridge to Nowhere*, Complete College America, 2012; *Inside Higher Ed*, http://completecollege.org/docs/CCA-Remediation-final.pdf; "NYC Announces 3 Early-College High Schools," *Crains New York Business*, August 16, 2013, www.crainsnewyork.com/article/20130816/TECHNOLOGY /130819918/nyc-announces-3-early-college-high-schools#; Diane Cardwell, "New Program Aims to Help the Poor Juggle Education and Jobs," *New York Times*, April 17, 2007, www.nytimes.com/2007/04/17/nyregion/17mayor .html?fta=y; Michael Winerip, "In College, Working Hard to Learn High School Material," *New York Times*, October 23, 2011, www.nytimes.com /2011/10/24/education/24winerip.html.

CUNY, for its part, introduced special programs . . . :

Donna Linderman and Zineta Kolenovic, *Results Thus Far and the Road Ahead: A Follow-Up Report on CUNY Accelerated Study in Associate Programs (ASAP)* (Brooklyn, NY: CUNY Accelerated Study in Associate Programs, 2012), www.cuny.edu/academics/programs/notable/asap/ASAP _Followup_Report_020112.pdf; Henry M. Levin and Emma Garcia, *Benefit-Cost Analysis of Accelerated Study in Associate Programs (ASAP) of the City University of New York (CUNY)*, Center for Benefit-Cost Studies of Education (CBCSE), Teachers College, Columbia University, May 2013, http:// www.cuny.edu/academics/programs/notable/asap/Levin_ASAP_Benefit _Cost_Report_FINAL_05222013.pdf.

Under mayor Bill DeBlasio, elected in 2013, . . . :

"De Blasio Plans to Get Rid of School Letter Grades, Bloomberg Says That's a Mistake," *NY 1 News*, November 13, 2013, www.ny1.com/content/news/1986

89/de-blasio-plans-to-get-rid-of-school-letter-grades—bloomberg-says-that
-s-a-mistake.

**KIPP, perhaps the most lauded group of charter schools in the nation, has
been going through a public reexamination . . . :**

The Promise of College Completion: KIPP's Early Successes and Challenges,
KIPP, April 28, 2011, www.kipp.org/results/college-completion-report.

Envision Schools:

Envision Education, Our Impact, 2012, www.envisionschools.org/impact.

In a community like Oakland, California . . . :

Jill Tucker, "Even Odds," San Francisco Chronicle, August 23, 2013, www
.sfchronicle.com/local/bayarea/item/even-odds-part-1-22785.php.

"Local control funding formula":

"An Overview of the Local Control Funding Formula," California Legislative Analyst's Office, December 18, 2013, www.lao.ca.gov/reports/2013
/edu/lcff/lcff-072913.aspx.

**In a few years, thanks to the spread of statewide longitudinal data sys-
tems . . . :**

Anya Kamenetz, "What Parents Need to Know About Big Data and Student
Privacy," NPR Ed., April 28, 2014, www.npr.org/blogs/alltechconsidered
/2014/04/28/305715935/what-parents-need-to-know-about-big-data
-and-student-privacy.

A California state bill and a federal bill . . . :

Andrew Ujifisa, "State Lawmakers Ramp Up Attention to Data Privacy,"
Education Week, April 15, 2014. www.edweek.org/ew/articles/2014/04/16
/28data.h33.html.

Education secretary Arne Duncan, for one, supports this approach:

Arne Duncan, "Robust Data Gives Us the Roadmap to Reform," Marce 2
2014, Archived: Secretary Arne Duncan Addresses the Fourth Annual IES
Research, Conference, www.ed.gov/news/speeches/robust-data-gives-us
-roadmap-reform.

Linda Darling-Hammond:

Her professional website is through Stanford University, at https://
ed.stanford.edu/faculty/ldh; Linda Darling-Hammond, The Flat World and
Education: How America's Commitment to Equity Will Determine Our Future
(New York: Teachers College Press, 2010; Linda Darling-Hammond, "Stan-
dards and Assessments: Where We Are and What We Need," The Teachers
College Record, 2003; Elle Rustique-Forrester and R. Pecheone, Multiple
Measures Approaches to High School Graduation, School Redesign Network at
Stanford University, 2005.

CHAPTER 7
A 2006 national comparison of scores on the NAEP . . . :
   Henry I. Braun, Frank Jenkins, and Wendy Grigg, *Comparing Private Schools and Public Schools Using Hierarchical Linear Modeling* (Washington, DC: National Center for Education Statistics, 2006), https://nces.ed.gov /Pubsearch/pubsinfo.asp?pubid=2006461.
PISA scores:
   "Private Schools: Who Benefits?" *PISA in Focus*, August 2011, www.oecd .org/pisa/pisaproducts/pisainfocus/48482894.pdf; Po Bronson and Ashley Merryman, *NurtureShock: New Thinking About Children* (New York: Twelve, 2009).
A 2009 Review of the research . . . :
   Derek C. Briggs, "Preparation for College Admission Exams," National Association for College Admission Counseling, 2009, www.nacacnet.org /research/publicationsresources/marketplace/documents/testprepdiscussion paper.pdf; John Hechinger, "SAT Coaching Found to Boost Scores—Barely," *Wall Street Journal*, May 20m 2009, http://online.wsj.com/news/articles /SB124278685697537839.
Wechsler Preschool and Primary Scale of Intelligence (WPPSI):
   Patricia Hayot, "Letter to Colleagues," Independent Schools Admissions Association of Greater New York, September 18, 2013, http://graphics8.ny times.com/packages/pdf/nyregion/ISAAGNY-letter-to-membership-Sept -2013.pdf.

Manage the Test
Providence Student Union:
   Valerie Strauss, "R.I. Adults Took a Standardized Test, and They Didn't Like It," *Washington Post*, March 17, 2013, www.washingtonpost.com/blogs /answer-sheet/wp/2013/03/17/r-i-adults-took-a-standardized-test-and-they -didnt-like-it; Bob Alexander, *MaxTheTest.com: Test Prep and College Admissions Help*, 2014, http://maxthetest.com.

Manage Your Emotions
Mindfulness and Meditation:
   Amy Saltzman's website is Still Quiet Place, http://www.stillquietplace .com; "Meditation in Schools (Quiet Time Program)," David Lynch Foundation, www.davidlynchfoundation.org/schools.html; "Scientific Evidence That Transcendental Meditation Works," David Lynch Foundation, www.david lynchfoundation.org/research.html; "Introduction," Center for Wellness and

Achievement in Education, http://www.cwae.org/solutions.php; David L. Kirp, "Meditation Transforms Roughest San Francisco Schools," *SFGate*, January 12, 2014, http://www.sfgate.com/opinion/openforum/article/Meditation -transforms-roughest-San-Francisco-5136942.php; Emily Campbell, "Research Round-Up: Mindfulness in Schools," Greater Good: The Science of a Meaningful Life, October 10, 2013, http://greatergood.berkeley.edu/article /item/research_round_up_school_based_mindfulness_programs.

. . . run through the following checklist:

"Child Sleep: Recommended Hours for Every Age," *WebMD*, 2012, www .webmd.com/parenting/guide/sleep-children; G. Curcio, M. Ferrara, and L. Degennaro, "Sleep Loss, Learning Capacity and Academic Performance," *Sleep Medicine Reviews* 10, no. 5 (2006): 323–337; *Kavanaugh's Vehicle for Content and Curriculum*, www.ncbi.nlm.nih.gov/pubmed/16564189; Andrea Petersen, "Pediatricians Set Limits on Screen Time," *Wall Street Journal*, October 28, 2013, http://abcnews.go.com/WNT/Health/story?id=1123055; "Family Dinner Linked to Better Grades for Teens," *ABC News*, September 13, 2005; "Family Meals Spell S-U-C-C-E-S-S," *Center for Families*, Purdue University, www.cfs.purdue.edu/cff/documents/promoting_meals/spell successfactsheet.pdf; Joseph E. Donnelly and Kate Lambourne, "Classroom-Based Physical Activity, Cognition, and Academic Achievement," *Preventive Medicine* 52 (2011): S36–S42, www.sciencedirect.com/science/article/pii /S0091743511000491.

The Collaborative for Academic, Social, and Emotional Learning (CASEL) has reported in their review of dozens of studies . . . :

Civic Enterprises, John Bridgeland, Mary Bruce, and Arya Hariharan, *The Missing Piece: A National Teacher Survey on How Social and Emotional Learning Can Empower Children and Transform Schools* (Chicago: Collaborative for Academic, Social, and Emotional Learning, 2013), www.casel.org/library/the -missing-piece.

CASEL asks parents to sign a pledge . . . :

CASEL, "Casel: Success in School Success in Life," 2013, www.Casel.org.

The full list is:

Focus on your child's strengths first before being constructively critical.

Follow up with consequences for misbehavior.

Ask children how they feel and be understanding of those feelings first before making suggestions.

Practice ways to stay calm when angry (like counting to ten, thinking of other things, finding the positive when it seems none exists).

Avoid shaming your child.

Be willing to apologize.

Give children choices where appropriate and respect their wishes if it really doesn't matter (gain authority by being firm on important matters).

Ask questions that help children solve problems on their own.

Read books and stories together.

Encourage sharing and helping.

Khan Academy . . . :

Anya Kamenetz, "This Simple Khan Academy Interface Hack Improved Learning By 5%," *Fast Company*, April 8, 2013, www.fastcompany.com /3007951/tech-forecast/simple-khan-academy-interface-hack-improved -learning-5.

Brainology . . . :

"Motivate Students to Grow Their Minds!" Mindset Works, www.mindset works.com.

Manage Self-Motivation

Andrea Kuszewski:

"Increase Your Intelligence: Five Ways to Maximize Your Cognitive Potential," *Scientific American Blog*, March 7, 2011, http://blogs.scientific american.com/guest-blog/2011/03/07/you-can-increase-your-intelligence-5 -ways-to-maximize-your-cognitive-potential.

Dopamine:

Susana Pecina et al., "Hyperdopaminergic Mutant Mice Have Higher 'Wanting' but Not 'Liking' for Sweet Rewards," *Journal of Neuroscience* 23, no. 28 (2003): 9395–9402, www.jneurosci.org/content/23/28/9395.full.

Kimberly Sheridan:

L. Hetland, E. Winner, S. Veenema, and K. M. Sheridan, *Studio Thinking: The Real Benefits of Visual Arts Education* (Teachers College Press: New York, 2007); Sylvia's Super Awesome Mini Maker Show is found at YouTube, www.youtube.com/playlist?list=PLFE6E8EADEDFC09DF; Dale Dougherty, "DARPA MENTOR Award to Bring Making to Education," Makerspace, January 16, 2012, http://makerspace.com/press/darpa-mentor-award-to-bring -making-to-education. For more on the maker movement, see Make Faire, http://makerfaire.com/ and http://makermedia.com.

Keith Sawyer:

His work can be found at KeithSawyer.com.

Self-authoring:

Anya Kamenetz, "Can a Writing Assignment Make You Happier, Healthier and Less Stressed?" *O: The Oprah Magazine*, December 2013, www .oprah.com/spirit/Self-Authoring-Health-Benefits-of-Writing.

Manage Your Tone

21.6 million:

Richard Fry, "A Rising Share of Young Adults Live in Their Parents' Home," Pew Research, August 1, 2013, www.pewsocialtrends.org/2013/08/01/a-rising-share-of-young-adults-live-in-their-parents-home.

Gever Tulley:

Gever Tulley, *Fifty Dangerous Things (You Should Let Your Children Do)* (San Francisco: Tinkering Unlimited, 2009). His TED talks can be found at www.ted.com/speakers/gever_tulley. His school is Brightworks http://www.sfbrightworks.org: "Brightworks is a learning community that strives to create a meaningful learning experience for students based on depth of inquiry, collaboration through trust and creativity, and development into capable, adaptable citizens of the world. We use real tools, real materials, and real problems to encourage students' love of learning, curiosity about the world, ability to engage, tenacity to think big, and persistence to do amazing things."

Suniya Luthar:

Suniya S. Luthar, "The Problem with Rich Kids," *Psychology Today*, November/December 2013, www.psychologytoday.com/articles/201310/the-problem-rich-kids; Suniya S. Luthar, Samuel H. Barkin, and Elizabeth J. Crossman, "'I Can, Therefore I Must': Fragility in the Upper-Middle Classes," *Development and Psychopathology* 25, no. 4, pt. 2 (2013): 1529–1549.

INDEX

Anya Kamenetz is NPR's lead digital education reporter. She's the author of two previous books, *Generation Debt* and *DIY U*. She is a former senior writer for *Fast Company*, has a nationally syndicated column with Tribune Media, and her work has appeared in the *New York Times*, *Washington Post*, CNN.com, *Slate*, *Newsweek*, *O: The Oprah Magazine*, and a wide variety of other publications. She has won two national awards from the Education Writers Association and appeared in the documentaries *Generation Next*, *Default*, and *Ivory Tower*. She lives in Brooklyn with her husband and daughter and can be found online at AnyaKamenetz.net.

PublicAffairs is a publishing house founded in 1997. It is a tribute to the standards, values, and flair of three persons who have served as mentors to countless reporters, writers, editors, and book people of all kinds, including me.

I. F. STONE, proprietor of *I. F. Stone's Weekly*, combined a commitment to the First Amendment with entrepreneurial zeal and reporting skill and became one of the great independent journalists in American history. At the age of eighty, Izzy published *The Trial of Socrates*, which was a national bestseller. He wrote the book after he taught himself ancient Greek.

BENJAMIN C. BRADLEE was for nearly thirty years the charismatic editorial leader of *The Washington Post*. It was Ben who gave the *Post* the range and courage to pursue such historic issues as Watergate. He supported his reporters with a tenacity that made them fearless and it is no accident that so many became authors of influential, best-selling books.

ROBERT L. BERNSTEIN, the chief executive of Random House for more than a quarter century, guided one of the nation's premier publishing houses. Bob was personally responsible for many books of political dissent and argument that challenged tyranny around the globe. He is also the founder and longtime chair of Human Rights Watch, one of the most respected human rights organizations in the world.

∙ ∙ ∙

For fifty years, the banner of Public Affairs Press was carried by its owner Morris B. Schnapper, who published Gandhi, Nasser, Toynbee, Truman, and about 1,500 other authors. In 1983, Schnapper was described by *The Washington Post* as "a redoubtable gadfly." His legacy will endure in the books to come.

Peter Osnos, *Founder and Editor-at-Large*